HIKING
THROUGH

HIKING THROUGH

One man's journey to peace and freedom on the Appalachian Trail

PAUL STUTZMAN

Revell

a division of Baker Publishing Group
Grand Rapids, Michigan

Published by Revell
a division of Baker Publishing Group
P.O. Box 6287, Grand Rapids, MI 49516-6287
www.revellbooks.com

Original edition published 2010 by Synergy Books

Printed in the United States of America

Library of Congress Cataloging-in-Publication Data
Stutzman, Paul V.
    Hiking through : one man's journey to peace and freedom on the Appalachian Trail / Paul Stutzman.
        p.   cm.
    ISBN 978-0-8007-2053-7 (pbk.)
    1. Stutzman, Paul V.—Travel—Appalachian Trail. 2. Hiking—Appalachian Trail. 3. Stutzman, Paul V.—Religion. 4. Appalachian Trail—Description and travel. 5. Wives—Death. 6. Bereavement. 7. Self-actualization (Psychology) I. Title.
GV199.42.A68S88 2012
917.4—dc23   2011047589

The internet addresses, email addresses, and phone numbers in this book are accurate at the time of publication. They are provided only as a resource; Baker Publishing Group does not endorse them or vouch for their content or permanence.

To protect the privacy of those who have shared their stories with the author, some details and names have been changed.

12   13   14   15   16   17   18   7   6   5   4   3

In keeping with biblical principles of creation stewardship, Baker Publishing Group advocates the responsible use of our natural resources. As a member of the Green Press Initiative, our company uses recycled paper when possible. The text paper of this book is composed in part of post-consumer waste.

To Mary
Our family still misses you so much,
and we look forward to the day we'll be reunited.

Contents

Author's Note

Additional photos from my Appalachian Trail adventure can be viewed at my website, www.hikingthrough.com. I hope they add to your enjoyment of this book.

In this book, I'll only be using "real" trail names if their owners have given me permission. This gives all you hikers opportunity for plausible denial when your spouse reads some of these adventures and says, "Hey, honey, that sounds like you. You did *what*?" You, my guilty trail friends, can just act innocent and say, "Nope. Not me. I would never do anything that dumb."

Prologue

Cautiously, I stepped on the narrow boards traversing the bog. Two weeks of almost constant rain had brought the water to the top of the wooden walkway, and at several points the path was completely submerged. A tenuous passage, this was the only route available through the swamp that stood between me and the peak of the mountain.

I was nearly to the top of Mt. Success in New Hampshire, and after crossing this bog and summiting the mountain, I would be less than two miles from Maine, the fourteenth and final state in my thru-hike of the Appalachian Trail.

The *click, click, click* of my hiking poles was the only sound I heard as I crossed the shimmering quagmire. Over the years, rain had accumulated here and created a primordial soup of water five feet deep, seasoned with decaying trees, vegetation, and insects. As I planted my left hiking pole on a half-submerged board, the tip of the pole slipped away and the momentum of the thirty-pound pack on my back destroyed my precarious balance. I heard my own shrill scream of "Oh God, no!" and the bog added a weary hiker as another ingredient in its murky depth.

I sank up to my backpack in the muck. Like a drowning man flailing for a lifesaver, I scrambled to escape, grabbing the board where I'd been walking just seconds earlier, leaning forward over its steadfastness, slowly wriggling my body out of the bog's grasp. As I lay frightened and gasping on the narrow wooden path, I saw the picture of myself covered in decaying muck and slime, and muttered, "Congratulations, Mom and Dad, it's a boy."

I lay there for several minutes, contemplating the journey that had brought me to this lonely spot where I was exhausted, indescribably filthy, and facing who-knows-what around every bend. I could have been warm and dry and well-fed at home. I could have been back at work, in a safe routine, productive, earning a paycheck. *Oh, wait—I gave all that up so I could be out here alone in this cold, rainy, godforsaken bog.*

The Big C

It always happens to someone else. A knock on the door late at night while parents lie in bed wondering why a child is not yet home. A call from the hospital saying a spouse is waiting in the emergency room and heart-wrenching decisions must be made. For me, it had always happened to someone else; death's bony finger had lifted people out of my sphere, but so far that grim reaper had only worked at the periphery of my life.

That all changed with one phone call.

My wife, Mary, called me at the restaurant I had managed for seventeen years. Her strained voice said, "It's malignant."

My mind raced—benign, malignant—which was good news, which was bad? I couldn't remember.

"What does that mean?"

"I have cancer." The words jerked out between sobs. I told Mary I was coming home, hung up the phone, dropped my head into my hands, and for the first time in years, wept.

The daily calendar on my desk caught my eye. On that day, August 30, 2002, the meditation came from the lyrics of an old song I had often sung growing up in the Conservative Mennonite Church, "God of Grace and God of Glory."

I ripped off the calendar page, thinking that I was indeed going to need the wisdom and courage spoken of in the song; but I did not know how desperately I would need help in the coming months. That page is still tucked away in my Bible.

At home, Mary and I held each other and determined to battle the disease together—my wife, with her faith and spirit, and me beside her every step of the way.

After my high school graduation in 1969, I worked as an orderly at a local hospital. Every morning, the night shift gave us reports and updates on the patients in our care. The charge nurse's habit was to use the letter C whenever cancer was in a report, so that became our lingo, never using the actual word *cancer.*

That word strikes fear in people from all walks of life and all economic brackets. However, if caught early and given proper treatment, many types of cancer can be cured or controlled; a diagnosis of cancer today is not always a pronouncement of imminent death. For Mary, it was breast cancer, and we would soon become all too familiar with its statistics. One in eight women will be diagnosed with breast cancer. It sounds more optimistic to say that seven out of eight women will never suffer with this disease. Yet almost everyone will surely know someone—maybe someone dear to them—diagnosed with breast cancer.

Unfortunately for Mary, the diagnosis came too late. With cancer in her family history, she had been faithful in yearly checkups and mammograms. Several years before, her mammogram showed a spot, but we were told it appeared to be only a calcium deposit. In retrospect, we should have sought another opinion, but regrettably we did not. We were oblivious to the growing danger, until menopause reared its ugly head.

Mary's difficulties during menopause had become frustrating, so she sought the counsel of a doctor recommended as an expert on menopause. But the menopause nuisances suddenly became secondary when the doctor learned about the abnormality in Mary's latest mammogram. She immediately ordered another test, followed by a biopsy.

And now the results were in: that big C was written on the chart of Mary's life. My wife was now that one woman in eight.

Our children must be told. The two oldest were living at home and were soon informed. But our youngest daughter was three hours away, at college, and Mary decided to drive to western Ohio and spend the weekend with her. Realizing that mother and daughter needed the time together, I decided to stay at home.

That meant a weekend apart from my wife, and we'd been dealt a numbing blow. I found myself reverting to one of my own stress-relievers, dreaming about hiking in the woods without a care. For years, one of my favorite daydreams had been about thru-hiking the Appalachian Trail (AT). I nursed the dream tenderly, but never thought it could become reality.

Mary knew how much I loved hiking, and I had often shared my dream with her. So with my wife's blessing, I did more than daydream. While she visited our daughter, I spent my weekend at Harpers Ferry, West Virginia, the headquarters for the AT.

Harpers Ferry is where abolitionist John Brown raided the U.S. Armory in his fight against slavery. Today it is also the location of the Appalachian Trail Conservancy. The state of West Virginia has only four miles of the 2,176 that make up the Appalachian Trail, and those four miles of trail go right through this little town.

I explored a small section of trail in both directions from town. A short distance south is Jefferson Rock, a high stone outlook where Thomas Jefferson once stood and admired the view of the Potomac and Shenandoah rivers rushing together in the valley below. I walked a little farther south to where U.S. Highway 340 crosses the Shenandoah River. There, the Appalachian Trail disappears up into the surrounding hills. What was up there, around the next bend, over the next mountain? I stood for a long time, contemplating what it would be like to hike the thousand miles from Harpers Ferry to Springer Mountain, Georgia, the trail's southern terminus.

I promised myself that one day I would come hiking out of those woods and down into Harpers Ferry. I'd cross town and follow the trail across the footbridge over the Potomac River and hike along the C&O Canal Towpath northward into Maryland, exploring every bend in the trail, soaking up every scene, with my sights set on the AT's northern terminus, mighty Mt. Katahdin in Baxter State Park, Maine.

Someday.

After stopping at the Appalachian Trail Conservancy, where I picked up some valuable trail information, I wanted to visit one more historical site. St. Peter's Roman Catholic Church, built in 1833, was the only church in Harpers Ferry to escape destruction during the Civil War. Its steeple soars above the little town, and the trail passes within several feet of the church's front door.

I'd never been inside a Catholic church in my life. But I felt compelled to enter this church to pray.

I was the only person in the sanctuary. I knelt and prayed for Mary and our family, for strength and wisdom for the journey ahead. I believed that God could heal my wife if He chose, and I pleaded with Him for that healing.

This Conservative Mennonite boy was on his knees in the old Catholic church, knowing how much we needed what only God could give.

We would fight. We determined to learn everything we could about breast cancer. We knew that the right treatment increased the survival rate for breast cancer patients. We were hopeful that would be the case for Mary. We researched, looking for the place to get the best treatment. We soon learned that health insurance coverage would define our choices.

Discussions with Mary's doctor and the insurance company determined that a mastectomy was necessary. The next week was full of meetings with staff and surgeons, one of whom was the plastic surgeon who would immediately construct a new breast, using both an implant and muscle tissue from Mary's back.

A mastectomy. Removal of the entire breast. But we discovered that the insurance company was required to pay not just for the reconstruction of a new breast, but also for any necessary procedure to then make both breasts symmetrical. At some point, Mary could have a nip and tuck done on her other breast. My wife was delighted—rather than focusing on losing one breast, she was excited about having two new ones. That was my wife.

We approached her surgery, which was scheduled for the first week of October, with optimism. Mary was convinced everything would be fine and refused to even use the word *cancer*. The surgery seemed to go well. We sat in her hospital room afterward, waiting for her oncologist and hoping that the worst was behind us.

The doctor arrived and took a seat by Mary's bed. The surgery had gone well, he reported, but they had also removed numerous lymph nodes.

Then the doctor got up, walked across the room, and closed the door. Dread washed over me.

The cancer had metastasized to Mary's liver. The prognosis was not good. The cancer was already stage IV, the final, extreme, worst stage of development. There would be no cure, no stopping the disease. The only thing that could be done was to contain it as long as possible.

Did I even want to know? Regardless, I had to ask. "How much time do we have?"

We were stunned by the reply: several months, maybe several years, depending on Mary's response to treatment.

The bottom dropped out of our lives.

The doctor discussed treatments and then left us alone to hold each other and cry. But later that night in her hospital bed, Mary awoke to a feeling she described as the hand of

God, reaching down and holding her. She was filled with incredible peace, and she was convinced God was going to heal her.

Through years of surgeries and setbacks, my wife never wavered from that belief. Chemotherapy left her sick and humiliated at the loss of all her hair. Countless blood tests and treatments made it increasingly difficult to locate good veins in her arms, so one surgery installed a port in her shoulder to allow insertion of a needle. But the port only worked temporarily, so another surgery removed it. Then there was an infection around her implant and another surgery removed that. Every setback that occurred was met with "All will be well" from Mary, and I marveled at her positive attitude.

Over several years, we adjusted to new routines. Our life was now built around chemotherapy, hospital trips, and blood tests. My wife had many good friends who helped out by driving her to tests and treatments, and sometimes life even felt almost normal.

But early in 2006, we knew that the battle was not going well. Mary's weight kept dropping, and she was growing weaker. It was gut-wrenching for me, a healthy man, to watch the girl I dated, fell in love with, and married, now weakening, fading away, shriveling. I begged God to either heal Mary, as we felt He had promised, or take her home. Mary never lost her faith in God or her belief that she would be healed. How I admired her courage.

The day came when the doctor called our family into his office and advised that it was time to consider hospice care. And wow! What a reaction from Mary! She informed us all that it was *not* going to happen, since hospice care was for people who were dying. Not until the final week of her life did she relent, and even then she declared *she* did not need it, but if *we* needed help, then she would allow it.

The first week of September 2006 was so very painful, as one by one, friends and relatives came to say their good-byes. Thursday evening, September 7, surrounded by myself and our three children, Mary took her last breath and then was gone from our lives.

What a harsh reality. My wife of thirty-two years was no longer alive. It had happened, but I almost couldn't comprehend the reality of it. I had watched her body deteriorate, but always I clung to the hope that God would heal her, that her dying and leaving us would never actually happen.

As our family sat and cried together, waiting for the funeral home to pick up Mary's body, I could not help but wonder what glorious things she was seeing. As a Christian, I believed that she was finally at rest, totally healed, seeing things and experiencing a life that my mind could not comprehend or imagine.

The following days were filled with the decisions we all postpone thinking about: choosing a coffin, finding a gravesite, writing an obituary, setting details about visitation and the funeral service. To make these decisions before your own passing is a great consideration for those you leave behind, who must deal with all those details at a time when thinking is numbed.

My family was on autopilot, moving through the days and decisions because we had to. Friends, family, and church surrounded us with care. On Sunday, September 10, we held a graveside service, followed by a memorial for Mary. It was an emotional time, and I realized how important the church family was to us and how fortunate we were to have a pastor and his wife who cared for their flock.

Reality hit that evening, after everyone had left my house. I knew then I was alone—completely, utterly alone. I had depended so much on my wife, and already I missed her terribly. In despair, I went to God. I knelt by my bed and thanked God for giving me thirty-two years with Mary. I asked for wisdom as I went on alone. And I prayed I could help others facing similar sadness and grief.

I did not know then what direction God would take me in. I only hurt.

But when I finished my prayer, the seed of an idea had been planted along the edge of my mind. That seed held the small beginnings of a plan.

2

The Plan

It seems to me that women handle grief better than men do. Perhaps women are more community-minded; they have a wider circle of friends and are willing to speak more openly about their emotions. Unfortunately, when pain descends upon us men we react as we've been taught: keep emotions in check and solve the problem.

Men may treat bereavement as just another of life's problems. We need to devise a solution—the sooner the better—and end the pain. And the solution for many men appears to be finding another woman to replace the lost loved one. (I'm convinced there are men who use the memorial service for their spouse as a screening tool for potential candidates.) Find another wife, re-create the life that has been lost, problem solved. Grief gone.

But stoicism and all our problem-solving skills cannot bring real recovery from grief. Until and unless we live through and understand our pain, we will never be a good partner to anyone in the future.

Good old Webster defines grief as "intense emotional suffering caused by loss." Right as he may be, it doesn't sound much like he's experienced that suffering. Here's my description, born of living through it:

grief (grēf) **1.** helplessness and hopelessness **2.** an elevator that only goes down **3.** a black hole of emotions that traps one in its vortex **4.** stepping out of an airplane without a parachute, welcoming impact as relief from the pain **5.** desperately wanting to have life return to what it once was.

Two voices clamor through the cloud of grief. One still believes that by some miraculous intervention of God, life might yet return to normal; the other voice replies that everything has been irrevocably changed forever. The road to recovery opens only after these two voices can be reconciled.

For me, as for everyone, that road to recovery wound through a landscape of regret. Reflecting on the years Mary and I had together, I mourned the time we had wasted on silly disagreements and lamented that I had spent too much time at work, leaving the task of raising our children to my wife. I sorrowed that I had, indeed, taken Mary and our life together for granted.

On my path through the pain, I read several books on grief, determined to understand what grief was, why we grieve, and how to recover. I also joined a grief recovery group at our church; I highly recommend such support to anyone who has lost a loved one.

Healing came in other ways as well. In the fall after Mary's death, my cousin joined me for two days of hiking in Utah's

Zion Canyon. I once again experienced the soothing and healing power of nature. I realized how helpful it was to discuss my feelings of loss and regret with another male and to trust another person with my thoughts and feelings. As I worked my way up the narrow but exhilarating Angels Landing Trail, I reflected on my marriage and how easily I had slipped into taking my wife for granted. I wondered how I would have been different as a husband if I had known that our days together would be over too soon.

On the flight home, I considered the balm brought by just two days of hiking and wondered if a much longer hike might translate into continued healing. And I wanted to somehow link such a hike to my new message for men: *don't take your spouse and family for granted.*

The plan was starting to take root.

One of the first lessons in Grief 101 is a caution against making any big, life-changing decisions for at least one year. That includes buying or selling your home, quitting or changing jobs, or getting remarried. Making major choices while your emotions are all jumbled up and you're unable to think clearly is opening the door to disaster. If you're fortunate enough to have some assets built up, there may be children, grandchildren, heirs, in-laws, outlaws, ruffians, and assorted vultures circling, eyeing a hoped-for endowment. Fortunately, I was not cursed with a great deal of money, so there were no grief groupies hanging around. I had three children who loved me, a church family that cared for me, and a good job. At least part of my life was still intact.

My job took on new meaning. No longer just a means to pay for house, cars, and college tuition, my work at the restaurant became the environment where I most felt a sense of normalcy. I had lost my spouse, but I still had a reason to get up each morning. Day by day, week by week, time dragged by; but the job routine was safe and predictable.

The route to work passed the cemetery where we had buried my wife. For several months, I thought of Mary as soon as that hillside came into view. One day, I realized I was a mile beyond the cemetery; I'd passed it and not felt my eyes drawn there. As the weeks went by, the one mile stretched to two, then three, until finally there were nights I drove all the way home without thinking about the gravesite on the hill. Those increasing distances seemed to measure my progress on the path toward recovery.

As the one-year anniversary of Mary's death approached, a road trip seemed like a good idea. Thinking I could leave the safety of my work environment, I planned a solo trip to New Orleans. But my timing was terrible. I left on the eve of the anniversary of Mary's death, and by the time I was sixty miles from home, loneliness hijacked all my plans. Memories flooded back, and driving away from my home and safe routine of work, I realized again how alone I was. Emotions overwhelmed me and the tears started to roll. I wasn't ready to be *this* alone. Crying like a baby, I turned the car around and went back home.

Yes, there had been much healing in a year, yet that one-year anniversary was a brutal reminder of all that I'd lost.

But I had survived a year, with its ups and downs, the hurt and the healing. I had survived the first year.

I had worked in food service for almost twenty-five years. There had been great satisfactions in those years, some simply from successful management of a busy place, but many also from relationships on the job. We often employed younger people, inexperienced and working their first jobs. I had the opportunity to be not only a boss, but also a mentor to young adults learning how to function in a workplace. One day, while I waited in a hospital with Mary, a young intern entered the room with Mary's oncologist. "Paul, what are *you* doing here?" the intern exclaimed. She was a young lady who had worked her very first job at my restaurant, and that day in the hospital she thanked me for encouraging her to pursue her dream of becoming a doctor.

But the years had also brought frustrating changes to the hospitality industry. Workplace issues arose that I had never imagined earlier in my career. We had to deal with tattoos, body piercings, sexual harassment, sexual identity crises, anorexia, bulimia, and those ever-present necessities for kids, cell phones and iPods. It was a whole new ballgame. "What do you mean *rules*? You expect me to work without talking on my cell phone?" And these kids were becoming legal scholars: they came to work with more metal protruding from their bodies than most modern cars, and couldn't understand a manager who insisted on following a silly employee manual. "You will hear from my dad's attorney," I was told more than once.

Customers were also becoming more demanding. It's the manager's job to handle unhappy customers. Most of those situations can be easily handled, and of course there are always a few legitimate complaints. But as most restaurant managers will attest, there are customers who visit your establishment with only one goal: a free meal. After long years in the business, I knew most of their tricks. The manager must be the arbiter of what is fact and what is fiction. After twenty-five years, customer complaints and employee issues had taken a toll.

The beginning of the end for me came on a Friday night, shortly after my aborted trip to New Orleans.

One of my servers informed me that we had an irate customer. He had ordered our largest chicken dinner, and—sure enough—that very last piece did not look good to him. I had observed his many trips to the salad bar, and I knew there was nothing wrong with his meal. I approached his booth and immediately recognized Trouble. Years of being in the people business had turned me into something of a self-made psychologist. (While my employees were becoming self-made attorneys, I was becoming the restaurant shrink.)

It is with mingled shame and pride that I admit to completely mishandling the situation. I sized him up. My problem was a vertically challenged, steroid-pumped weight lifter. Please note that I have no problem with weight lifting, bodybuilding, or any attempts to improve one's body. But this guy was obviously addicted to his bodybuilding. You know the type—short in stature with a protruding chest, above which his neck had somehow melted into his shoulders. He should have worn a sign: "I need attention. I am very insecure."

"What's the problem?" I asked.

That little head swiveled on the steroid-enhanced shoulders, face livid, veins bulging. And Trouble informed me his chicken was "no good." I made him aware that I knew of his many trips to the salad bar, and I was also certain there was nothing wrong with his chicken, especially since he had already eaten most of it.

Not the response he wanted. He unhinged. Swollen arms flailed. In a rage, he cursed and screamed, "Are you calling me a liar?"

Yes, I agreed with him, he was a liar. Must have pushed the wrong button there too, because then he offered to kill me. By then, every Christian tenet I had ever been taught (such as *love thy enemy*) had left me, and I was savoring the idea of tearing him apart, limb by overinflated limb. But I thought better of it, since he could have squeezed the life out of me like a boa constrictor.

He hurled more invectives, went through another round of profanities, and then left, shouting to the entire dining room that he would *never* come back to this restaurant. I assured him that never would be too soon.

Later in the evening, my own rage past, I reflected on my new approach to handling customer complaints. My response was the result of years of cumulative stress. The whole scene had been like a final pounding of the gavel that told me, "It's time to leave."

That night as I passed the cemetery I looked toward Mary's grave and whispered, "I think it's time."

Mary and I had always thought we would work hard, get out of debt, retire early, and then enjoy doing some mission project to benefit others. In May of 2006, I made our last house payment. I took the envelope with the final payment to the hospital where Mary lay.

"This is it, Mary. No more debt."

"That's wonderful!" she replied.

Wonderful, indeed, but what price had we paid? Within four months, my wife was dead. All those things we were going to do together were now impossible. We had spent a lifetime working toward that distant goal, making promises to ourselves that now we could never fulfill. Sure, it's important to plan for the future, but think about this: You've had the gift of yesterday and you are living today with its choices and opportunities, but who knows if you will have tomorrow? You've heard it time and again, but I will tell you—and I know it's true, because the painful lesson is etched into my yesterday—no one has a guarantee of tomorrow. That's why it is so important *today* to tell our spouses and loved ones what they mean to us.

On the night the enraged weight lifter faced the equally enraged restaurant manager, I took a look at my life. If I was serious about taking each day that God gave me and utilizing that day to help other people, then I would need to make a very difficult decision.

Driving to work the next morning, I asked God for a sign, some confirmation that it was time to leave the restaurant.

Early in my shift, I was called to the front desk. This time, the complainant was a middle-aged man delivering another profanity-laced tirade about the quality of our bacon. I curtly told him I would see what could be done about improving the lifestyle of the sacrificial hogs, and I walked away, shaking my head in disbelief that with all the problems facing humanity, I was dealing with a temper tantrum over pig fat!

In two consecutive shifts, I'd encountered the two most difficult customers of my restaurant career. *God, I know I asked You for a sign. But did You have to go this far?* Of course, in my case, the shock treatment was probably necessary, because my fear of the unknown was greater than any discomfort in the present. It's why we often stay in jobs we don't find fulfilling and why people stay in abusive situations; we are frozen in place, unable to give up our known misery even for the promise of a happier tomorrow.

There was no doubt that I needed to step away from my position, but I also realized how important my job was. It was my identity and my safety net. I knew by then that my unknown tomorrow would involve hiking the Appalachian Trail. What would people think of my giving up a good job to go hiking in the woods?

The two customer encounters had brought everything into sharp focus for me, but there were also gentler pushes.

I'm at the age where I read obituaries. Beyond checking to see who is gone, I find the content of obituaries fascinating. What did people accomplish in their allotted years? What was important in their lives? Those long lists of organizations and activities—are people truly living, or just filling their schedules?

One day, with the two terror customers still raw in my memory, I finished reading that day's obituaries and pictured someone reading a column about my own demise in the hopefully distant future. What did I want those lines to say? That I worked all my life and was found dead in my office chair, done in by some crazed weight lifter? No, I wanted something much more interesting—both for me in life and for the readers of my history—something like: "After a successful restaurant career, Mr. S retired early and followed his dream of thru-hiking the Appalachian Trail and writing a book about everything he learned."

I once again asked God about the wisdom of leaving my job. I was still debating, but a question waved in my mind, a quiet, gentle question that I'm convinced came from God. *Would you give up your job if you knew I wanted you to?*

Of course I'd do it, was the automatic reply in my head. *It's time. Go. I will be there with you.*

The internal debate was over. I finally had the peace I needed to make this life-changing decision. I would quit my job. I would hike the AT. I would use the walk to deliver a message to men: *Don't take your spouse and family for granted. Enjoy today fully. Don't assume you have tomorrow to tell your loved ones what they mean to you.*

I would deliver the message whenever I could. But I had no way of knowing that on the trail God would deliver an even greater message to me.

One thing remained: my letter of resignation. Until this letter was written and sent, I could back away from this crazy idea. Even my dad, eighty-three years old and still working every day, questioned the wisdom of my decision.

I wanted to begin my hike by the end of March, and my company required a two-month notice to have an orderly transition of management. I waited until the last possible day, and wrote the letter.

I was convinced this decision was right; why was it still so difficult? I sat at my desk, the email to my boss composed, waiting on the computer screen in front of me. Fear and doubt paralyzed me; I could not hit that send button.

Instead, I wandered through the restaurant on a pilgrimage of memories through every department: bakery, kitchen, banquet rooms, dining rooms, wait stations, dish room, hostess station, and even the Dumpster room. Long hours, customer complaints, and employee issues no longer filled my mind. Now I was reliving good times spent with great employees and wonderful customers. How could I survive without them? What was my life, if not the restaurant?

I can't quit.

You must quit.

Can't.

Must.

For several hours I vacillated. During my years of managing this place, my decisions had always been predicated on what was best for the restaurant. Now at last the question was: What is right for me? With tears streaming down my face, I sat down at my desk once again and hit *send*.

3

The Narrow Path

Every year, several thousand believers answer the call to make a pilgrimage from Springer Mountain, Georgia, to another mountaintop 2,176 miles away. Of these thousands, only several hundred are chosen to finish.

Chosen? Yes. If you are ever one of those solitary Appalachian Trail thru-hikers and you somehow survive three hundred daunting mountains, precarious river crossings, difficult rock climbs, discouraging illness and loneliness, and punishing weather, and you stand at last at the summit of mighty Mt. Katahdin, then you will indeed know what it is to be one of those chosen few.

You are then forever part of the brotherhood and sisterhood of the AT. Whether you are God-fearing, agnostic, or atheist, you are irrevocably changed. Some of the changed are better equipped to deal with society; some never find a place to fit. Only your trail brothers and sisters will understand the transformations within you. As much as you want friends and family to know how and why you have changed so dramatically, you cannot describe where your wilderness journey has taken you.

But still, we try. More books have been written about the Appalachian Trail than any other trail in America. Something life-changing and unique happens to thru-hikers on the AT that makes this one trail almost mythical and compels us hikers to write about our journeys.

I am convinced it's all about community, our interaction with fellow hikers and those folks we meet in trail towns. It's also about being alone, the solitude always coupled with knowledge that safe harbor is never too far away.

There was much to do. Most hikers spend at least a year planning this hike; I had two months. Decisions about equipment, clothing, food, shoes, and water supply loomed large. Weight was a big factor. I'd carry everything on my back for the next five months. Twenty years before, comfort might not have been a consideration; but now my body demanded a vote on tent, sleeping pad, and sleeping bag. For every piece of equipment, I found so many different companies and models (all claiming superiority) that I felt overwhelmed by information.

My smartest move was finding an outfitter with an employee who had completed a thru-hike. Based on his assurance that I would encounter cold and snow in April, I purchased a five-degree MontBell down sleeping bag. There are reasons to avoid down-filled bags, and in hindsight, I actually would not recommend them; but this heavy bag did keep me from turning into a popsicle on cold nights in the Smoky Mountains.

Many hikers spend much time drying and packaging their own food; I had neither the time nor the desire to do so. Instead, I bought freeze-dried food. Cooking dinner would mean boiling twelve ounces of water, pouring it into a foil bag containing four ounces of food, waiting ten minutes, and then relishing a one-pound meal. That meal would supply five hundred calories, and additional nutrition would come from trail mix, energy bars, breakfast bars, candy bars, and Little Debbies. I planned to carry a week's supply of food, and I would call my trail boss with instructions on where and when to send each subsequent food box.

Ina, my friend and co-worker, would be my trail boss. Support at home is crucial for conquest of the AT. Small details can have large repercussions. For example, if a food drop arrives at a post office on Saturday but the hiker doesn't arrive before noon, chances are that the food can't be picked up until the post office opens again on Monday; thus an entire day is lost. Planning food deliveries also involves choosing the best pickup location, whether a post office or hostel.

I found myself paralyzed by uncertainty and doubt. *Can I hike through fourteen states and over two thousand miles?* After much mental jousting with my fears, I knew my choice must be to *believe*. The AT was teaching me before I had left a single footprint on the trail.

Had I known all the results of my choices, all the details of the next months, all that waited for me on the trail, I probably would have rapidly backed away from a path so difficult. But I would also have missed the most incredible journey of my life. It was not only an incredible journey on my own two feet wandering through spectacular creation, but also a journey of discovery through the landscape of my mind and heart.

Preparation for a long-distance hike should include building an appropriate degree of physical fitness. Although I was not a total ball of flab, twenty-five years of pies, pastries, and rich restaurant food had created twenty pounds more of me than was necessary. Winters in Ohio are not conducive to any kind of exercise regimen. Hence, my only physical preparation for the trail consisted of several trips up and down the stairs with my loaded pack.

How difficult could this be, anyway, this idyllic footpath, this extended walk in the park? Sure, I'd have extra weight on my back, but I reasoned that every pound of body weight I lost would be like an extra pound taken out of my backpack. My math reassured me; if I carried a thirty-five-pound pack, but lost twenty pounds, it would feel like I was carrying only fifteen pounds.

Oh, my math was so wrong.

Saturday, March 29, 2008. Two months had passed quickly and my final day at the restaurant had arrived. Normally, our Saturdays were very busy, so I went about my routine, trying to keep a sense of normalcy. Doubts had crept in countless times since I had sent my resignation letter. Was this what God wanted me to do? Could I change my mind? But there was no turning back. A new manager had already been hired. I was free to go.

My mind raced through jumbled thoughts and emotions, some logical, some philosophical, some wildly irrational. *How could anyone replace me so quickly? This place can't survive without me. How can I give up everything here to become a jobless bum?* But some rational brain cell came forward and admonished me, *Just leave already. There is probably someone in the dining room choking on a piece of bacon right now, while the new manager has to explain to an irate customer why the eggs turned green.* I took one more sentimental journey through every corner of my stress factory. I'd already said my farewells to loyal friends and co-workers, so I finished my memory walk, turned my back on my safety net, and walked away.

I couldn't give myself one unoccupied moment, or I would have to face the fact that I was unemployed. I decided to leave for the trail that very day. My backpack was ready, and in a few hours I went from maintaining a job and a house to lugging around a thirty-five-pound bag that held everything I'd need to survive in the wilderness.

Amicalola Falls State Park, twenty miles east of Ellijay, Georgia, was my destination. Amicalola Falls is a series of seven falls dropping a total of 729 feet down a rocky mountainside; the name itself is Cherokee for "tumbling waters." At the base of the falls, I stood wrapped in a blanket of mist. Taking comfort from the sound of the falling water, I felt a kinship with this river. My life, flowing merrily along, had suddenly arrived at an abyss where everything fell away and the waters tumbled and crashed over the edge. But after the abrupt, headlong plunge down the cliff, the river quiets itself in pools and then moves on steadily and unhindered. I wanted the same for my life.

I was finally here at the southern terminus of the Appalachian Trail. Tomorrow I would take my first steps on the trail that had held my dreams for so long.

Thru-hikers stop at the visitor center in the state park and sign their first register on the trail. These notebooks log hikers' progress and record their thoughts along the way. Hikers leave information, warnings, encouragement, or gripes for those coming after them. I browsed back through several weeks of entries, looking for names I recognized from reading the Trail Journals website.

The Trail Journals site was created for hikers to post journal entries so family and friends can follow their progress; folks at home can also send messages to a hiker. The site is a great place to gather information; for several years, I'd hiked vicariously with thru-hikers. Now I was no longer a reader of Trail Journals; I would be one of the writers.

I entered my name in the register and officially became hiker number 391 attempting to walk from Georgia to Maine.

In my room at the Amicalola Lodge, I spread out my equipment. Nervously, I packed and repacked my backpack. Should the tent go in flat or upright? Two liters of water or three? I filtered water from the room faucet, just for practice. The night was restless and long.

A blanket of fog dropped before morning, making visibility almost zero. It delayed my departure for a few hours, which I filled by needlessly unpacking and repacking several more times. The fog at last lifted, and I set out to find the trailhead somewhere at the top of Springer Mountain.

An eight-mile approach trail leads from the lodge to the trailhead on the mountain. It is a blue-blazed trail, which means it is not an official part of the Appalachian Trail, which is marked with white blazes. I could either hike or drive to the summit trailhead, where I would start my thru-hike. My trail boss, Ina, had driven to Georgia with me to return my car to Ohio. And since she had not yet departed with my car, I chose to drive to the trailhead. As it turned out, it would have been easier to hike the eight miles. U.S. Forest Service Road 42 was made for a four-wheel drive vehicle, not my family sedan. We bumped around, over, and through ruts and rocks and arrived at a sparsely graveled parking area at Big Stamp Gap.

Another vehicle was unloading hikers. Someone was giving them directions: head south for the start of the trail. *That can't be right. Maine is north.* I hadn't even taken my first steps on the trail, and already I was confused. I realized then that the trail went right through the parking lot, with one path leading north and one leading south. The official beginning of the AT did indeed start one mile south of where we stood. So the first mile of my hike would be south to the start of the trail, and then I'd hike back to this parking lot again and continue through it, northward.

Since I would be hiking back to this spot, I convinced Ina to hike those first two miles with me. I had persuaded her to take a day off work to deliver me to Georgia, and now I was going to squeeze two more miles out of her. Actually, it was just a ploy to delay the loneliness that I already sensed was waiting for me just a few steps into those woods.

A cluster of gnarled trees and an outcropping of rocks greeted me when I arrived at last at the southern terminus of the Appalachian Trail. On one large rock was the first white blaze of the trail. For the next 2,176 miles, those small two-by-six-inch painted white marks would be my road map, almost 80,000 of them on trees, rocks, signs, buildings, and even railroad ties. Adjacent to the first blaze, a bronze plaque embedded in the rock bore the image of a hiker and the inscription,

> Appalachian Trail
> Georgia to Maine
> A Footpath for
> Those who seek
> Fellowship with
> the Wilderness.

I posed for a photo at the first blaze and then signed the register. Enclosed in a plastic bag, the fat notebook contained entries from optimistic hikers, often bold or brave statements. My entry simply read, "Apostle, heading to Maine."

We finally arrived back at the parking lot, one mile of the trail under my feet. With a heavy heart, I hoisted my pack. The time had finally arrived. Just when I had thought this day could not possibly get sadder and more depressing, it started to rain. I dropped my pack again, and for the first of many times in the months to come, I put on rain gear. I was scared. I wondered if this was the worst decision of my life. My friend and I had said good-bye, and there was nothing more to say. As I watched the car disappear down that dirt road, I felt more alone than I'd ever felt in my life. The raindrops and my tears fell together as I turned and trudged into the woods.

After sniveling along for a short distance, I stopped to compose myself and take stock of the situation. *Let's see*

. . . you quit your job, you are standing alone in a woods in Georgia, and you plan to hike 2,176 miles to Maine. You have never camped for more than a weekend in your life, and you intend to live in a tent for almost five months. Yes, indeed, that does make a lot of sense. Now get moving.

It took some time, but my emotions finally settled down, and I began to notice my surroundings. I was walking on a carpet of pine needles, through a stand of Cathedral Hemlocks. Stover Creek flowed to the right, and the song of running water soothed my saddened spirit. For several miles, the trail was the idyllic pathway in the woods of my dreams.

Several hikers had overtaken me. We paused to chat, and as they moved on I wondered if we would meet again in the days to come. My start date determined who I would meet on the trail. Beginning one day earlier or one day later would have changed my personal interactions all the way to Maine. Who was I destined to meet when I chose March 31 to begin walking north?

Several miles later, I stopped for a lunch break and experienced for the first time that great relief of slipping the heavy pack off my back.

Another eight miles brought me to Hawk Mountain Shelter. It was only four o'clock, but the next shelter was seven miles away. I approached this shelter with the intention of stopping but soon realized it was already full. If I stayed here, I would have to set up my tent nearby. While I considered my options, two hikers left the shelter, having decided the building was too full and it was too early to stop. Their plan was to hike several more miles and then set up camp in the woods. I asked to join them, and was graciously received.

"What's your trail name?" one of them asked.

"Apostle," I replied. "Apostle Paul. I'm hiking to Damascus, hoping for an enlightening experience. Damascus, Virginia, that is. Then on to Maine."

They found the humor in my biblical reference, and introduced themselves as Marathon Man and Lion King. Most hikers are known by trail names. In earlier years, a hiker would often gain such a moniker as a result of some stupid or habitual action on his part, and the nickname would follow him forever on the trail: "Nose Picker" or "Gas Bag" or sometimes something much worse. Most thru-hikers today choose their own names before setting foot on the trail, as a means of avoiding this potential denigration by fellow hikers. I'd chosen Apostle, not only because my name was Paul, but because the definition of *apostle* is "one sent forth on a special mission."

The three of us hiked several more miles and stopped at Horse Gap, just a small clearing in the woods with a creek running along one side. We would set up camp here. It was time to unfurl Big Agnes.

Big Agnes was my tent. Shopping for my home away from home during those two frantic months of preparation, I knew I wanted something big enough to hold myself plus all my worldly possessions. I chose a Big Agnes Seedhouse SL2. This two-person tent weighed nine ounces more than the one-person model. I agonized over adding those extra nine ounces, but in the end, I chose the luxury of additional space. By the time I got to Maine, I realized that nine ounces of luxury carried 2,176 miles translates into lots of extra exertion.

With our tents pitched and meals eaten, it was time for us to hang our bear bags. We were hiking through bear country and had been advised to hang our bags from a sturdy tree branch, out of any prowler's reach. I realized in dismay that the only appropriate branch was directly over my tent. Just great. The bear could use my tent as a launching pad to reach those food bags. It was not a comforting picture. Rather than relocate my tent, we headed farther into the woods, searching for a suitable branch. I know what you're thinking: *You're surrounded by trees; shouldn't there be branches everywhere?* But, as I would learn, finding a good branch for bear bags is never easy.

We made many attempts to hurl a weighted rope over a good branch. I must report, our throws were mostly unsuccessful; we broke several perfectly good branches in the process. Finally, we lassoed our branch and hung our three food bags, a tantalizing buffet we hoped was out of the reach of any forest marauders.

The rain had started again and was coming down hard by the time I finished filtering my water. It was eight o'clock—hiker midnight, as it's known on the trail. I scrambled out of my soaked clothes and snuggled into my fluffy, down-filled sleeping bag. The first day of my lifelong dream was complete. I was utterly weary, from both the physical and emotional ordeal of the day. But I had survived one day.

I got very little sleep that night, kept awake by raindrops pinging on my tent and my still-churning emotions of the day. I wondered what lay ahead of me on this narrow path to Maine.

The Narrow Way

Every year, approximately four million people visit Ohio's Amish Country, hoping for a respite from their busy lives. They come to enjoy the scenic beauty and the slower lifestyle of the Amish and Mennonites. I grew up as part of that community, insulated from the outside world.

But the quiet, rural community I knew as a child was transformed by the wealth tourists brought to town. Tourist dollars became a vital source of income for area residents, and restaurants, shops, furniture stores, inns, flea markets, and cheese factories soon dotted the landscape.

Most of these shops are closed on Sundays. Consequently, most of the tourist crowd leaves by Saturday night and is deprived of witnessing our number one industry: religion.

Unlike most communities that appear to have a mix of bars and churches, the community of my childhood had only churches. That was fine, since no one had a thirst for alcohol (or so I thought). Churches sprouted up everywhere. In my community, spreading the gospel sometimes meant moving down the road a few miles and building a new church. Often this migration was prompted by disagreements within a congregation on superficial things like dress, color of vehicles, and other vital issues that determine eternal destiny.

In this mix of churchology, I formed early beliefs and learned lessons about life and leadership. It was very clear that my outward appearance mattered more than my inward condition. Sure, we were taught "salvation," but salvation was contingent on obedience to a strict regimen of rules. The straight and narrow path that was intended to deliver me to life everlasting seemed as narrow and precarious as a balance beam.

Shortly after I was born into an Amish family, my parents decided to leave that church and, as the saying goes, "jump the fence." The fence we jumped was quite low, and we landed in a conservative Mennonite church that was not far removed from our previous Amish beliefs.

Now we could travel by car instead of horse and buggy, and we were soon the proud owners of a Studebaker. To this day, the Studebaker is on my short list of the ugliest vehicles ever made, but that first car did expand my horizons, since now we could travel farther and visit other churches. Visits to other congregations were pretty much the extent of our exploration of the wider world.

As time passed, riding in the old Studebaker became dangerous. Sometimes the right rear door popped open if a passenger was forgetful enough to lean against it. After my sister fell out of the car one day on our way to church, Dad realized the old car had to go.

At the car dealer's lot, a 1956 Pontiac captivated my dad. A thing of beauty, it gleamed with shining chrome; Chief Pontiac himself perched on the front hood. There was a problem, though. Our church strictly forbade two colors on our cars. This shiny Pontiac would be labeled a sinmobile. After discussing this dilemma with the car salesman, Dad agreed to a compromise; the price was adjusted so that we could afford to repaint the car.

We drove home in bliss, swathed in yellow and chrome, with the magic sounds of the radio drifting from the dashboard. Of course, the church would not permit a radio, so we would have to remove the antenna with a hacksaw. Somehow I convinced my dad to delay that amputation for a few days, and I would sneak into the garage to enjoy stolen moments of the wonder of radio. This was just one of the enticements to adventure that would beset me as I lived out years of convoluted attempts to stay on the straight and narrow way. Dad soon discovered my malfeasance, and I watched with sadness as the hacksaw removed my connection to the outside world.

We waited for the body shop to schedule the paint job, and I took great joy in the delay. I rode up front whenever I could, hoping all my friends would see me in this beautiful vehicle. But my dad parked it behind the church on Sundays, attempting to hide it from judgmental eyes. On the day the yellow chariot was painted, it left our house a thing of beauty but returned in the evening a dark blue version of its former glorious self.

Maybe the church was right. That two-toned car did have me feeling mighty proud—and wasn't pride a sin?

One day I made an exhilarating discovery. It was Saturday, our routine car-washing day. I brought out the green hose and laid it on the ground, waiting for the sunshine to make the vinyl pliable enough to unroll. Then I climbed into the car and fiddled with the radio controls. Of course there was only static; even so, I still enjoyed pressing the buttons and moving back and forth across the dial. Later, as I washed the front fender, I heard a voice coming from inside the car. I had inadvertently rested my hand on the sad little nub that was all that remained of the radio antenna. When I pulled my hand away, the sound of the radio died. I touched the nub again, and the voice came from the dashboard. I was a human antenna. Never has there been an inventor more thrilled with his discovery.

After several hours of forbidden entertainment, I smugly joined my family at lunch with no intention of revealing my discovery. But it wasn't long afterward that Dad came into the house, bewildered. The car wouldn't start. Dead battery, he thought. Oops. I knew the cause, but I would not be confessing. Instead, I noted that if my secret entertainment was to continue, I would have to start the engine occasionally to keep that battery charged.

Of course, it's impossible to keep secrets of this magnitude for very long. I couldn't resist passing on my knowledge to friends at church, and they also became human antennae and were thus exposed to evil worldly influences like Cleveland Indians baseball, sports shows, mind-corroding country music, and seductive beer jingles.

Unfortunately, one of us Mennonite Marconis was eventually busted, and the preachers discovered our secret. A new edict came forth: whenever a car was purchased, the entire radio must be removed. Cars in the church parking lot now sported gaping holes in the dash.

The new policy came too late—we had been exposed to the influences of the world. There was no return to our pre-radio innocence. I was further modernized when a cousin in great emotional distress offered to sell me his eight-transistor AM/FM radio. Evidently the preaching had convinced him of his sinfulness, and under deep conviction he offered me the offending device for six dollars.

This was even better than secret sin in the Pontiac. Best of all, I was now mobile. In the woods, behind the barn, even climbing trees—I was never without my connection to the outside world. Yes, I confess: I listened to every Indians game and knew all the country music tunes. On Friday and Saturday nights, I would hide downstairs in the fruit cellar to listen to the Grand Ole Opry from Nashville.

But the constant sermonizing against the wiles of the devil eventually prodded me into compliance, and I decided it was time to end my disobedience. My rehabilitated conscience contrived a plan to destroy the evil thing.

My father, now a bona fide Pontiac man, had traded the '56 for a newer, bigger '59. I was allowed to drive the car on our property. I decided to crush the tempting radio by backing over it with the Pontiac. After one farewell twirl through the dial, I laid the offensive thing in the gravel behind the rear wheel and proceeded to back over it. For good measure, I drove forward and then backed over the defenseless little radio again. The poor thing was now completely smashed. I picked it up, and the 9-volt battery dangled by two wires connecting it to the transistor board. The white plastic body was completely destroyed, but the guts of the radio still clung together, tenaciously grasping at survival. On a whim, I flipped the on button, and to my surprise the radio came to life. "It's a miracle!" I yelped. "God must not hate this radio after all."

That was the sign I needed. The radio had survived the crushing weight of a monster '59 Pontiac, and thus it must not be wrong for me to keep it. So I did. I carried the wounded thing in a little box to keep all the parts together.

Besides worldly cars and poison-spewing radios, there were many other insidious evils out to destroy us. We heard constant warnings from the pulpit. Television, for example, was moving into more liberal Mennonite churches but was strictly forbidden in our congregation. Our minister heard of a Mennonite family that actually had a TV in their basement. He predicted it would just be a matter of time until that television climbed those basement steps and settled into the living room. "Sin is creeping in," was his constant lament. He was right, of course, and by some mysterious power that TV did eventually climb those stairs. Those preachers were right just often enough that I wondered if maybe they actually did have a special spiritual insight.

Another pulpit prophecy concerned head coverings and women's hairstyles. Our church taught that outward appearance was to set us apart from the world, but I observed that the ladies carried the burden of this nonconformity requirement. The men were hardly discernible from their worldly neighbors, but the women were obedient from head to toe, to the point of wrapping themselves like mummies. The ladies may have looked happy, but I always thought their hair was combed and bobby-pinned so tightly that their smiles were stretched into place. And over this tightly bound coiffure, every woman was required to wear a head covering.

Once again, the liberal Mennonites in the community proved the prophetic foresight of my preacher. He predicted that when women were allowed to wear their hair down, in no time the hair would be cut and head coverings would get smaller and smaller. What he failed to see was that coverings would disappear altogether in many Mennonite churches. Today when you visit Amish Country, you'll witness an amalgamation of religious headgear of all shapes and sizes.

As I matured, I began questioning the teachings of the church. For example, the preacher talked often about inviting Jesus into our hearts. I was a literal thinker and just could not grasp such a concept. Would He bring a moving van and set up residence in my physical heart? I recalled a young man in our church who went to the altar to receive Jesus into his heart almost every time an altar call was made. What had happened to Jesus? Was it so easy to lose Jesus that you had to ask Him repeatedly to return to His heart-home?

And I was troubled by a new fear. Preachers talked about the second coming of Jesus. Even when I thought I finally understood the concept of Christianity, I was not quite ready to accept it and live it. Now I was hearing that Jesus could return the second time before I had even accepted Him the first time.

One night when I was sixteen, I drove alone to church. (Dad was generous with the car, as long as my destination was church.) A visiting minister from Nebraska was holding a series of revival meetings, and he was a real pulpit-pounder. That memorable night, my body was in the pew, but my mind managed to escape and went roaming around the outside world. A sharp rapping on the podium brought mind back to body at once. That preacher had knuckles of steel. I have never heard such a riveting sound as those knuckles rapping on the wooden podium. Then, grasping both sides of the podium, he leaned forward and nearly shouted, "Jesus is coming soon! Get ready! He may come back tonight!"

That preacher and his rapping knuckles managed to scare several of my friends into the kingdom, but I held out. As I drove home later, gripping the wheel with both hands, I looked nervously up into the night sky, expecting Jesus to burst through at any moment. I was scared. I begged Him not to come back just yet. I still wanted to experience a number of things, and I doubted that Jesus would want to be anywhere near my heart while I was testing life.

That first rainy, sleepless night on the AT, I reflected on the restrictions I still felt on my path to everlasting life. I had left my parents' church and married a "liberal" Mennonite girl, who did indeed cut her hair and phase out her head covering. I owned a television and bought any kind of car I could afford. I went to Cleveland Indians games and even movies. I embraced Christianity in a form different from the conservative church's. Yet still I felt precarious, on that balance beam, fearful of any misstep.

I had a vague expectation that the Appalachian Trail might lead me through experiences that would push out the tight boundaries of my life. In the early hours of the morning, I made my resolution. On this trek, I would submerge myself in the traditions and life of the trail, and openly meet new thoughts and ideas.

And I would leave behind my lifelong traveling companion, Guilt.

5

My New Life

A thud brought me out of fitful sleep. Marathon Man had deposited my food bag outside my tent. I was not ready to get up; even though I had slept little, my aching body was cozy and warm in the sleeping bag, and I could still hear rain bouncing off the tent cover.

Reluctantly, I unzipped the tent and stuck my head out to greet my second day on the trail. Rain and mist swirled through the small clearing. I moved my food bag into the tent and retreated again into the warmth of my sleeping bag. I knew the trail saying, "No rain, no Maine," but my daydreams had painted a trail warmed with sunshine. I was not mentally prepared to hike in rain at the outset of my journey.

Voices broke the silence of the wet morning. Marathon Man and Lion King were collapsing their tents. Reluctantly, I shed the warm comfort of my sleeping bag and slipped into my rain gear.

After all those trial packings and unpackings as I prepared for the trail, I had decided to stow my tent at the bottom of my backpack. So this morning I stashed all my other belongings beside a tree, exposed to the rain, and as quickly as possible collapsed and folded Big Agnes, wiping off most of the water with a chamois cloth. Even so, I was still carrying an extra pound or two of moisture when I finally hoisted the full pack.

Lion King also had a restless night; his tent had not sealed properly and his sleeping bag was now waterlogged. "Happy April Fools' Day," I mumbled to myself. It was the first day of April, and only a fool would have quit a good job to hike out here in this rain.

Several climbs lay ahead of us that morning, but none appeared too difficult. Sassafras and Justus Mountains were both in the 3,300 foot elevation range. The trail would stay at an elevation of 2,500 to 3,700 feet until the following day, when towering Blood Mountain awaited us.

Although the trail was not muddy, the rain had created slippery conditions and I moved cautiously. Wet leaves and slick rocks waited everywhere to trip me up. In all my previous hikes in Zion and the Grand Canyon, I had never used hiking poles. Fortunately, my outfitting advisor had convinced me hiking poles were essential. The morning hike was barely under way, and the poles had already saved me from several tumbles; I silently thanked him for his advice.

On the path to Maine, the Appalachian Trail passes through six national parks and eight national forests. We were hiking through the first of the forests today, the Chattahoochee National Forest.

We tapped Lion King, the eldest in our group, as our leader. At seventy, he was the second-oldest hiker I'd encounter on my hike. He was also in incredible shape, and Marathon Man and I had to hustle to keep up with him.

Lion King had set his sights on Maine, and I wondered why he was on the trail. His answer was one I would hear numerous times during my hike. "My wife passed away recently, and I'm trying to find peace and healing." Although this man owned several homes in Hawaii and was quite wealthy, his possessions and money mattered little now. In search of contentment, he had traveled across America, living out of his car. Finally the call of the trail brought him here, where he sought the healing that was so elusive. He carried a palpable sadness and loneliness, and I felt a kinship to his sorrow. His story was a reminder that the message I carried held universal truth. We spend a lifetime working hard to accumulate homes and possessions that we believe are vital for comfort and security, only to discover those material accumulations are quite meaningless in our darkest hour of sadness and need.

Another thing made us kindred spirits—Lion King had owned several restaurants, and so we both understood the demands of the business and knew the personal price paid for such a career. We chuckled over stories and commiserated over frustrations.

By noon we arrived at Gooch Mountain Shelter. Over 250 of these primitive structures are scattered at intervals along the trail. My small thru-hiker's handbook showed each shelter's location, many fairly close to the AT, some up to half a mile off the trail. Most are three-sided structures with a lean-to roof and an open front. When possible, the shelters were constructed near a spring or other water source and also offered the small luxury of a nearby privy. This early in the hiking season, the shelters would fill up early in the afternoon, especially on rainy days.

My guidebook said the Gooch Shelter was two hundred yards from the trail, with a spring nearby. Ready for a break, we settled on Gooch as a lunch stop. Just a short distance down a side trail, we found the small spring; fresh water bubbled out from beneath a rock formation. This part of Georgia had been very dry the past winter, and hikers were concerned about the availability of water. However, recent rains had filled every spring and small brook, and we never suffered lack of water in Georgia.

One of the greatest pleasures on the trail is that first drink of cold, filtered spring water. When you've hiked for hours, body aching and throat parched, nothing is better than the splash of that fresh water as you tip your bottle upward and coolness flows down your dry throat and refreshes both body and spirit.

Back at the shelter, I rummaged through my food bag for lunch. Breakfast had been one Pop-Tart. I'd never eaten a Pop-Tart before, but the picture on the wrapper had looked promising. It was not nearly as good as I had imagined.

A thru-hiker will burn anywhere from 5,000 to 7,000 calories a day, requiring intake of several pounds of food. My pre-hike calculations led me to believe that I could do with considerably fewer calories, since I was carrying those extra twenty pounds. Those calculations were in serious error, and I needed to adjust my calorie intake plan quickly.

While we relaxed on the shelter floor, a newcomer appeared. He had started his hike a day before ours, hiking the eight-mile approach trail. The newcomer introduced himself as hailing from Michigan, but I thought something about his speech pattern suggested that Michigan was not his original home. As we prepared to leave, he asked to join our group; none of us objected, so we now numbered four.

Solo or partner? It's a key decision when planning a long-distance hike. There is no "best" way; each choice has advantages. Partnering with another hiker gives the obvious benefit of shared common items, such as tents and cooking equipment. That translates into less weight each hiker must carry. A hiking partner can ease the loneliness that lies in wait along the trail. But unless you choose a partner wisely, your partnership may not survive the trials and tribulations of a thru-hike. Suppose, for example, you wish to hike twenty miles in one day, but your partner is finished at ten?

Going solo can cause anxiety, but you'll likely encounter fellow hikers with whom you are comfortable, and you'll hike stretches together simply because the company is enjoyable. Many different personalities and characters walk the trail, everyone with a unique hiking style. You'll welcome the company of some hikers; others will drive you crazy.

There are a few strategies to politely separate yourself from a hiker who makes you uncomfortable. One ploy is to drop back and hike so slowly that your unchosen partner initiates the separation himself, out of the frustration of waiting for you. Or, at the end of the day, when your unwanted companion is dead tired and has his tent already set up, kick into a jumping jack routine and declare that you're not tired and are going to hike several more miles. If you're close to town and need to resupply, the strategy might be to take a zero day. (A zero day on the trail is when a hiker does just that—zero miles.) That will put some distance between you and the offensive hiker. Sadly, a true hanger-on will probably also decide to take a zero with you. You may have to resort to honesty to gain your freedom, but sometimes even blunt truth goes unheeded. In such an extreme instance, you'll have to bring out the ultimate weapon: a crazed look (practice this look in advance) will cross your face, and you'll tell him, brokenly, that the many years spent in solitary confinement in prison turned you into a loner, unable to interact acceptably with other humans. You'll be free of your hanger-on. You'll also likely be free of *any* future personal interaction—the trail grapevine works its magic quickly.

I felt myself fortunate; I hiked with many different partners and never took offense if anyone hiked away from me. Although I had a definite mission and a goal to achieve, I also believed I could find joy in each mile of the journey; the many interesting personalities I encountered only added pleasure to my trek.

Our newcomer was approximately my age. His trail name was Sailor. "I've enjoyed sailing ever since I was a boy on Cape Cod," he said. That explained the accent. It also took me back many years to several wonderful days Mary and I had spent exploring the coastline of Cape Cod, all the way to Provincetown at the very tip. Meeting Sailor and listening to that accent awakened many precious memories from a time long ago, when life seemed uncomplicated.

Sailor and I would hike together for the next 740 miles. I have no idea of his social status or if he was wealthy or broke. Social status does not matter in the woods and mountains. The trail is a great equalizer. We were all simply thru-hikers with a single goal: reach the summit of Mt. Katahdin, two thousand miles away. And although I knew nothing about

Sailor's bank account, I do know he was the richest man I met on the trail. Those riches were not dollars, but precious experiences on the AT with his family. Several times on his thru-hike, Sailor was met by his two sons who both hiked with him for extended periods. His wife hiked through New York with him. Those gifts of the trail cannot be measured in dollars.

At Woody Gap the trail brought us into a clearing within sight of Georgia Rt. 60 and easy access to the towns of Suches and Dahlonega. For any hiker ready to throw in the towel and give up the trail, this is the first good chance to escape.

Resting on boulders along a parking area, we took a short break, unaware that here we would meet our first trail magic. Trail magic is an unexpected gift of food or drink from strangers, and comes at some of the most unlikely times and locations. Trudging along in the woods, hikers suddenly come upon a large container full of drinks, candy bars, or even beer. In areas without a water supply, a kind person will leave several gallons of water. One morning, in the middle of the woods, we found pastries and a large thermos of hot coffee. Often trail magic is the work of former hikers who understand how wonderful and appreciated these treats can be. Many times a journal accompanies the gift, explaining who has left the magic and the reason for the kindness. Hikers sign the journal with their thanks and names, and in turn many of the Good Samaritans follow the hikers in logs kept on the Trail Journals website.

Hikers have another way of snagging treats, a far cry from trail magic. This is the trail practice of yogi-ing. It refers to a hiker's attempt to approach a person with food and make a pathetic attempt to get food without begging. This should only be done as an act of desperation, although in some cases a hiker will yogi only to see if he can rise to the challenge of getting someone to hand over some food. A fine line separates subtlety and stupidity, and sadly, some hikers cross that line.

While we rested, a woman and her daughter approached and asked if we were thru-hikers. "We intend to thru-hike, but we've only walked twenty miles so far," one of us replied. They asked if we wanted cold beverages. Coca-Cola is my favorite soft drink; I craved it many days on the trail. Sure enough, she had a Coke. My first trail magic consisted of a cold Coke and a banana.

Refreshed, we crossed the parking area and started the one-mile climb up Big Cedar Mountain. Nearing the top, we stopped at Preaching Rock, a rock formation that gave us our first panoramic view of the area we were hiking.

By the middle of the afternoon the rain finally stopped, and hiking conditions and our spirits both improved considerably. Spring had not yet reached this elevation, and with no leaves anywhere we were afforded great views of our surroundings. We arrived at Miller Gap just as dusk settled in. A strong spring flowed nearby, so we set up our tents in a small clearing adjacent to the trail. We had hiked thirteen miles that day and were now twenty-three miles closer to our goal.

After my delicious meal of rehydrated Spanish rice and beans, I began the nightly ritual of hanging our food bags with a search for a suitable limb to hold our cache. Out of the thousands of trees that surrounded us, the best candidate was a limb hanging directly over the AT itself. The branch was not large, but it was supple enough that it did not break when the weight of four food bags was suspended from it.

After a brief discussion about tomorrow's plans, the four of us headed to our respective abodes. My clothing and other gear were drying on a nearby bush. I brought everything into my tent and slipped my exhausted body into my sleeping bag. Every muscle in my body ached. If I could only sleep this night.

But I lay awake and relived my first two days on the trail. I was finally here, out in the woods, jobless, doing what I had dreamed about for so long. Several hours passed while I solved all of the restaurant's problems and then moved on to the world's problems. My body may have left my job, but my brain was still in business mode. Sometime around midnight, my mind admitted it was as exhausted as my body, and I drifted off to sleep.

A shrill screech close to my tent jerked me awake. For the next several hours, none of us slept as two owls shrieked incessantly. One screeched from one side of my tent, and seconds later the other replied from the other side. We had surround sound with owls. Yipping animal sounds came through the night too, but nothing reached the decibel level achieved by those owls.

I managed to doze off several times, only to be awakened at dawn by more loud hooting—this time, hooting laughter from Marathon Man and Lion King. I unzipped my tent and saw the joke. The branch holding our food bags had betrayed us during the night. Apparently not as strong as we thought, it had slowly given way to the weight, and now our food was at eye level, drooping low over the trail itself, inviting any passing bear to partake. Unwilling to have our sad attempt at food-hanging ridiculed by other hikers, Marathon Man and Lion King quickly brought down the bags. The scene would have provided good trail gossip for veteran hikers to share at shelters.

The day promised excitement; we'd be hiking out into civilization again. We planned to hike only eight miles to Neels Gap, where the Appalachian Trail passes through a building housing a hiker hostel and an outfitter known as Mountain Crossings. The building is known as the Walasi-Yi center, using a Cherokee word referring to a giant mythical frog that supposedly guards the gap on Blood Mountain. The thought of a shower and laundry at the hostel gave us enough courage, though, to face any mythical beast.

A larger obstacle than the frog was Blood Mountain itself. At 4,461 feet, this mountain is the highest elevation on the Georgia section of the AT. From our campsite, we had a five-mile hike to reach the summit, five miles that included numerous PUDS (the trail acronym for "pointless ups and downs").

Traversing the PUDS before Blood Mountain, we caught up with a Vietnam veteran lugging a pack weighing close to sixty pounds. Hiking uphill, he lagged far behind us, but on the downhill slopes the weight of his pack propelled him forward. He told us he was contemplating a thru-hike but was not yet certain of his plans. Considering the weight he carried and his seeming lack of purpose, I doubted his chance of success. Most hopeful thru-hikers are well aware of advice from Dan "Wingfoot" Bruce, respected hiker and former author of *The Thru-hiker's Handbook*, who cautions that your hike must be the most important thing in your life at the moment, or you probably won't finish. Whether my own motivation was wise or selfish was unclear to me, but I did know that nothing was more important to me at that time than finishing the trail to Maine.

As we neared the summit of Blood Mountain, we sometimes lost our focus on the white blazes. Instead, our eyes were constantly drawn to the incredible views in every direction.

At the Blood Mountain shelter, we dropped our packs and took a break. This structure is a two-room stone building erected in 1934 by the Civilian Conservation Corps. The mountain's history fascinated me. Its name supposedly dates back to the 1600s, when the Creek and the Cherokee Indians battled for control of the area and the mountain "ran red with blood." The name could also have been inspired by the colorful red lichens covering the rocks near the summit. I preferred the more peaceful explanation, but other names in the area also told violent tales, places like Slaughter Gap and Slaughter Trail.

We were on our 2.4-mile descent to Neels Gap when we met hikers with good news. On the patio at Mountain Crossings, a church group was grilling hamburgers for hikers. Could we be lucky enough to have trail magic on two consecutive days?

Mountain Crossings at Neels Gap sits directly across from U.S. Highway 19/129. Two images immediately caught my attention. The first was smoke billowing from the charcoal grill, promising food. The second was possibly the best business plan ever conceived: an outfitting store sitting—literally— on the Appalachian Trail. The AT passed right through the building.

What a perfect location for this business. Every year, two thousand hikers attempt to thru-hike this trail, many of them carrying too much weight or the wrong equipment. Almost all of these hikers become customers here, out of necessity. The store has everything a hiker could ever want, and they do know what hikers need. The staff will go through your backpack (at your request, of course), sort out all unnecessary weight, and ship it home. Although 20 percent of hikers stop here and give up dreams of a thru-hike, many other pilgrims find aid and encouragement that make it possible to continue.

But first, the aroma of grilled burgers drew us to the patio, where a local church group used a meal as an opportunity to share God's love with us hikers. They didn't need to preach a sermon; three cheeseburgers and a cold Coke spoke more to me than words ever could.

The Vietnam vet had joined us, and I suggested he take his pack to the staff at the outfitter and let them lighten his load. He was ready to do just that. Our little group also took advantage of the laundry, and then luxuriated in hot showers.

Lion King was feeling the effects of three days of hiking in the rain and trying to sleep in a wet tent and damp sleeping bag. He and Sailor decided to spend the night at a cabin nearby. Marathon Man and I debated the merits of sleeping in bunks at the hostel or hiking a few more miles and then camping for the night. The real question was whether we wanted to risk being kept awake by owls or by human snores. The owls won; we decided to move on to find a campsite along the trail. Lion King and Sailor would leave early in the morning in hopes of catching us the next day.

I checked on the Vietnam veteran. At the back of the store, he and a staff member had laid out everything from his backpack, sorting into "keep" and "send home" piles. The pile going home was larger than the pile to keep. He carried knives of all shapes and sizes and a collection of books that weighed almost as much as my pack. If I stayed close to him, his knives, and his library, I would never have to fear for my safety or worry about boredom.

Alas, he decided to stay at Mountain Crossings, possibly for several nights. I never saw him again, or heard whether or not he continued hiking. Perhaps he was using one of those distancing techniques; perhaps he had already found his peace and contentment after only thirty miles on the trail. Perhaps his heavy load had exhausted his determination.

The Appalachian Trail runs through the breezeway connecting the hostel and the store. Marathon Man and I walked through it and once again entered the woods.

We hiked for an hour and arrived at a clearing called Bull Gap. We set up camp, and in the course of the evening, other hikers joined us. There were ten of us, old and young, sitting on logs around the fire, eating, comparing equipment, talking about our hiking goals and dreams. It had not rained for hours, I was dry, and my clothes were clean. The sun set over Bull Gap, and my body begged for rest. Contentment soaked through my spirit as I left the circle around the fire and strolled to my tent; the trail was becoming my home. I climbed into my sleeping bag and willed the owls to screech quietly.

6

A Cold, Rainy, Miserable Mess

Out of sheer exhaustion, I slept most of that night. The hoot birds woke me several times, but they were not sitting on every corner of my tent this time; they screeched their conversation somewhere off in the distance. Marathon Man and I were the first out of camp, a routine we continued throughout our days of hiking together. In accounting terms, we were LIFOs. Last In, First Out was a hiking style that suited us both.

We walked into a wild battle between man and the elements. It was not a good day in the woods.

Heavy morning fog was our mildest adversary. As we climbed the highest elevation of the day, Levelland Mountain at 3,942 feet, high winds brought rain that changed to stinging sleet. For the next ten miles, we struggled against battering winds and rain mixed with ice. We were blown over several other mountains, finding brief respite only in the gaps between.

We crossed mountains Cowrock, Wildcat, and Poor, and cut through gaps Tesnatee, Wide, and Low. Visibility was at best only fifty feet; we saw the trail underfoot but could only assume we had indeed climbed those mountains and threaded the gaps.

There were no morning breaks. Stopping would only allow cold and misery to overtake us. Shortly after noon, we reached Low Gap Shelter and gratefully stopped for a rest, a snack, and a chance to filter more water. The shelter protected us from the rain and sleet, but the howling wind blew cold blasts through the front opening, extinguishing any hope of warmth.

The wind also blew in Sailor and Lion King. All of us were weary of the battle, so we agreed to hike just a few more hours and then set up camp and take refuge for the night. Before leaving the shelter, I put on every article of clothing in my bag, hoping for more insulation.

We climbed no more big mountains in the afternoon, but several more hours of wind, rain, and sleet exhausted us more than any climb. At five o'clock, we stumbled into a small clearing near Red Clay Gap and set up camp in record time. By six, we were all in for the night. On a day when most intelligent people stayed inside, we had covered fifteen difficult miles.

I peeled off layers of wet clothes and welcomed the warmth of my sleeping bag. My tent refuge was comforting; I was dry and safe from the storm raging outside. And the presence of my three fellow hikers allayed the fears that surely would have prowled through my night if I had been alone.

The rain pounded most of the night, but I had the best rest since taking to the trail, probably because the night was so miserable that even the owls stayed indoors. Lion King was not so fortunate and spent another night fighting the elements trying to invade his tent. He was also suffering from a worsening cold.

The morning brought more rain, with no letup in sight. Our first substantial climb was 4,025 feet over Blue Mountain, followed by a 1.4-mile downhill slide to Unicoi Gap. The trail was now a wet and slick obstacle course, with every rock and root the enemy. Staying upright was a challenge, and my hiking poles saved me countless times when I slipped on wet leaves. Marathon Man hiked without poles, and although he did an incredible balancing act, nature often won and a loud thump announced another wipeout.

We reached Unicoi Gap without breaking any bones. Here the trail crossed Georgia Rt. 75; the town of Hiawassee was eleven miles west. Lion King decided that he must get off the trail and buy new equipment if he had any hope of continuing his hike. He planned to hitchhike to Hiawassee, get a motel room and take time to recover from his cold, and then find a ride back to Neels Gap to buy a better tent and backpack. We could either join him or move on without him.

Apparently Sailor, Marathon Man, and I had not yet had enough misery. We opted to continue on, confident that Lion King would catch up with us soon. But we never saw him again. Several days later, a hiker passed us and in conversation told us about the seventy-year-old he had encountered in Hiawassee. They had met in town and split the cost of a motel room. He reported that Lion King had new equipment but was staying in town a little longer to wait out the rain. Unfortunately, 2008 was one of the wettest years in Appalachian Trail history, so, for all I know, my friend may still be in the motel in Hiawassee, waiting for the rain to stop.

I had enjoyed my time with Lion King; we shared conversations about life and death and missing our spouses. I can only wish for him the peace and healing I found on my journey north.

Our group was now reduced to three. Marathon Man, our new leader, was sixty-three and defied every description of a hiker. He hiked without poles, had a pack made in 1969, and traveled in blue jeans. He was oblivious to modern technology, but he was in great shape, and that seemed to compensate for everything else. Seventy marathons had prepared Marathon Man for this rigorous hike; he had finished one just before starting the AT. Sailor had marathon background too; he had speedwalked the Chicago marathon. Sailor became our anchor man. I trudged in the middle.

Both of them had been Boy Scouts too, so they knew how to tie those knots to hang our bear bags. The only knot I could tie was in my shoes, since my boyhood church had frowned on joining such worldly groups as the Scouts or 4-H clubs. There I was, Apostle, hiking between two adult Boy Scouts; me, an out-of-shape restaurant manager who couldn't tie knots, being pushed and pulled over these mountains by a marathon runner and a speedwalker. I was well aware that any time they chose, the other two could hike away and leave me to my own pathetic camping skills. But they allowed me to hang around, and because of their patience and my stubbornness, I ended up covering miles much faster than I thought possible.

We climbed high and then slid downward, climbed and slid, all day. After Blue Mountain, Rocky Mountain was a 1.3-mile climb followed by a 1.2-mile descent to Indian Grave

Gap. We climbed and slid over several lesser obstacles and then faced Tray Mountain and a 2.5-mile uphill struggle to the highest elevation of our day. Shortly before we reached the summit, we came upon a wonderful sight. A local Boy Scout troop had parked a small camper beside the trail and offered hot chicken noodle soup and lemonade to hikers. But there were no Boy Scouts in sight. We couldn't blame them, in this horrible weather. We served ourselves and took stock of our day.

It was early afternoon and we had slipped, staggered, and stumbled close to ten miles. Should we set up our tents and avoid more punishment, or keep fighting the wind and rain to make more miles? Seven more miles would bring us to Deep Gap Shelter. The name itself appealed to us; we envisioned a refuge deep between the hills where the wind could not reach us. It seemed like the right choice, and we were fortified by the chicken soup.

We crossed a three-mile ridge crest called the Swag of the Blue Ridge. Under normal conditions, this would have been an easy walk, with little elevation gain or loss. That day, we were battered by strong winds and blowing rain as we struggled across the ridge. After that, Kelly Knob almost stopped me. At 4,275 feet, the climb was so steep and slippery that at times I thought I could go no farther. Mercifully, that was the last mountain of the day. We fell into Deep Gap Shelter around six o'clock.

In ten hours of nasty weather, we had hiked seventeen miles. We were either true hikers or we were idiots. I had never been this exhausted or gasped and wheezed so much in my life as I did in my climbs that day.

Somewhere on the trail, perhaps on that wet and slippery day, I started a habit that stayed with me all the way to Mt. Katahdin. When I slipped or stumbled, but recovered without falling or twisting my ankle or breaking a limb, I heard myself say aloud, "Thank You, God" or "Thank You, Jesus." That day, I was probably thanking the Good Lord all day long.

All my life I had been taught it was possible to communicate with God. But was that reality? Did He have a hand in what was going on in this world? Where was He while Mary suffered through those years of cancer and then died? Was there a reason God took her away from me, or did it "just happen"?

Of course I prayed—don't most people pray in some way, on some level? And yes, I truly believed that God had said He would be with me on this trail, but . . . I wanted more. I needed to know if God was who He said He was. *Are You in control of events, God, or do things on this earth just happen randomly?* I wanted to know. If it was true that humans could communicate with the deity, then I determined to talk with God on this hike as if He were trudging along beside me.

Deep Gap Shelter is a relatively new structure and has four walls instead of three, with an opening about five feet wide in the front wall. This meant no wind or rain would blow in during the night. We could spend the night within the protection of a roof and four walls, rather than fight the wind to set up tents in the rain. I anticipated the new experience. *This will be great*, I thought, *my first night in a shelter.*

I picked a spot in the corner farthest from the front opening and emptied my backpack. Before shedding my rain gear,

I made one final trip out into the rain to filter several liters of water. Back inside, I stripped down to my Patagonia long johns. In several minutes, I had a pouch of cooked spaghetti ready to eat, but was so exhausted I didn't have much of an appetite. I ate only half, and gave the other half to a grateful hiker across the floor.

Other hikers had arrived; it would be a full house tonight. Several of the men were section hikers with a church group. I met many section hikers on my way to Maine. Some come back year after year, each year hiking a different section of the AT. A few section hikers actually cover the entire trail in this way. Some, like the men's church group at Deep Gap Shelter that night, are only out for a few days to enjoy nature and hiking camaraderie. Ten of us filled the lower floor and another four hikers took the upper loft several feet above me. It was seven o'clock and the start of one of the worst nights of my life.

I was uncomfortable the minute I wiggled into my sleeping bag. My Patagonia underwear was still moist from my perspiring on the difficult climbs of the day. None of my other clothing was dry, so I squirmed out of the damp underwear and now lay in my sleeping bag naked as the day I was born. Some folks may prefer to sleep this way, but not me; it was most uncomfortable.

I could not ignore another irritation. During my shower at Neels Gap, I had felt a stinging sensation in the groin area when water hit my skin. Now my skin was on fire. I had read about hikers' problems with chafing, but never imagined how severe this problem can be. Chafing, caused by clothing rubbing against sweaty skin, is a painful fact of the trail; most long-distance hikers, both male and female, will have to contend with it. I met hikers who actually had to leave the trail for days because they were suffering so much.

Chafing can be prevented or minimized by wearing tight-fitting clothes and applying a cream before hiking. Some men wear a kilt so air can then move freely through the area in question. I do grudgingly admire an outdoorsman who is willing to wear a skirt to avoid this pain.

If you can't prevent chafing by cream or kilt, the only balm for the itchy pain is to dry the area and keep it dry. I came up with a plan to dry my medical emergency. For the next hour, I pushed up my sleeping bag with both legs and both arms, then released it—up, down, up, down, up, down. And it worked. Like a giant bellows, I created enough air movement to dry out the chafed area.

Alas, the air movement also brought to the surface all the aromas trapped in the heavy sleeping bag: body odors and the smell of wet feathers from the moist down filling. Lying on the floor in the corner of a crowded shelter, enveloped in repulsive stink, I admitted it to myself: for the first time, I regretted quitting my job in exchange for this misery. In the loft, I heard Sailor echo my own thoughts, lamenting to someone that this hike was not what he had signed up for. He thought he was taking a spring hike; he never expected this cold, rainy, miserable mess.

For several hours, I tried to sleep with no success. I was so tired I could not relax. I couldn't get comfortable on the hard floor. Sleep was not coming anytime soon. My watch said it was only eleven o'clock. Four miserable hours in this stinking bag and sleep was no closer.

Just try to shut down your mind, I told myself. *You have to get some rest.*

But I'm naked and stinking and uncomfortable, complained another part of my brain.

My conversation with myself was interrupted by a horrible sound nearby. "Whaaaaa . . . flump . . . whaaaaa . . . flump." The sound was coming from a church hiker. The man sounded like he was dying, giving out a horrible, guttural wheezing. How could he sleep through it? Soon the man beside him joined in and chainsawed through the night. Occasionally the first snorer gasped in mid-rattle and I thought maybe he had indeed passed away, but then "whaaaaa . . . flump," and the song started again. From the upstairs loft, a third voice joined the choir, a high-pitched, tenor snore. Sleep was impossible.

A persistent cough peppered the snore chorus. One hiker coughed for thirty minutes, then thought to remedy his condition by standing in the doorway for a smoke. The smoke was not as irritating as expected, since it helped mask another aroma that now wafted through the crowded room.

In hospitable brilliance, the leader of the church group had prepared a large pot of Western chili bean soup, and the group had shared it with the rest of the hikers. I had thought the night could not possibly get worse, but it did. The natural gas production began.

Nearly every sound a human body could make emanated from Deep Gap Shelter that night, and there was nothing I could do except wait out this night of misery and plan an escape at the first light of day. My journal entry the next day noted: "I would have welcomed a bear eating me."

At seven in the morning, we had enough visibility to gather our things and hike out into fresh air—and more rain. Yesterday, I would never have imagined that being out in the downpour once again would be such a relief.

We set out in anticipation of the next highway crossing the trail. At Dicks Creek Gap, the AT intersects with U.S. 76, and our guidebook showed a famed hostel just down the road. Everyone on the trail spoke highly of the Blueberry Patch, a Christian ministry run by Gary and Lennie Poteat. We desperately needed time to dry our gear.

My shoes were soaked. The choice of hiking shoes is one of the most important decisions a thru-hiker makes. At one time, almost everyone wore some form of hiking boot. This is no longer true. Today, many hikers wear a lightweight hiking shoe. I had chosen New Balance 950 GORE-TEX shoes. The GORE-TEX is supposedly waterproof, but most thru-hikers find it necessary to stomp through places that will soak any shoe. The GORE-TEX shoes stay dry longer than most, but when they get wet they also take longer to dry. Many hikers I met had problems with shoes; one went through five pair. I used two pair; the first pair survived until we reached Harpers Ferry, where I then switched to the other shoes. The second pair was pretty much destroyed in New Hampshire and Maine, when monsoon season turned my last four hundred miles into a muddy quagmire.

Before we reached Dicks Creek Gap, we crossed Powell Mountain, where the elevation allowed my cell phone signal to reach Blueberry Patch hostel. I made reservations and arrangements to be picked up at a road crossing.

In several hours, we were at the hostel, drying out. While we took hot showers, Lennie did our laundry. I noticed an odd contraption with two upside-down legs and protruding feet. A shoe dryer! I cannot describe how good it felt to have warm, clean clothes and dry shoes.

In a short time, we had moved from the outhouse to the penthouse. This happened many times on my hike. When I was discouraged and miserable, a kind deed came around the corner to lift my spirits. The Blueberry Patch folks don't beat anyone over the head with Scripture or theology. Gary and Lennie just live their belief, and their living speaks loud and clear.

The next day, we'd leave Georgia and enter North Carolina. I had hiked six days and sixty-eight miles. Five and a half of those days we had hiked in rain. But for now, I was safe and dry at the Blueberry Patch.

Gary even allowed me use of his car that afternoon. I took a group of hikers to Daniel's Steakhouse in Hiawassee, where we indulged in the first AYCE buffet of our hike. AYCE is the trail acronym for "all you can eat," and did we ever eat! I discovered that on the trail I could eat any time and any amount I wanted and never gain weight.

I spent the night in the hostel bunkhouse in conditions I previously would have considered primitive. Now I thought my accommodations luxurious, and I fell into a good night's rest.

An eight o'clock bell announced breakfast at the main house, a feast of pancakes, sausage, and eggs. Oh, boy, this day was starting out right.

And could it be possible? The rain had stopped.

Before leaving, I took a quick look through the hiker box. Every hostel has one of these treasure boxes. Hikers put extra or unwanted food, gear, books—anything you can imagine—into a community box. I met one man who outfitted himself with whatever he found there, living on the trail from one hiker box to the next.

Reluctantly, we took leave of the Blueberry Patch and were driven back to the trailhead at Dicks Creek Gap. Several big climbs awaited us that day, but we also knew we would leave Georgia and move into our next state. Nine miles later, we spotted a small metal sign on a tree, telling us we were at the Georgia-North Carolina state line. One state down, thirteen to go.

In the Nantahala National Forest at Bly Gap, a gnarled oak tree welcomed us to North Carolina. The twisted tree trunk appears to recline, branches reaching upward as if begging for help, in a pose so unusual that it is a much-photographed landmark on the AT. We lay on our backs by the tree and took a break, celebrating entry into our second state.

Toward evening, we passed a trail intersecting the AT called the Chunky Gal Trail, which led off to Chunky Gal Mountain. The Chunky Gal is a Cherokee legend, supposedly a rotund young maiden who left her disapproving family to follow her lover through these mountains. If the story is true, she may have started her journey as Chunky Gal but she surely must have lost her plumpness on the steep slopes.

Our first day in North Carolina ended in the woods close to Forest Road 71. It had been a good day. No rain, and we had finished Georgia. Things were looking better, and we congratulated ourselves on surviving one week on the trail. We went to bed early, knowing that big climbs the next day would demand all the energy we could muster.

Standing Indian Mountain glared at us from an elevation of 5,498 feet. We conquered it and then moved briskly over lesser mountains and gaps. Albert Mountain, though, forced us to stop and consider our choices.

The climb to the summit of Albert Mountain is rocky and strenuous. A blue-blazed trail skirts around the mountain, eliminating difficult rock climbs. Blue blazes frequently mark other trails off the AT, and they are usually easier routes. However, taking a blue-blazed trail means missing part of the Appalachian Trail. We decided to go up and over Albert Mountain.

Up to this point, I had not made a conscious decision to hike as a purist. A purist is a hiker who passes every white blaze on the Appalachian Trail. Individual interpretations assign different levels of purity. I know this sounds silly, but with so many eccentric people on a small path for 2,176 miles, some measure of silliness will always surface. I believed this was a once-in-a-lifetime opportunity; and so, when faced with blue blazes, my own stubborn standards demanded that I hike as a purist. My interpretation of *purist* became this: pass every white blaze with my full pack, with no slackpacking.

Some hikers choose to slackpack when they want credit for hiking the miles but do not want to carry full packs over difficult terrain. At many hostels, hikers ask someone to drive them ahead fifteen or twenty miles and then hike back to the hostel carrying only a light daypack. Obviously, carrying less weight means you can cover more miles. This also gives a hiker just a little more time at the hostel, which is almost always an enjoyable and sociable place. I was separated from several likable hiking partners because of their slackpacking habits.

For the next hour, we scrambled up a steep rocky slope, grabbing roots to pull ourselves upward. The almost-vertical ascent would have been a strenuous climb without a backpack,

Above, the first white blaze; *below*, trail sign; *top right*, entering the Great Smokies; *center right*, cold day in the Smokies; *bottom right*, stile crossing

but that extra thirty-five pounds hanging on my back made this the most difficult climb I had experienced. When we arrived at last at the summit, a spectacular view spread before us. We climbed a fire tower to look back at the mountains we had already crossed and forward at what lay ahead.

Much of the trail was lined with rhododendron bushes; at many places we walked through a tunnel of green. I could imagine how beautiful this would be later in the spring when all those bushes burst into flower. I camped that night under a large tree, surrounded by a wall of rhododendron bushes.

The next morning, we hiked one mile and then celebrated a landmark: one hundred miles! If I did this twenty-one more times, I could go home.

Studying my thru-hiker's handbook, I realized we were only nine miles from Winding Stair Gap. There, a state road crossing the AT would take us ten miles east to Franklin, North Carolina. Franklin was known as a hikers' town, mostly through the efforts of Ron Haven. This was a side trip we all wanted to make.

Ron Haven runs several motels in Franklin, and his short yellow bus shuttles hikers between the Appalachian Trail and the town several times a day. Haven's knowledge and services are a valuable resource for AT hikers. His motels offer great rates, and his yellow bus taxis hikers around town to the outfitter, the grocery, or the post office. Hikers take this opportunity to resupply or get a night's rest in a motel.

Early in the day, I found a spot with cell service and called Haven's Budget Inn. Ron himself answered.

"I'll be at Winding Stair Gap in the parking area at eleven. I'm returning some other hikers to the trail, and I'll see you then," he said. Fortunately, trail conditions were good and climbs were few, so we knocked off those nine miles quickly, reaching speeds of three miles per hour. At Winding Stair Gap we descended a series of log steps to a parking lot, and just minutes later the bus pulled in.

It was a reunion of sorts between hikers coming off the trail and those who had spent the previous night in Franklin. Every day, hikers reconnect with others they have met somewhere before on the trail. As Ron's bus emptied, I recognized several people I'd hiked with on previous days, and I saw a few new faces I would meet again later on the path north. It was a friendly meet-and-greet and information exchange with my new hiker community.

"Let's go!" boomed Ron in his Southern drawl, and we boarded the bus while others returned to the trail. Immediately, the stories started. Ron is an entertaining storyteller, and his tales about Franklin's history and people had us laughing all the way to town.

Marathon Man, Sailor, and I agreed to split the cost of a room. For very little money, we had two beds, a hot shower, and laundry facilities. Marathon Man insisted on sleeping on the floor; even if another bed had been available, he preferred the floor.

We took a short walk to an AYCE barbeque joint, where we did considerable damage. Later in the evening, Ron drove us to the outfitter and a grocery store. When he dropped us off at the motel, he told us that the next morning First Baptist Church was serving a free hiker breakfast for anyone interested. A van would stop by the motel to pick us up.

Could it get any better than this? We were dry, our clothes were clean, and in the morning we'd have a free breakfast.

In our room, I slipped under clean sheets. In the few moments before sleep, I realized a new, growing sense of freedom. Like my extra twenty pounds that were fast disappearing, I had carried the stresses of my old life onto the trail with me. Now they too were slowly melting away.

Butterflies

The aroma of frying bacon welcomed us into the fellowship hall at First Baptist Church of Franklin. We surely did appreciate the church's mission of feeding us poor, hungry, homeless wanderers. Friendly banter between hikers and pancake flippers started the day on a pleasant note.

We met our daily calorie requirement with just one meal and were driven back to our motel, where the short yellow bus waited for more passengers. Ron was in peak storytelling form, and our ride back to Winding Stair Gap passed too quickly. At the parking lot, a repeat of yesterday's reunion—with different faces—brought us up-to-date on all the trail gossip.

Ahead of us that day were Siler Bald and Wayah Bald. Normally, "bald" brings to mind a hairless head, but in this case it meant a treeless mountain summit. A stone tower topped Wayah's 5,340-foot summit; we climbed the tower for an astounding view. Mountain ranges marched in every direction. Wondering which of those we would be crossing in the days to come, we identified the highest mountain in the distance and suspected that was probably our destiny.

A lake sparkled in the distance. The Little Tennessee River flowed freely until 1942, when some great thinker believed the river should be harnessed to produce electricity. A giant concrete plug, 480 feet high and 2,365 feet wide, had turned the innocent little river into a 10,000-plus-acre pond for the pleasure of humanity.

Many times these dams are foisted on us as flood control devices. Perhaps we shouldn't be building or living in areas that flood so quickly? Maybe I'm too cynical, but I believe to accurately understand the motivation behind the building of these dams, you'll need to follow trails that are marked with dollars, trails that lead to some politician's doorstep.

But this sad state is only temporary. The plug is, after all, man-made; everything man builds eventually deteriorates. I am no kin to Nostradamus, but my prediction is that someday all the great and small rivers of the world will flow freely as God intended. Nor am I an anarchist or a wacko environmentalist, but only a voice in the wilderness speaking for rivers wishing to flow freely.

It was Wednesday. Our goal was to reach Fontana Village by noon Saturday. Sailor had a mail drop at the post office there, and I had a bounce box waiting for me. Before leaving Springer Mountain, I had mailed a box with extra food and supplies to this location. I would resupply from the box, and then mail (or "bounce") it to a location approximately a week ahead of us. We wanted to arrive at the post office before closing on Saturday, so we pushed for extra miles, running on energy from our huge breakfast.

We put nineteen miles behind us, our biggest day thus far. But the sun was setting, and we had not found a suitable camping spot. Finally, at Tellico Gap, we had no choice but to stealth camp, setting up in an area not meant for camping. On uneven ground, beside a series of power lines running through the gap, we settled in for the night.

The following morning, we stopped at the Nantahala Outdoor Center, which houses an outfitter, a small grocery, a whitewater rafting center, and a cozy restaurant hanging over the river's waters. Hamburgers at River's End Restaurant are legendary, and with our burgers we downed several energy drinks, fortifying ourselves for the climb we knew was ahead.

Cheoah Bald was eight miles away, a long, tough uphill climb. We stopped one mile short of the bald. Too tired to set up our tents, we braved the Sassafras Gap Shelter that night. Friendly people, a covered porch with a skylight, and only minor concerns about resident mice made my second shelter stay considerably better than the first.

The next morning, Friday, it turned cold and windy. Six miles brought us to a small clearing at Stecoah Gap, where several men had set up a grill and offered hikers hot dogs, candy bars, chips, and beverages. The Good Samaritan this time was a former thru-hiker. Those additional calories helped us knock off the next twelve miles quickly, and we knew we'd meet our deadline. We were less than five miles from the Fontana post office and the comforts of the Fontana Lodge when we stopped for the night just past Walker Gap.

I pitched Big Agnes in a clearing only three feet from a small stream. The little creek was so close I could almost filter water without leaving my tent. I settled in for the night, relaxing into the murmuring of the brook, the sound a balm for my tired body and spirit.

I thought I could hear the soft voice of God in the music of the brook. *Apostle, did you see Me today?*

"Yes, God, and thank You for springtime!" The valleys and mountains were bursting with new life. At higher elevations, buds were starting to appear. In the gaps, flowers waved as I walked by. The earthy smell of spring was everywhere.

How about the butterfly? Did you see the butterfly?

"Dear God, that was awesome! It stopped me in my tracks."

That morning, a beautiful butterfly had floated above my head, sailed ahead on the path, then circled back and fluttered around me. As I walked, it drifted along beside me for a while. I had watched it with amazement. "Yes, God, and today I remembered that other butterfly You sent my way."

Mary had loved butterflies, especially Monarchs. The Monarch is sometimes called the milkweed butterfly, because most of its life cycle takes place on milkweed plants. Every year, my wife drove out into the country, located a stand of milkweed, and searched for a caterpillar marked with bright yellow and black stripes. The chosen caterpillar would be housed in a mason jar topped with screen, furnished with twigs and plenty of milkweed leaves. Then the waiting and watching began.

For about two weeks, the caterpillar did nothing but eat and eliminate. But then the excitement started. Mary never missed it, and she made certain we didn't either. Her excited call would round up the family, and we'd watch that caterpillar start to spin. Hanging upside down from a twig or the bottom surface of the screen, the caterpillar spins until the exterior skeleton slips off and the chrysalis forms a jade green shell.

For the next several weeks, the chrysalis hung immobile. If we went on vacation during that time, the jar of hope traveled in the front seat with us. As the butterfly developed inside, the green sheath slowly changed color and became thin and almost transparent. When the chrysalis finally started to move gently, Mary again gathered our family to watch the drama unfold. Soon a wrinkled, deformed butterfly emerged. For several hours, this sad-looking creature would hang on to its former home, slowly moving its wings up and down in an effort to dry and strengthen them.

Then came the ceremony of release. To the front porch we all went, and with Mary's encouraging words, "Fly, little butterfly," the now-beautiful creature was set free.

In the week before Mary left us, she spent both days and nights in her chair in the living room, enduring considerable pain, not wanting to move between the chair and bed. Finally, we convinced her to move to her bedroom. As I lifted her from the chair to a wheelchair, someone exclaimed, "Look out there!"

Outside our glass door, a tree branch curved over the balcony, and a caterpillar inched along that branch, ten feet from the ground. In seventeen years of living in that house, we had never seen a caterpillar on that tree. None have been there since that day. This little messenger crept along the branch, then onto a smaller twig, inching closer to the sliding door. I wheeled Mary over so she could get a better view.

I had no doubt God was showing us that Mary was going through her own metamorphosis. She would be set free to fly away, just like all the butterflies she had released into the sunshine.

I settled Mary in her bed, then went back to find the caterpillar. But it had disappeared. Later, I related this little story to our pastor. He did not seem surprised; he said he had often seen God reveal Himself, especially at difficult times.

Following Mary's funeral, I gave some of the flower arrangements to the local nursing home and several friends. I still had a living room full of flowers, so I decided those would go to my sisters and Mary's friends who had been so helpful during her illness.

The day after the funeral, a friend of Mary's brought me a twig with a chrysalis bound to it. I stuck the twig into a flower arrangement. One of my sisters had told me she had never seen a butterfly emerge, so I would give her this one to enjoy.

That evening, I fell asleep in my chair in the living room. At two in the morning, an unfamiliar sound woke me. A mysterious fluttering whisper was coming from the assortment of plants and collectibles on the shelf above the kitchen cabinets. I stood dumbfounded as a Monarch butterfly emerged from the plants and danced around me in the living room. It had abandoned its chrysalis before I could deliver it to my sister. I watched in wonderment, not quite believing what I was seeing.

Now it was my turn to grant freedom. The Monarch did not seem eager to leave, but was attracted to the light in the living room. I turned off that light, and turned on the kitchen light. *Follow the light, little butterfly.* It came to the kitchen. I shut off the kitchen light and flipped on the light in the foyer. The butterfly followed. I opened the front door and snapped off the foyer light while turning on the porch light. *Go, little butterfly, fly away. You are free.* The butterfly winged through the front door and disappeared.

In my tent beside the brook, I remembered the unexpected caterpillar and the night visit of the Monarch butterfly. And before I realized it, I was talking aloud, talking with that voice of God in the brook. Correction, I was talking *to* the voice, because once I got started, I was on a roll and didn't give much chance for reply.

"Yes, God, I understood the symbolism that night. You set Mary free. So You were there all along? I often questioned whether You cared about what was happening to us. If You care, why did she suffer so, and die?"

I didn't want glib, churchy lines. I wanted answers.

"Is there a reason for all this sickness and death? If You are in control of everything, why is the world in such a mess?"

Was He listening? Was He there?

"I need to know if You are firmly in command. I could make a case that You do not control events and everything happens at random. But if I can convince myself that You do have a plan, then maybe I could believe Mary died for a good reason."

If God cared but let us suffer anyway, then I was angry and would be a bit brash with Him.

"How can You know how much pain we went through? Do You know what it's like to lose a wife or a mom? Oh, yes, You lost a son once. But You were only apart for three days. Even I could bear just three days of separation."

An answer came back, cutting through my pent-up questions and frustration.

You are missing the point, my dear Apostle.

A storm warned me of its rapid approach. Lightning crackled around the campsite and thunder rumbled and echoed through the mountains. The sound of raindrops drowned out my conversation with the brook. Another thunder clap seemed to shake the very ground under our campsite. God had apparently moved from the gentle brook to the powerful storm.

"Wow, God! You *can* talk loudly!" I said at last—when I could speak again.

You're a funny one, aren't you, Apostle?

"Created in Your own image, I believe. Perhaps I am missing the point, but that's why I'm out here. Sure wish I'd always hear You this clearly. Oh, and thanks for the butterfly today. I'll look for You tomorrow on the trail."

8

The Smoky Mountains

Several storms rolled over us during the night, but by six o'clock the next morning the rain had stopped and we were on the trail, headed for Fontana Dam. I had called ahead to the Hike Inn, a hostel near the dam, to check on available space. They were full; many hikers were out on the trail for the weekend.

Plan B was to stay at Fontana Lodge in the Fontana Village Resort. Just when we had become stinking, honest-to-goodness woodsmen, a resort was tossed our way to soften us up again. The village, a few miles off the trail, also offered a small grocery, an outfitter, and a post office. Fontana Dam was built during World War II, when the war effort demanded more electricity; the cottages in the village housed up to five thousand workers during construction of the dam. Now those cottages are vacation rentals and time-shares.

The rain brought fresh signs of new growth. Everywhere, vegetation was changing. One small sentinel of spring met me, a morel mushroom, standing alone in the middle of my path. Climbing hills and scouring woods in search of those tasty morsels is one of my favorite springtime rituals. I had to force myself to keep hiking.

The morning's hike would be an easy one, just two and a half miles downhill to the dam, then another two miles off the trail and into the village. Our path soon brought us to a parking area close to the dam. Fontana Dam marks the southern boundary of Great Smoky Mountains National Park, so we were required to fill out a park permit at the visitor center. It was a simple form, requiring only basic information and no fee.

A car pulled into the parking area and unloaded a hiker. We discovered the driver was the owner of the Hike Inn, returning one of her guests to the trail. She apologized for not having a room for us, but offered to drive us the remaining two miles to the village, dropping us off in front of the Fontana Lodge. We checked in and found a beautiful lodge, a comfortable room, an exceptional restaurant, and a Coke machine. Oh, yes, life was good.

At the post office, Sailor picked up a food box from his wife, and I resupplied from my bounce box, taking things I judged necessary for the next hundred miles and sending the remainder ahead to Hot Springs, North Carolina. After a stop at a laundromat, we went back to our room for what would become the food box ritual. Sailor's wife always sent far more food than he could possibly carry, so he dumped out the box, took his choice first, and then granted Marathon Man and me the extra fruit and candy.

At the Mountview Bistro in the lodge, we met another group of hikers, and in the usual exchange of information we learned that our path across the dam was closed. The Appalachian Trail follows a roadway that crosses over the top of the dam, but a defect had been discovered, construction crews were set up to repair it, and the dam was closed to all traffic. A defect in this concrete monstrosity? At 480 feet, this was the highest dam east of the Rockies, and backed up thirty miles of water to create the lake. A defect could not be reassuring to folks living downstream.

I was intrigued, though, by another option. If we were brave enough, we could try to sneak across the dam. A three-hundred-dollar fine was meant to discourage anyone from ignoring the "Closed" signs, but several hikers who had crossed and were subsequently caught assured us their fines had been only one hundred dollars.

I wanted to attempt the crossing. If caught, I would just consider the penalty a fee for my travel, like a toll booth on an interstate. But Marathon Man stubbornly refused to go across that dam. Maybe it was because the fine also came with a night in jail.

The next morning, we took a shuttle to the trailhead at the northern end of the dam. It was decision time.

If the Appalachian Trail is closed for any reason, the marked alternate route is considered the official AT. Since the trail across Fontana Dam was now inaccessible, a two-mile, blue-blazed trail circled the concrete wall, connecting to the AT once again on the northern side. That blue-blazed detour trail left the AT back at the parking area on the southern end of the dam, where we had hitched a ride to the lodge yesterday. Many of the other hikers who had stayed in the village just took the shuttle to the northern end, picked up the AT there, and avoided the two-mile detour. If I started hiking at this northern point, I could no longer claim to be a purist hiker.

I could not cheat. I asked the van driver to take me back to the parking area by the marina, where we had left the trail yesterday, and I would pick up the blue-blazed detour there. My Appalachian hike would be two miles longer than the official miles listed in the handbook.

Sailor and Marathon Man detoured with me. Sailor was also still a purist hiker, and Marathon Man knew that his plans would take him off the trail in a few days, so his choice was to keep our company a bit longer. We left the parking lot, and a few steps down the trail we came to the Fontana Dam Shelter. The hiking community knows this place as the Fontana Hilton; it's one of the more modern shelters on the trail, with two levels that sleep twenty-four, a smooth wooden floor, running water, and nearby restrooms. We stopped to read the register and catch up on trail happenings.

Two miles later, we rejoined the AT at the northern end of the dam, where a welcome sign ushered us into the Great Smoky Mountains National Park. My outfitter back in Ohio had predicted cold nights and possible snow in the Smokies; but even with his warnings, I had no idea what we were heading into.

Our Great Smoky sojourn began with Shuckstack Mountain, a four-mile climb. For the next seventy miles, we would be hiking high in the mountains, at elevations between four and six thousand feet. Three miles beyond Shuckstack, we walked into a spring scene that etched itself into my memory.

At Doe Knob, large patches of white wildflowers covered the forest floor. The white, fringed phacelias were small and delicate, but so plentiful that the pools of blossoms looked almost like a covering of snow. The air was getting colder, and as we approached the area of the flower-snow, small round ice pellets began to fall, bouncing like hail. Little white balls bounced up and down in the field of fringed blossoms, everywhere a movement of white. The entire expanse of tiny flowers seemed to dance in excitement, waving and welcoming us to the Smokies.

By four o'clock, we had put thirteen uphill miles behind us and were tired and cold and ready to end the day. In the Smoky Mountains, the risk of bear encounters is considerably higher, and all hikers are required to overnight in shelters. Most reserve spots in advance, but thru-hikers cannot know exactly when they will reach any given point, so each shelter holds four spots for the first thru-hikers who arrive. If the shelter is full, park regulations do permit hikers to set up camp outside, as long as tents are within protection of the building.

We were only a short distance from Mollie's Ridge Shelter, and we met a ridge runner who advised us to spend the night there. We learned from him that a large number of hikers were out, weather conditions were deteriorating, and shelters would fill up early in the afternoon.

Someone had put a canvas covering on the front of this building, offering some protection from the cold wind. We three quickly claimed our spots inside, and I ventured out into the cold one more time to filter water at a nearby spring, one liter for my meal that night and one for my pack the next day. Hikers trickled in throughout the evening. Those arriving later had to pitch their tents outside in the cold.

That night, I silently thanked my salesman at the outfitter for selling me a five-degree sleeping bag. Even wrapped in the warm sleeping bag, I again wore every article of clothing I had with me, trying to keep the cold at bay.

Extreme cold the next morning prompted a quick start. It was snowing hard, and we needed to keep moving just to stay warm. I had gloves, but they were little protection against the cold. I warmed one hand under my coat, against my body, while holding both hiking poles in the other. Then I'd switch hands, trying to keep my fingers thawed. I grabbed the water hose coming from my pack for a drink of water, but there was nothing. My drinking water had frozen. Finally, I resorted to eating the shining ice crystals covering the trees and foliage all around me.

The first cold climb of the day was a short bump over Devils Tater Patch. Stones resembling potatoes protrude from the ground everywhere, giving this area its name.

Thunderhead Mountain straddles the state line between North Carolina and Tennessee, and we crossed one of its peaks, Rocky Top. The view from the 5,441-foot summit was spectacular. Mountain slopes glittered with new snow, and we could see Fontana Lake lying behind us.

At two in the afternoon, Derrick Knob Shelter was in sight. We'd only hiked twelve miles, but the heavy snow had soaked and chilled us. Our socks and shoes were wet from trudging in six inches of accumulated snow. We decided to stop for the day and were among the first hikers to arrive.

Happily, this shelter had not only a canvas cover protecting the front, but also a stone fireplace. We took turns warming by the fire, drying our socks and shoes.

The shelter filled with frozen, weary hikers. Derrick Knob is listed as a twelve-person building, but on that cold, miserable night, close to thirty hikers crammed into it. We lay body-to-body on the bunks and the dirt floor, unaware that even more hikers—at least a dozen tents—had camped outside in the snow.

At five in the evening, I climbed into my sleeping bag fully dressed, wearing even my now-dry shoes. That began a miserable twelve-hour sleeping bag marathon, with no escape and very little sleep. I had elbows in my ribs on both sides, and found it almost impossible to turn over or to wiggle into a comfortable position without bumping into other arms, legs, and heads. There was nothing to do but wait for morning. I pulled the bag over the top of my head, drawing the string until only my nose stuck out. I couldn't sleep, but at least I was no longer cold.

And of course there was a snoring champion who showcased his talent that night. He was probably the only one who slept. By four in the morning, hikers were packing up and leaving, complaining that it was impossible to sleep with the noise. Sailor, Marathon Man, and I left at five. There was no reason to punish ourselves when we could be on the trail making miles.

We trudged over Cold Spring Knob as the morning sky started to lighten. Just as the sun made its appearance, we topped Silers Bald and stopped, dazzled by the view. Clean, glittering snow covered endless miles of mountain ranges, and sunlight sparkled from ice crystals on every tree and bush around us. What a gift. Weather conditions had conspired to hinder our hiking, but this morning we were treated to a glittering show of wonder.

Clingman's Dome, the highest elevation on the entire Appalachian Trail, reaches 6,654 feet heavenward, and every branch and bush on its heights was covered with a thick coat of hoarfrost and snow. We were climbing a huge ice castle, everything frozen and dazzling, framed against a brilliant blue sky. The sun gradually warmed us, but also created a messy trail. Snow became icy slush that once again soaked our shoes and socks. Only the spectacular views could take our minds off our cold, wet feet. We climbed the observation tower at the top of Clingman's Dome and contemplated the ranges of mountains ahead of us, as far as the eye could see. At least we knew we were on the trail's highest point, and there was nowhere to go but down.

Our reward for the early morning departure was just ahead. The incredible snoring machine had forced us onto the trail earlier than planned, so by midafternoon we were already at the trail leading to Mt. Collins Shelter. The shelter was a half-mile off the trail, and none of us was excited about another night's stay in a cold, crowded shelter. Four more miles on the trail would bring us to Newfound Gap, where the Tennessee-North Carolina line runs through a parking lot beside U.S. Rt. 441. Sixteen miles west on 441 was Gatlinburg, Tennessee. Should we go a few more shivering miles and hope to hitch a ride to Gatlinburg? I took the lead, and we hustled toward Newfound Gap.

The trail led through a stand of mature hardwood trees, a grand, majestic growth of towering elder statesmen of the forest. A storm had felled many along our path, uprooting and toppling the giants. They lay in sad defeat, with large root systems exposed, still clutching the ground and the large rocks to which they had entrusted their lives.

Going downhill all the way, sometimes crossing narrow boardwalks that protected fragile plant life, we arrived at Newfound Gap in less than two hours. Our day had been eighteen miles soaked with cold and slush and brilliant sunshine.

At the state line, we took a celebratory picture and then set about finding a ride to Gatlinburg. There were several cars in the parking lot, but no one was interested in picking up three bedraggled hikers. Sailor suggested we walk out to the highway and try our luck at hitchhiking.

The first vehicle in our sights was a pickup truck occupied by a middle-aged couple. They slowed down. "You fellows are welcome to jump on the back if you want a ride to Gatlinburg," the man said. "Where do you want to be dropped off?" he called back through the open window.

Our ride dropped us across the street from a hiker-friendly motel on Ski Mountain Road. Hiking eighteen miles of slushy mountain trails creates extreme appreciation for a hot shower. What luxury!

Once we were clean and warm, the urgent need was food. After my limited menu of dried dinners, it was incredible to walk busy sidewalks and have so many choices of eateries. We settled on a steakhouse.

In less than an hour, we were transported from a remote snowy mountain forest to one of the gaudiest tourist meccas in the United States.

After many cups of coffee, eggs, and pancakes the next morning at The Flapjack House restaurant, we were back on the trail.

Several miles brought us to a protruding rock formation called Charlie's Bunion. Atop this high perch, we had views of both Mt. Le Conte and Mt. Kephart and a panoramic view of gorges and valleys stretching out in every direction. We were hiking on top of the world.

At four o'clock, we reached the intersection of the Hughes Ridge Trail and the AT. Half a mile down Hughes Ridge was Pecks Corner Shelter. We did not like the thought of hiking that far off the AT, but the next shelter was over five miles away. The sunshine was fading, the falling temperature turning the slushy trail to ice. Every step that afternoon had required great care, and we had made only ten miles.

We opted for Pecks, located in a grove of beech trees. One large tree had fallen close to the shelter, and we positioned our wet shoes and socks on its large trunk, hoping to dry them in the last rays of sunlight.

Our hike began the next morning with only one goal. Weary of the treacherous conditions, we were determined to get as close as possible to the northern boundary of the Smoky Mountains. This day was just as difficult as the previous two.

Hiking over the slopes of Mt. Sequoyah, we plowed through snowdrifts several feet deep. Guyot Spur was 6,320 feet high, and after that climb we slid downhill for fourteen miles. Snowdrifts and icy trails made every step precarious.

As the day warmed, melting ice sent little streams running down the trail. We gradually descended from six thousand feet to five thousand, then to four thousand, where the snow and ice turned to mud. As the snow disappeared, more drifts of spring wildflowers decorated the forest, their color and freshness lifting our spirits.

We all agreed that views in the Smokies were unsurpassed, but we had seen enough. We wanted to get these mountains behind us, so we doggedly kept hiking until we reached Davenport Gap, Tennessee. Finally, at the modest elevation of 1,980 feet, we bid good-bye to the Great Smoky Mountains.

We had survived a seventy-mile test of endurance. To celebrate our status as seasoned hikers, we added three additional miles over the Pigeon River, under I-40, to Green Corner Road where the Standing Bear Hostel congratulated us on our escape from the mountains. Standing Bear is an old homestead that was converted to a hostel, with several cabins and a rustic bunkhouse. A hot shower, a whole pizza, several candy bars, two cans of pop, and one liter of water later, I was a contented hiker.

That night, around the community fire ring, I spotted a young hiker I had first met at the Blueberry Patch.

"Muskrat, how did you get here ahead of us?" I asked in surprise.

"Oh, I've been here several days already. I'm doing a work-for-stay." Many hostels along the trail give hikers a free stay in exchange for work. This makes it possible for hikers to stay on the trail, even on a tight budget. He explained, "After leaving the Blueberry Patch, I wanted to catch up with some hiker friends ahead of me, so I skipped the entire Smoky Mountains and hitchhiked up here."

He was a yellow-blazer. The phrase refers to the yellow blazes down the center of a highway. And although purists would never say it aloud, we also think it represents a yellow blaze down the back of a hiker who refuses to tackle difficult sections of the AT, like the Smokies. But I bit my lip, as any purist would do when meeting a yellow-blazer. I knew what

Muskrat's reply would be if I took the bait and commented on his hiking style. The reply, "Hike your own hike" is heard time and again on the trail, and it's just a polite way of saying, "Shut up and mind your own business."

To many hikers, the journey is more about memories than miles. As I blazed a path to my bunk that night, I thought about what I would have missed if I had skipped the Smokies. Yes, a lot of pain, but also infinite pleasures. Fields of flowers with tiny snowballs bouncing among them had welcomed us to the Smokies, and beautiful expanses of wildflowers had bid us good-bye as we departed.

Most enjoyable of all was the excitement of meeting new people who were like flowers scattered along the path of my life.

9

Let's Go Left

What a pleasure to start the next day with clear skies and trails free of snow and ice.

For a week, we were never quite certain which state we were in, since the trail wove along the North Carolina and Tennessee border. One hour we were hiking in our third state, and the next hour we dropped back to the second state we thought we had finished.

At these lower levels, spring had already arrived. Our attention to the trail was constantly diverted by wildflowers of many species and colors. A solitary dandelion caught my eye, and I was delighted by its beauty. Most homeowners consider the lowly dandelion a nuisance, a plague to be stamped out. But out here, growing alone in the woods, this drop of sunshine was a thing of beauty, perhaps not as delicate as some of the woodland beauties, but almost indestructible.

Surely the dandelion knows secrets of stubborn survival that the giant trees we had seen toppled in the Smokies did not.

It was our nineteenth day on the Appalachian Trail. Our bodies were taking on hiker resiliency and stamina, but the difficulties in the Smokies had drained and wearied us. Almost 250 miles had passed under our shoes, and we needed a zero day, a day of rest. The AT led through Hot Springs, thirty-three miles ahead of us, and we planned to take our first zero day in that town nestled in a mountain valley.

The trail again went upward, climbing above 4,000 feet. Snowbird Mountain waited in the distance, and long before we reached its slopes we spotted a white, shimmering UFO that had landed on the mountaintop. It was a five-mile climb to the summit, where we were prepared to meet the little green men, but found only an unusual FAA tower perched atop the mountain.

Nine more miles of climbing took us to the highest elevation of the day, Max Patch Mountain. This bald summit, covered by 350 grassy acres, is part of Pisgah National Forest and is a favorite spot for day-hikers, picnickers, and kite-flyers. The AT traverses the top of the bald, and I felt as though I were on the mountain meadow with Julie Andrews singing in *The Sound of Music*. The 360-degree view of mountain ranges stretching to every horizon was even more impressive than I had imagined; I understood why Max Patch is called the "crown jewel" of the Appalachian Trail. That night would be the first full moon of my trek, and I imagined the joy of camping on the bald's meadow with a big moon shining above. Such a plan was impossible, though; the winds would have snatched our tents and transformed them into Max Patch's own unidentified flying objects.

Roaring Fork Shelter was one mile farther and one thousand feet lower, and we made that our destination. Sailor, Marathon Man, and I reached the shelter at four o'clock and were the only hikers there. It seemed the perfect opportunity to try a plan we had been discussing. I wanted to do a night hike, traveling by the light of the moon. Since we were alone in the shelter, we could retire early, sleep until three in the morning, and then start our moonlit hike. An additional bonus to the plan was that we could knock off the last eighteen miles to Hot Springs and arrive in town even earlier than we had hoped.

But our plans quickly hit a snag.

We unpacked and unrolled our sleeping bags. I was boiling water for my evening meal. Sailor sat in a corner, reading the shelter register and catching up on trail happenings.

"Hey, fellows. There's a reason no one else is here. This shelter has bear problems!"

The register recounted the stories. A renegade bear had found his new food source in the packs hikers obligingly carried into the woods for him. The bear climbed the trees at night and knocked down food bags, eating everything, including toothpaste. One hiker noted the bear had even eaten his toothbrush, and if anyone should find a blue toothbrush in a pile of bear poop, yes, please return the toothbrush.

The bear had paid a visit just the night before. One hiker awakened in the night, feeling a tug on his sleeping bag, and was jerked to full alertness when he realized a bear had his front paws on the shelter floor and was tugging at his sleeping bag.

I was imagining the exciting story I could take home if we did indeed have a bear visit that night. Marathon Man instantly geared for flight; he had an intense fear of bears. I was not quite as ready to run, but then I remembered a joke about several hunters being chased by a bear. One hunter turned to the other and said, "I don't have to run faster than the bear, I just need to run faster than you." Reality convinced me. I was hiking with a marathon runner and a marathon walker. It would be my rump the bear would be chasing.

I had lost my interest in taking home a bear story. "Hey, guys, let's get going!"

Three more miles brought us to the site of the old Roaring Fork Shelter. No longer in use, the shelter had a new name posted on a sign: "No Camping Permitted." Unusual name for a campsite, we thought, as we set up our tents.

Still committed to a walk by the light of the moon, we rose at four in the morning and were soon on the trail. However, another minor glitch cracked our plan. The moon had vanished and a storm front was moving through, pushing heavy clouds. There was no moonlight for our moonlit walk. Only our headlamps lit our way. The trail passed directly in front of the Walnut Mountain Shelter, where three young hikers were awakened by a noise outside shortly after four. They watched in amazement as three headlamps bobbed up and down through the darkness and disappeared down the trail.

We were beginning to see notes in shelter registers about our group of three. The hiking community had dubbed us The Early Riser Crew.

Our no-moon moonlit hike started a day of descent from 4,260 feet in the mountains to the main street of Hot Springs in the valley at 1,325 feet. We walked into town at noon, hoping to stay at Elmer's, a famous hostel in town. Again we were disappointed; Elmer had no vacancy.

The day was rainy with a forecast of more rain for the next few days, and many hikers were staying in town. We walked through the town, looking for a good spot to take our zero day, finally discovering a comfortable cottage beside a stream. We shed our gear and relaxed, enjoying the prospect of our rest day.

At Bluff Mountain Outfitters, I weighed myself and found I had lost close to a pound for every day on the trail. At this rate, I would finish my hike weighing about the same as my backpack.

For the next day and a half, we rested and made numerous trips to both the Smoky Mountain Diner and the Paddlers Pub, in a quest to consume as many calories as possible. At both eateries, I sat and watched, enjoying the atmosphere and the interaction between employees and customers. I did miss my old life at the restaurant.

The zero day rejuvenated us, and we were eager to get back to the trail. One last meal at the Smoky Mountain Diner filled us with a huge breakfast and enough caffeine to propel us over any mountain.

White blazes led us through town, over railroad tracks, and along the road for a short stretch. A bridge took us over the French Broad River. Then we lost the trail. Back and forth we went along the road, looking for that elusive white marker. We finally resorted to checking our thru-hiker handbook and found that immediately after the bridge, the trail dove over the guardrail and down an embankment to wind along the river. Even after nearly three weeks of watching our blazes, we had missed the path.

After following the river for a short distance, the trail climbed again. It was a wonderful day to hike. The rain had stopped and the sun was breaking through the fog as we hiked through Pump Gap. Spring was bursting out around us. Trees showed hints of fresh green, and wildflowers bloomed in abundance. Yes, this was indeed better than any day at work.

Several miles into the morning, we stopped and dropped our gear. Sailor and Marathon Man rested against a fallen log, and I stretched out on the ground, head on my pack. Just to my right, a cluster of the little white-fringed phacelias fluttered in the breeze, waving at me. I watched them lazily, and then was suddenly gripped by "the feeling."

Many years ago, Mary found our youngest daughter, age three, sitting in the foliage of a large potted plant I had been nurturing for years. When her mother asked why she was sitting in the middle of Daddy's plant, our little girl replied, "I just got the feeling."

Now I understood what had happened to her that day. Watching those delicate flowers sway in the sunshine, I was seized with curiosity—how would they taste? Checking to make certain my friends were not watching, I reached over, plucked one little bloom, and popped it into my mouth. That day, I started my own trail tradition of munching a sample whenever I discovered any new wildflower.

At a road crossing later in the day, we found a notice nailed to a post: any hiker was welcome to a meal at the house half a mile down the road.

We followed the directions to a lovely log home. The husband and wife team had thru-hiked themselves several years before, and the trail had worked its magic on them. They purchased this home and made it their Christian mission to witness to hikers. We were presented with conversation on good old-fashioned Bible-Belt salvation. This was no problem to me; I had heard this all my life. Three weeks into my hike, I would have been willing to walk barefoot through fifteen feet of burning embers for a good home-cooked meal. And the meal was good: homemade waffles and pork stew and all the Coke I could drink, topped off with an ice cream brownie sundae.

I might even have done thirty feet of burning embers for that meal.

Seven hikers dined at the table in the log home, Motor-mouth among them. We had met him before, hiking with two other men, all in their twenties. Motormouth's name was well-deserved; he never shut up, except when he coughed, which he seemed to do almost as much as he talked. He claimed his lungs had been damaged by a harrowing trip on bad drugs taken while he was in Mexico.

Among the seven of us, there was quite a diversity of religious opinions. We covered everything from reincarnation to agnosticism. Our host asked thought-provoking questions about the existence of God, and Motormouth seemed to have all the answers; his parents had enrolled him in a Jesuit school for many years. I was content to let him run on unhindered, since it gave me more time to enjoy my ice cream sundae. Our hosts even shared books with us; we were encouraged to take a book along, on the condition that we would read it. I declined; I didn't want the extra weight, and I had already read many of them. Motormouth, though, did choose one and packed it away.

On the way back to the trail, we crossed the North Carolina-Tennessee line. We had actually hiked out of state to get that free meal. Two more miles brought us to Little Laurel Shelter, where we hung our bear bags and went to bed.

We had not gone far the next morning when we came to a fence running through the woods, and hanging from a nail on the top board was Motormouth's book in a plastic bag. Was he a speed reader, or had he sat up all night reading with his headlamp? We drew other conclusions, since the book was in perfect condition, looking as if no one had ever opened it.

Our next goal was to reach Erwin, Tennessee, in three days. This would require some serious hiking. We worked our way through several difficult rock climbs; White Rock Cliffs was the most strenuous and unforgettable. The path was a difficult mile of climbing over and through jagged white rocks running along a ridge that gave views into Tennessee on one side and North Carolina on the other. If it hadn't been such hard work, that mile would have been a spectacularly beautiful stroll.

We had decided to hike several miles past Bald Mountain Shelter before camping for the night, so that our destination at Erwin would be within reach the next day. But late in the afternoon we met a trail maintainer busy with repair work. His backpack was overly large and lay nearby. We stopped to chat about his work and this section of the trail, and he told us that his pack held soft drinks, bananas, bratwurst, and Little Debbies. He was planning a cookout that night for anyone staying at Bald Mountain Shelter, a mile down the path. Our plans immediately changed.

We arrived at the shelter, bearing the good news of the cookout to hikers already settling in for the night. Delicious food and an unexpected party lifted everyone's spirits, and it was an unusually pleasant shelter stay.

Much too early in the morning, I felt a tug on my sleeping bag, and my startled yet sleepy mind could only think, *Could that bear have tracked us here?* But it was only Marathon Man, with our wake-up call. *Go away! Can't I have just one more hour of rest?* But he did not relent, and we rolled out, assembling our gear quickly and quietly by the light of our headlamps.

We were at an elevation over 5,000 feet until we reached Little Bald in early morning light. After that, it was all downhill, a sixteen-mile descent that would take us to Erwin, Tennessee. By midmorning, we were only a few miles away from our destination and caught great views of the town below us and the Nolichucky River winding through the valley.

At noon, the trail abruptly deposited us on River Road, less than one hundred feet from Uncle Johnny's Nolichucky Hostel. We booked a small cabin for the night and headed for hot showers. Food was the next item on our agenda, and we caught a shuttle from the hostel to an AYCE pizza place with a salad bar. For the second time in a week, I ate my greens.

Later in the afternoon, Sailor and I set out to find the post office and a pharmacy. I had bounced my food supply box here from Hot Springs, and Sailor needed supplies to treat his blisters that were growing to monstrous proportions.

At the hostel, we had noticed a number of bikes left in a rack for hikers to use whenever they wished. I concluded that Erwin must not have any problems with crime, since such a row of unattended, unlocked bicycles could be a tempting target.

After hiking over three hundred miles, we thought a bike ride would be a welcome change from walking. We borrowed small day packs from the hostel and headed for the bike rack. It was soon obvious why these bikes were safe. Any thief stealing one of these bikes would never be able to reach speeds high enough for a getaway; in fact, he might possibly return the bike and lodge a complaint. My bike was stuck in fifth gear, so it took some gusto to get rolling. Sailor's bike broke down a half-mile from the hostel, and he had to push it back and choose another.

Once I got my bike up to speed, I felt like lightning on two wheels. Still, I arrived at the post office only five minutes before closing time. I tore open my box and grabbed what I thought I would need in the next eight days. "You have one minute left," said an ominous voice from behind the counter.

"I want to send this box to Damascus, Virginia," I said, hastily repacking and closing the box, with the precious minute ticking away.

"If you send it first class, I'll tape it for you," said the voice. I handed over the box with payment. The "Closed" sign hit the door at the same time I did.

I pedaled down the street, met Sailor at the pharmacy, and we headed back to the hostel. My bike slowly cranked up to speed, and as I was opening up the throttle on the bike path between the railroad tracks and I-26, I was reliving another bike ride on a fateful night long ago.

My friend was fourteen, and I was fifteen. We had pedaled our bikes down the long dirt lane to my uncle's old farmhouse for a sleepover with my cousin. At eleven that night, we were still wide awake and full of youthful energy. My friend suggested a night bike ride. Agreeing that a ride through the dark countryside might be exciting, we all pedaled back out the driveway to the quiet country road. Overhead, a gibbous moon was shining brightly.

We stopped at the intersection of the lane and the country road, debating which way to turn. To the right, the road lay level and easy. To the left, we'd have a hard climb up a steep hill, but the ride back down would be free and exhilarating. My friend's words still ring in my ears: "Let's go left." Almost a mile later, we stopped at the top of the hill, panting from the climb. We paused to catch our breath, then turned our bicycles, and with a rush of excitement headed back down the hill.

Near the bottom of the hill, something suddenly went wrong. My friend was no longer beside me. We had just crossed a bridge, and he had vanished.

A cry for help came from somewhere in the darkness below the bridge. My friend's bike had veered off the road and he'd lost control on the gravel berm. While we flew across the bridge, he and his bike had gone down the bank, the momentum carrying him completely across the little stream and smashing him into the wooden retaining wall on the opposite side. He stumbled up toward the road, and we saw blood covering his face, running from a gash above one eye.

His bike was mangled beyond driving, so we positioned him on the front of my cousin's handlebars and carefully drove up the long driveway back to the farmhouse.

My uncle rushed us to the local hospital, but during the night my friend slipped into a coma and was transferred to a larger facility. I was able to visit him only once, briefly, since he was unconscious and on life support.

For the next two days, I prayed harder than I had ever prayed before. I begged and pleaded with God to let my friend live. I imagine I literally prayed without ceasing, as the Scriptures tell us to do. It was unthinkable that God would not heal him.

I even offered God a deal. If He would let my friend live, I vowed, I would become a missionary. This was the absolute sacrifice for me; I had often heard missionaries speak about their work and had long ago come to the conclusion that mission work was not for me. Leaving friends and family to travel to another country to preach to people who didn't wear many clothes would be the worst possible life I could imagine. Yet I was willing to do this, if only God would let my friend live.

My father was the one who told me my friend had died. "It's not possible!" I sobbed. "How could God let that happen?" I had never before known such anguish or felt so betrayed.

One small, seemingly inconsequential decision. *Let's go left.*

My friend was far too young to die, and I was too young to grapple with thoughts of life after death and the sovereignty of God. The only certainty I knew was that when I had needed God, He didn't seem to be available.

A blaring car horn jolted me away from the painful ride through my memories. We were almost back to the hostel, and my hands had a death grip on the handlebars. I had once again been racing down that hill under a huge, shining moon.

Choices. We make hundreds of them every day, each decision holding the potential to lead to pain or pleasure, joy or despair. That one left turn taken so early in my life had an effect that still rippled through my whole being many years later.

Is God in control of our lives? That question had taken root in my mind when I was fifteen, the consequence of an innocent moonlit bike ride.

The question still whispered to me now, decades later, in the mountains of North Carolina.

10

Words Have Meaning

Morning in Erwin, Tennessee, saw ten of us hikers crowded around a lunch counter in the back of a little grocery store. The trail grapevine had recommended breakfast here. Several elderly ladies took our orders and prepared our food right in front of us. There were only a few stools, so some in the group stood. It was a scene Norman Rockwell might have painted.

We could have been ten stockbrokers or lawyers or any other group of men meeting for breakfast anywhere in America on that Friday morning in April. But we were ten thru-hikers, discussing equipment, shelters, and the upcoming terrain. No deadlines, no big deals to hammer out, just ten hikers, each with his own personal agenda. Motormouth was talking constantly, but no one paid much attention to anything he said. His two hiker buddies were conspicuously absent.

The shuttle took us back to our hostel and we packed up, getting a very late start on our day. I enjoyed these town stops; the amenities and kindnesses rejuvenated both body and spirit.

Several miles down the trail, we met one of Motormouth's friends taking a break at the Curley Maple Gap Shelter. "Hey, what happened to you guys this morning?" I asked. "I saw Motormouth at breakfast, but you two were missing."

"Well, it's like this," he began in his Southern drawl. "The three of us shared one room last night. Motormouth was talking all night long, and my friend attempted to drown out the noise by drinking. The more Motormouth talked, the more my friend drank. He must have had ten or twelve beers. Didn't stop the talking, but at least he wasn't in any shape to listen. Wasn't in any shape to hike today, either." He added that Motormouth was taking a bus back home for a family function today.

"So that means we won't have to listen to him anymore?" I had high hopes.

"Nope. You're not quite that lucky. He's estimating where we'll be in several days, and he'll yellow-blaze his way back to meet us."

We did not start hiking until almost noon that day and decided to push on until dark. The afternoon included several big uphill climbs, a rest to enjoy the beautiful vista from a bald called Beauty Spot, and the conquest of Unaka Mountain. These climbs soon drained any strength I had regained during the town stop in Erwin.

At seven thirty, we pitched our tents at Cherry Gap Shelter. I lost no time in filtering my water, cooking a meal, and sliding into my sleeping bag. I wanted as much rest as possible, knowing that the next day would be our biggest climb until we reached Mt. Washington in New Hampshire. Roan Mountain rises over 6,000 feet, and we had heard much about the difficulty of summiting this mountain.

Roan Mountain exceeded its reputation. Two peaks of the mountain rise to the west, and three grassy balds stretch over seven miles on the east. Carvers Gap sits between these two parts of the mountain.

We climbed for several "endless hours," as I later wrote in my journal. This was a *climb*, not just a casual uphill walk. I struggled over rocks, grabbing tree roots on the steep trail to pull myself upward, my lungs protesting and aching for a rest. I talked to my body, trying to push it upward. *Okay, leg, step onto that mass of roots. Now, other leg, get yourself up over that rock. C'mon body, get up there with the feet.* The climb was harder than anything I'd imagined in my daydreams of the AT. And the thirty-five pounds on my back seemed to have doubled its weight, conspiring with the mountain to keep me from making the summit.

At the top, I doubled over in pain and exhaustion. A brief rest, then onward. But a short distance later, the trail abruptly turned upward again.

"What's this?" I asked Sailor in dismay, looking up the almost vertical path. "I thought we just hiked over Roan Mountain."

He consulted his hiker handbook and gave us the bad news. We had just crossed Beartown Mountain and still had close to a mile and a half to the summit of Roan. And before the summit, we must cross the two humps of Roan High Bluff and Roan High Knob, until we would finally reach the high point of 6,285 feet.

When at last we crossed Roan High Knob, our hopes for rest were frustrated yet again. We located a shelter, but it was filling up fast; because the dense forest crowded closely, there were very few tent spots outside. We debated. A few more miles would take us through Carvers Gap and on to one of the balds. Jane Bald was not as dramatic as Max Patch, but it would certainly be interesting to camp on one of those open grassy areas. We moved on.

In Carvers Gap, at a road crossing, we stopped for a moment at a parking lot that straddled the state line. Roan Mountain had completely drained our energy and we had drained our water supply. We'd been hiking for eleven hours and still had a mile to go.

A car pulled up. "Are you guys thru-hikers?" We assured the driver that our intent was to become thru-hikers.

"Great. I come out here one day each year to do trail magic. I've been here several hours, and you're the first thru-hikers I've met. I was almost ready to give up and head home. I've got bananas, tortilla chips, and blueberry turnovers," he said, starting to unpack the goodies.

Our new friend had hiked half of the trail one year but could not finish. Someday he wanted to complete the hike, but until then, he kept in touch with the trail and its magic by meeting and feeding thru-hikers. We offered to wait for him if he wanted to go home, get his pack, and join us. All three of us knew those "somedays" seldom arrive.

We devoured most of his food, saving only a few bananas for breakfast the next day. Refreshed, we crossed the road, and the mile to Jane Bald melted away quickly. The sun was disappearing over Roan Mountain as we set up camp in the waning light.

The balds created a world different from the steep, forested mountains. Clear of trees, covered mostly with grasses and wildflowers, the rounded knobs gave splendid views in every direction and we rolled over them with delight. The trail-magic bananas at breakfast added to our energy.

We climbed Little Hump Mountain and then Hump Mountain. Hump Junior was only one hundred feet shorter than Hump Senior, so both required some of that extra banana energy. Since leaving Erwin, our climbing skills and endurance had been tested and stretched, and we were ready for a shorter, easier day. According to our hiker handbook, we would cross U.S. Rt. 19 in the afternoon; from there, we could follow the highway just a short distance east to the Mountain Harbour Bed and Breakfast, recommended to us by several hikers. Rumor had it that we might also get a home-cooked meal.

The morning's hike brought more trail magic. Tacked to the railing of a wooden footbridge, a handwritten note told us, "Trail magic in creek. Please take trash out." Attached to the note was a bag filled with Hostess Twinkies, and in the clear mountain stream lay a chilled six-pack of Coca-Cola.

With renewed vigor from the sugar buzz, we soon emerged from the woods and headed down the road to Mountain Harbour. The B&B was in a beautiful house with a long porch and rock gardens, set in a clearing crisscrossed by a stream and split-rail fences. The hiker hostel was in the barn.

Lest you make incorrect assumptions about the hospitality here, let me add that the upper level of the barn had been designed as a hiker cabin, complete with a wood burning stove, a kitchen area, modern bathroom fixtures, and a hot shower. It was both comfortable and comforting. Rain had started again, and we were happy to be under a roof. In the evening, we walked to the main house where our hosts served us a huge meal of barbecue ribs and chicken. They treated us like family, and I realized that I had indeed become part of a family that kept growing larger as I traveled north.

Rain on the tin roof lulled me to sleep that night. On the floor below me were three horses and a goat. We were sleeping in the stable. There was no Baby Jesus, but we were certainly three wise men.

The rain was still coming down when we awoke, adding to the discomfort of a cold mountain morning. We left our cozy cabin in the barn reluctantly and lingered over a hot, satisfying breakfast at the main house. But finally we could delay no longer, and off we went, into the wind and rain. At least the terrain was easier that day, in the 3,300 to 3,600-foot range, with no dramatic changes in elevation.

Late in the afternoon, we arrived at Moreland Gap Shelter and stopped to debate staying there or pushing on another mile and camping in the woods. We hiked on. However, the rain began again and we could find no suitable campsite. Constant thunder and lightning around us suggested we were not three wise men after all.

Finally, in desperation, we set up our tents in a lane running through a field, a path probably used by a farmer to move farm equipment from one field to another. We hoped the weather was bad enough to keep him and his equipment inside that night.

The temperature fell during the night—and so did the rain. When I tried to open my tent in the morning, I no longer had a tent flap, but a hatch. I pushed open the rigid piece of canvas and realized that Big Agnes had frozen into an igloo, completely coated with a layer of ice. I pounded the igloo with a stick, trying to remove as much ice as possible, then bent the material enough so that I could shove it into my pack. We were almost as frozen as our tents and had only one thing on our minds: find a warm place to thaw out.

Less than four miles away was Dennis Cove Road and the Kincora Hiking Hostel, where we stopped to defrost. An hour passed quickly while we visited with other hikers, deiced our tents, and warmed our bodies.

Another easy mile brought us to Laurel Fork Gorge, where a flight of rock steps took us down the side of the gorge to the base of a waterfall, a lovely spot with a pool perfect for taking a dip—if the temperature had been eighty degrees higher. Then the trail followed the river, squeezing between the water and the tall, rocky wall of the gorge, now and then crossing wooden footbridges to the opposite side.

The climb out of the gorge was much steeper than we expected. A sign told us we were in the Pond Mountain Wilderness, part of the Cherokee National Forest. None of us had heard of this climb, and with no forewarning we were ambushed by its difficulty. Shouldn't a mountain called "Pond" be an easy climb?

By midafternoon, we had hiked close to fourteen miles and were standing at another road crossing. To our left on U.S. 321 was Hampton, Tennessee, home to the Braemar Castle Hostel. The hostel owner ran a grocery store and old-time hardware across the street, and we knew a restaurant was also nearby. Record cold was in the forecast and we did not wish to repeat the previous night's misery, so we decided to hitchhike to town, two miles away. No one picked us up, so we walked the entire distance to Hampton.

The Braemar Castle Hostel is a fifty-room office building constructed by the Pittsburgh Lumber Company in the early 1900s. The exterior of the all-wood structure was enhanced by river stone in the 1930s, giving it the appearance of a castle. Now it's a hiker hostel. We went from a barn to a castle in two days.

Sailor, Marathon Man, and I were the only guests that night, and as we walked up several flights of wooden steps, they groaned and creaked a welcome. No alarm system was needed here; those wooden stairs would announce any intruders long before they reached our room.

During the night, the temperature did drop to record lows, but we were warm and dry in our castle, reassured that we three wise men could still occasionally make good choices.

The next morning, the hostel owner shuttled us back to Shook Branch Picnic Area, where we had left the trail the previous day. The owner of the Kincora Hostel, where we had thawed the day before, was dropping off slackpackers at the same spot. As we hiked away, the two hostel owners were leaning against the back of the pickup, engaged in laughter and friendly banter. Competitors perhaps, but partners in their love of nature and the trail. Two more good people in my ever-growing list of trail friends.

We followed the shoreline of Lake Watauga. The town of Old Butler lay somewhere nearby, a town steeped in history. Many early pioneer families settled and farmed here; Native Americans were peaceful neighbors; Daniel Boone even spent time in Old Butler. I enjoy early American history, and I thought perhaps I should visit this historic town while I was in the neighborhood.

How do you find Old Butler? Jump in a boat, go to the middle of the lake, then go straight down several hundred

Above, Wautauga Lake; *below,* McAfee Knob; *top right,* trail in Virginia; *center right,* foggy morning on the trail; *bottom right,* suspension bridge

feet. Yes, another government-created reservoir, this one an earthen dam creating a lake covering 6,430 acres. The victims this time were the Watauga and the Elk rivers and historic Old Butler itself. Over seven hundred homes in Old Butler were flooded to create the lake. I wondered how the displaced families felt flood control was working for them.

The AT crosses over the top of the large earthen embankment, 1,000 feet long. Surrounding mountains still show scars where dirt was gouged from their slopes to create the stopper. As I crossed the dirt wall holding back the huge man-made puddle, I tried to ignore the ten square miles of water pushing at the soil and silt under my feet.

Safely across, we tackled a 2,000-foot climb over Iron Mountain. The day was filled with wildflowers and green fields, a perfect springtime hike. We made camp that night beside a little spring, on a small uphill grade.

Twenty-two miles made a good day, but the evening was bittersweet. This would be our last night with Marathon Man. Tomorrow we would reach Damascus, Virginia, where he planned to end his hike and return home. We would be losing our leader, a singer of songs, who had introduced us to the birds along the trail. His hiking leadership had pushed me quickly into shape, he loved books as much as I did, and his agile intellect had sharpened mine as we bounced ideas back and forth.

Relaxing alone in my tent, I thought about the month I had spent on the trail. I'd seen and done so much, everything far removed from my previous life. I had learned to accept the friendship of others quite different from myself, and I was beginning to be happy being me, even with all my shortcomings.

Every day, it seemed that God revealed more of Himself to me. Perhaps it was because I wanted to hear. Several days before, I had been following a young man on the trail. When I was within speaking distance, I attempted a conversation with him, but was ignored. I realized he had earbuds in and was focused on his music. Everywhere these days, people are plugging their ears and depriving themselves of good conversation. That earpiece is like putting up a "Do Not Disturb" sign. This ear-plugged hiker shut out not only all conversation with fellow humans, but also all the sounds of nature. He could not hear the singing birds or the whispering pines.

Apparently he could not even hear approaching thunder. The ear-plugged young man had a hiking partner who was a short distance ahead of him. Thunder had been rumbling around us, and raindrops started to fall as we crossed a road. The unplugged hiker had heard the warning rumbles; catching sight of a country church down the road, he dashed to the refuge of its little porch. But the other hiker marched on, head down, watching the trail and concentrating only on his music. His friend stood on that dry porch, calling, but the hiker never saw his friend leave the trail and certainly did not hear his name called out. He was soaked by the rain and separated from his partner. I wonder how far he walked before he realized he was alone.

Though I watched with amusement as this little scene played out, I felt an inner nudge that said, *That's you, you know.* And I got it. I saw myself in church on Sunday mornings, hoping to hear from God but letting so many worries and distractions clog my mind that I never could hear Him, even when He stood there calling my name. I saw the times

I had knelt for a quick prayer at night and then immediately tumbled into sleep. How could God talk to a sleeping person?

Now I had finally removed everything plugging my ears and my head, and I felt willing and able to listen to God.

"Words have meanings." We often heard this maxim from Sailor, and since I had lots of time to think as I hiked, those three words rattled around in my head daily and took on real meaning for me.

Our words hold great power. That pointed little bit of membrane in our mouths that gives voice to our hearts can energize or soothe or destroy.

As I hiked, I had an amazing number of conversations about the loss of a loved one. Still, it should not have surprised me—after all, it was *my* reason for being on the trail, and every family, nationality, creed, and color shares the experience of death.

One of those conversations was with a hiker who was a young man when his father died. We spoke about grief and regrets and what we wished we could do differently. He told me his story. On the night his father unexpectedly passed away, they had an angry shouting match. The son fired some very harsh words at his dad. Later that evening, the father suffered a massive heart attack and died. His son carried painful regrets for his words, and the argument was still vivid many years later. He sadly told me that he could not erase those angry words from his mind.

We never know which conversation with our spouse or children will be our last. Once spoken, words have the power to linger forever. "I hate you," screams a wife, or "I never wanted you," says a husband. Words can be cutting and cruel, rejecting and crushing. Words do have meaning. They can and do determine our destiny.

Our sons and daughters are listening to our words. How they interpret our words, our tone, our intent, will play a large role in shaping their own characters. Our words affect our children's destinies too.

What if we chose our words more thoughtfully?

I make no claims to being Husband of the Year. I was never even in the running. Realistically, on the husband scale, I was probably average. My school report card sometimes came home with the teacher's note, "Does not live up to full potential," and that was probably a fair assessment of my husband skills too. Yes, my grief included regrets, and some of those regrets might have distressed me for a lifetime if I had not listened to a voice inside me.

My conversation with the hiker haunted by his last words to his father put me back in Mary's hospital room. She had been admitted to the hospital in an extremely weakened state, and I had spent the evening with her. Leaving, I went dashing through the rain to the parking garage. Before I reached my car, a voice inside me spoke up firm and clear. *Paul, go back up to her room and say it.*

I knew exactly what I needed to do. Back through the rain and up to her room I went, and quietly called her name.

"Paul, what are you doing back here?" Her weak voice was almost a whisper.

I took both frail hands in mine and, with tears spilling, asked my wife's forgiveness for all the times she needed my help, all the times she needed me, but I wasn't available. My one goal in life was to be wealthy. And in my pursuit of that goal, I had too often ignored what my wife needed from me.

129

"Forgive me for all the times I was such a thoughtless husband," I said.

Her words came like a balm for my pain: "Yes, I will forgive you. And I also need forgiveness for not always being the wife I could have been. You'll forgive me?"

Any burdens we carried were gone. I left for home, and the last words I heard that night were, "Good night, dear. I love you."

Forgiveness and *love*: words that can soothe and heal a troubled soul. You, my reader, might also have some powerful words that need to be spoken. Don't put it off; you may have less time than you realize. Take it from someone with experience: words do have meaning.

11

Instead, I'm Happy

My four thirty alarm sounded: an early bird chirping into the quiet of the morning. Soon the woods would fill with sounds of other feathered friends waking up and starting their day.

One morning at three thirty, I'd heard a solitary bird begin his morning song. It sounded like my four thirty bird, but this one was an hour early, with just a few short chirps. There was no response; the woods remained silent. The early chirper fell silent too for another hour.

I lay in my sleeping bag, luxuriating in its warmth and the peaceful morning sounds of the woods. I could hear Marathon Man rustling about, packing up his tent for the last time.

When I finally flipped back the tent flap to greet the day, the morning had a colossal feel to it. Early light filtered through the trees into our little clearing. I grabbed my water bottle, and at a cold and clear spring bubbling out of the ground,

I cupped my hands in the pool and splashed my face. The shock brought all my senses to life. I had never been an early morning person, but out here on the trail, I'd fallen in love with the newness and freshness of spring mornings. I could smell spring in the air; on this morning it seemed all of nature heralded the arrival of a new day and promised: *this will be a good day.*

This is it, Marathon Man. Lead us home to Damascus.

The sun glinted through the bare trees, slanting sunbeams across our path as we worked our way toward the town. We had nineteen miles to our destination, most of it at 3,000-plus elevation, no serious climbs or descents, a fairly easy walk with time and spare energy to think.

We hiked in silence most of the morning, each lost in his own thoughts. Three men from diverse backgrounds had met on a narrow trail. We were all searching for something, with no agenda except to hike. But we had become a team, and now the team was about to disband. Our silence honored the brotherhood we three had forged.

I reflected on past weeks and all I'd observed about people and myself. In one month, I had gained more insights on life than I had in many, many years past. I'd traveled the sad road of death and grieving; it was time to find my path back to life and living. My mind had finally released the accumulation of years of job-related stress and now felt as clear as the spring by my campsite. I was Apostle, not just a reactor to disgruntled customers and difficult employees and demanding business situations and the sadness of bereavement. Now I was Apostle, hiking to . . . what? What lay ahead of me on this trail? Where would this journey take me? I did not know, but I did know I was shedding the old and hiking toward the new.

Our hiker handbook noted that by the time a thru-hiker reached Damascus, he would probably be in close to peak hiker shape. By this time too, all blisters should be healed. I had not yet been plagued by blisters. Whenever I felt a hot spot (an area where friction is occurring) on my foot, I had treated it immediately. During breaks, I had taken off my shoes to dry my feet. Those precautions had saved me thus far from the pain of blistering.

For a long time, the trail had followed the state line, and we were often uncertain if we were in Tennessee or North Carolina. But now as we began the last four downhill miles toward the town, we knew we were in Virginia at last. State number four.

Georgia, North Carolina, and Tennessee had been beautiful, with rugged mountains and panoramic vistas. Those mountain climbs had toughened us and shaped us into true hikers, but we would welcome easier terrain. We'd been told the hiking in Virginia was less difficult, but even without that prospect, we were excited about exploring a new state.

What I didn't know then was that it would take as long to hike through Virginia as the combined time we'd spent hiking the first three states. Virginia has the longest section of the AT, totaling 550 miles; it also held the promise of many interesting days on the Skyline Drive and the Blue Ridge Parkway in beautiful Shenandoah Valley.

At the edge of Damascus, the trail made a sharp right turn; we walked between two houses, and we were suddenly on Mock Avenue in the Friendliest Town on the Appalachian Trail. White blazes led us down Laurel Avenue, and then I realized I was hiking with an intruder—in my shoe. The steep downhill hike had produced my first blister. Thankfully, we planned to take our second zero day in this town, so I would have time to properly treat it.

Our first stop was at Mt. Rogers Outfitters, where I had bounced my box from Erwin, Tennessee. Then on to the post office to pick up the food box my trail boss Ina had sent. I toted both boxes under my arms as we searched for a place to stay. Damascus has earned its "friendliest town" moniker by playing host to hordes of wanderers every year, since the Appalachian Trail, the Virginia Creeper Trail, the Transcontinental Bike Trail, and the Daniel Boone Memorial Trail all weave through this town. Now we were searching for The Place, popular with hikers and cyclists, which offered lodging in an old house that was somewhere behind a Methodist church.

A woman's voice called to us and interrupted our search. The owner of the Montgomery Homestead Bed and Breakfast invited us to her front porch and sold us on staying at her B&B for the next two nights. The B&B was more costly than The Place, but we splurged because Marathon Man's time with us was almost over. It was a good decision; we had a wonderful stay at the lovely home.

Later in the day, I returned my bounce box to Mt. Rogers Outfitters. I was planning to return to this town soon, so there was no point in mailing it ahead. Every May, Damascus hosts Trail Days, a yearly hiker festival that draws ten to fifteen thousand hikers and dozens of vendors of outdoor products. It's the hiker equivalent of Woodstock, and thru-hikers will hitch rides for long distances to participate in the event. I had promised myself the full Appalachian Trail experience, and so I intended to come back to Damascus for this gathering of the trail community.

Early the next morning, I walked with Marathon Man back to the outfitter, where a ride waited to return him to Springer Mountain to pick up his car and head home. Sailor stayed at the B&B, nursing horrible blisters. I did not enjoy good-byes—I'd had too many of them lately—but I was not going to forgo one last walk with my friend. Marathon Man had made me a better hiker. He was the reason we had made Damascus in record time. The three of us were not only a hiking team; we had also become good friends. We would miss Marathon Man.

That evening, Sailor and I walked to The Mill Restaurant for supper. Pathfinder soon walked in, and I thought surely this surprise must be a godsend, a consolation for losing Marathon Man.

I had never met Pathfinder, although I'd followed his hike on the Trail Journals website before I began my own journey. He had started a thru-hike in January, in the dead of winter. When he reached Damascus, he abruptly left the AT, but promised to return later to resume his hike. Pathfinder had done numerous thru-hikes and was quite knowledgeable about the trail. I'd been intrigued by his journals and had wished that our paths would cross sometime on the AT. But what were the odds of such a meeting, with hikers strung out over two thousand miles and five months?

Now the well-known trail figure walked into The Mill Restaurant where we sat at supper. I recognized him from photos I'd seen, and Sailor invited him to join us. Pathfinder accepted our invitation, and we fell into the easy and quick fellowship of the AT community. I couldn't wait long to ask my question: "Pathfinder, you hike the AT year after year. Why?"

"Well, Apostle, my wife died of cancer about five years ago—"

I interrupted. "Say no more. I know exactly why you're here."

The conversation that followed was one I would have many times with other men on the trail. The stories were deeply personal yet all possessed universal threads. We had lost a spouse and thus had lost our lives; we came seeking peace, harmony, and restoration. Pathfinder's story of losing his wife to cancer was uncannily similar to mine. As he told his story, every detail resonated with my own pain and loss.

He and his wife had been athletic people, both marathon runners. The Big C had robbed them of many activities they had once shared as it slowly drained his wife's strength and energy. Returning home one evening, they drove through Dicks Creek Gap, close to Hiawassee, Georgia. Pathfinder never even knew the Appalachian Trail passed through this gap and had never hiked on the AT, but that night he saw the trail sign and pulled over.

He told his wife he wanted to walk up the trail a bit. He walked a short time, lost in thoughts about the cancer and what it had done to their lives. When he finally turned to go back to the car, he saw that his wife had followed him a short way up the trail. From a distance, he caught sight of her, a frail shadow leaning weakly against a tree, breathless and too exhausted to go farther. Overwhelmed by what they had lost and filled with compassion for her, he gently picked her up and carried her back to the car. She said to him, "You're going to hike this trail after I'm gone, aren't you?"

"Shortly after that, she did pass away. I sold my construction company and came to the trail," he told me. "And I've come back every year since to thru-hike. Apostle, I sold my company at the height of the building boom. If I'd kept my business and not done that hike, I'd be a rich man today. Instead, I'm happy."

Pathfinder's story sounded so familiar, so like my own—but there was one thing I could not comprehend. He had never finished that first thru-hike. As he approached the sign at the top of Mt. Katahdin, marking the end of the trail, he stopped ten feet away and could not go on. He broke down in tears, turned away and never reached that sign on his first hike.

I could not understand how one could stop short of such a hard-won goal. I had only been on the trail for a month, but already I knew something of the price any thru-hiker pays to reach Katahdin's summit. Right now, that was all that mattered to me. I wanted to finish this hike, kiss that sign, and go home.

Later that night, I stopped at a Dollar General store and bought a bottle of Vitamin I. More commonly known as ibuprofen, this is a hiker's best friend. Several weeks before, I'd started taking one tablet each morning to ease the pain in my aching feet and legs. A box of Little Debbie snacks also seemed like a necessary purchase; I flipped it over and found that each cake had almost 270 calories I could not pass up.

Back at the house, Sailor and I packed our bags for an early morning departure. We had hiked 461 miles, and the next day would begin our second month on the trail.

Before leaving in the morning, we checked the weather channel and the report promised an 80 percent chance of storms by the afternoon. "What are the chances those words have meaning?" I asked Sailor as we headed outdoors.

"Oh, probably about an 80 percent chance."

We headed north. For almost a mile, we shared the trail with horses and bicycles. The AT was blazed along the Virginia Creeper Trail, a converted railroad bed that runs thirty-four miles from Abingdon, Virginia, to the North Carolina state line. It was Saturday morning, and already there was much activity on the bike path. After more than four hundred miles of hiking in lonely woods on a narrow dirt path, it was a strange sensation to have bicycles whizzing past us.

We hiked over Feathercamp Ridge and Straight Mountain, the AT never straying far from the Virginia Creeper. Early in the afternoon, we stopped at Lost Mountain Shelter for a break. We had walked in light rain several times that morning, but it looked as if we would avoid the nasty weather that had been predicted. We had already hiked over fifteen miles, and we could probably still get in another ten before quitting for the day.

Before we could hoist our packs again, however, the 80 percent hit us. Lightning shot through the sky, thunder shook the shelter, and rain came in torrents. Sailor and I looked at each other wordlessly, grateful that we were safe and dry. We unrolled sleeping bags, and at two in the afternoon our hiking day was done. We spent the rest of the day in the shelter, relaxing and watching the storm.

The storm brought another person seeking shelter and gave us a new hiking partner. Litefoot had just graduated from high school and was hiking the AT as a graduation present to himself. He had been homeschooled, raised with strict religious training, and still carried an innocence not found in many of today's high school graduates. Skinny, soft-spoken, and serious, he reminded me of myself at that age.

Litefoot had convinced his worried parents to let him do this hike to explore the world. But already he had found the world not much to his liking. The buddies he had been hiking with were drinking and partying, and he'd separated himself from them. We three were all trapped in the shelter for the afternoon and night, so our introductions were lengthy and thorough. Sailor and I liked the young man, and when Litefoot asked politely if we would mind if he hiked with us, we assured him we would be happy to have him join us.

We were three again. By six in the morning, we were on our way to Mt. Rogers. On Buzzard Rock, a slope of Whitetop Mountain, a fog bank engulfed the mountainside. Sailor was barely visible several feet in front of me, and shrubs and bushes appeared and disappeared eerily in foggy mist as we wound around Whitetop.

Then the breeze picked up and nature astonished me once again. That huge bank of fog became a living entity that gathered itself and took flight, swiftly and silently retreating. It moved from my left to my right, like a huge cloud scudding across a clear sky. The entire hillside on which I stood came into view as the cloud of fog rolled down the slope, up another hillside beyond us, and then disappeared in the distance. No fog in Ohio has ever done that. I stood and watched in awe. The air was now crystal clear.

"Can you believe what you just saw?" I yelled ahead to Sailor, who had also stopped to watch the show. *Wow, God,*

You're on the job early today. That was a treat. With an opening act like that, this will be a great day.

We crossed Virginia Rt. 600 at Elk Garden and hiked through open pastures on our way to the summit of Mt. Rogers. The world was increasingly green, and I was finding more and more wildflowers to sample; I munched all kinds and colors of offerings from my salad bar in the wild.

It was a pleasant surprise to find that the Appalachian Trail did not go directly over the 5,729-foot summit. Rather, the trail traversed the shoulder of the mountain, a half mile below the peak. A blue-blazed trail led to the top, but a sign also told us, "No Views."

Soon after squeezing through a natural rock tunnel called Fat Man's Squeeze, we arrived at one of the prettiest spots in Virginia. The Wilburn Ridge and the Grayson Highlands are dotted with pink and red rock outcroppings, with clusters of evergreens scattered throughout open fields on the rolling hillsides.

Herds of wild ponies graze these highlands. Although hikers are encouraged not to feed the ponies, many of the animals were so tame that they nuzzled us, looking for a handout. The ponies roam everywhere in Grayson Highlands State Park, including shelters and camping areas. We passed the Thomas Knob Shelter and spotted three of them at the picnic table, scrounging for food like park chipmunks or squirrels.

The three of us set up camp that night on a grassy bald, next to a large rock outcropping below the ridge crest of Pine Mountain. That day had been a wonderful twenty-two-mile hike. Our second day in Virginia gave us a rogue fog bank, the three highest mountains in the state, scenic hikes through unique rock formations, and those wild keepers of th/ terlands, the ponies.

As dusk settled over the highlands, I summoned enough energy to scramble up one of the rock formations and watch the last glimmers of the setting sun fade behind the rolling peaks. From my roost on the rock, I looked over our three tents arranged on the green grass of the bald, and found myself smiling at the absurdity of this moment of my life.

I am sitting on a rock somewhere in Virginia. I quit my job. All I do is walk all day. I should be lonely—and often I am—but something is very different. Something that has been eluding me for years has finally overtaken me. Contentment. I've been living life too fast. But now that I'm traveling at two miles per hour, contentment has caught up with me. God, why do we make our lives so difficult, trying to find contentment?

I scrambled back down from my rocky perch, back across the grassy bald to my tent. Inside, I relaxed, leaving the tent flap open; the vista of sky and peaks was too good to block out. Only after darkness set in did I reach out and zip up the tent flap. Couldn't have those wild ponies sneaking in and stealing my food.

And I heard Pathfinder's voice in my head. *I could have been rich. Instead, I'm happy.*

By six the next morning, our grassy bald was fully lit with morning sun and we were ready for another day of adventure. An hour into our hike, we stopped at Old Orchard Shelter to filter water and have a celebratory snack. We had reached the 500-mile point of our trek. Trail conditions were easy and the miles slipped by quickly. Litefoot's company was pleasant and companionable; I looked forward to many days of conversation with him.

By eleven o'clock, we had hiked twelve miles and were in Dickey Gap. Virginia Rt. 650 crosses here, and a car was just dropping off a hiker as we arrived at the highway. It was good timing. The driver was the owner of Jerry's Kitchen and Goods, a small grocery store and restaurant several miles away in Troutdale, Virginia. He offered to drive us there for a hot meal and then return us to the trail. It was almost as amazing as trail magic—we stumbled out of the woods onto a little country road, and within one hour we had a hot meal at a restaurant and were back on the trail again.

That hot meal seemed to cast its magic on the afternoon. Sun soaked our path, log bridges took us over beautiful streams, and wildflowers bloomed in abundance. Good conversation and easygoing humor flowed like the many waterfalls we passed, and even our mountain climb seemed as gentle as its name: Brushy Mountain.

Our goal was to reach Partnership Shelter by that evening. That would require our longest day yet on the trail, but we felt energetic and optimistic. Our determination was undoubtedly bolstered by the incentive of pizza. Yes, pizza on the Appalachian Trail. The shelter was close to the Mt. Rogers National Recreation Area headquarters building, where a local pizza place had taped a menu to the outdoor pay phone, promising delivery. The imagined taste of cheese and spicy sauce kept us hiking at a good clip.

At six o'clock, we arrived at the shelter. Another great day. We'd hiked 26.4 miles in twelve hours, passed our five-hundred-mile mark, enjoyed a hot meal for lunch, and would possibly have pizza for supper. Could life get any better?

Partnership Shelter is one of the most comfortable shelters on the entire trail, a two-story log building that can easily sleep sixteen. It boasts a solar shower and piped water to a washbasin behind the shelter. Just down the trail, we found the headquarters, the pay phone, and the pizza menu. Things were looking good. Sailor and I ordered two pizzas and went back to the shelter to await delivery.

And then it happened. A goddess of stunning beauty sashayed from the shelter and took a seat at the picnic table in front of the building. Life could get better, it turned out. She had just emerged from the shower and was attired in her evening wear. Of course, being sociable folks, Litefoot and I sat down with the beauty.

On a whim, Bubbles had decided she wanted to do a section hike. She bought new equipment and headed down the trail. Five days later, she still had not figured out how to set up her tent. Every night in camp, men had offered to set it up for her, and of course she was happy to let them do it. I'll just say it: men can be stupid and gullible at times.

When God created Bubbles, He must have taken extra time, because it was a job well done. Every curve was in its proper place, and Litefoot was entranced by the whole package. No, no, no, Litefoot! It's a trap! You must resist the spell!

Our pizzas arrived, and later as Sailor and I headed for our tents, he speculated that Litefoot probably would not be hiking with us on the morrow. *Come on, Sailor*, I thought, *have some faith in our innocent young hiking partner.*

Early the next morning, Sailor and I were getting ready to leave. All was quiet in Litefoot's tent. "Hey, Litefoot, wake up!" My call got no response, and I grabbed one of my hiking poles and gave his tent a good rap. "You coming with us today?"

After a moment of silence, a hesitant voice came through the canvas.

"Ah . . . you guys go ahead without me. I'll catch up with you later."

Sailor gave me an I-told-you-so grin over the tent as we hoisted our packs for another day. I clung to the hope that Litefoot would escape the spell cast at the picnic table and rejoin us later in the day. Alas, we never saw him again. Several days later, we met a hiker who had also stayed at the shelter that night.

"Do you know what happened to Litefoot?" I asked, hoping we might still reconnect with our young friend.

"Sure do. He left the shelter that morning, hiking away with Bubbles."

As surely as Bubble rhymes with Trouble, Litefoot was now on a trail fraught with danger. After only a few days with us mature, sensible adults, he had jettisoned us for the first fair maiden to cross his path.

However, now that I think about it, we should have been forewarned. It was, after all, Partnership Shelter.

12

Choices and Consequences

Sailor and I had once again lost a hiking partner, but it was a splendid day in Virginia. We rolled through open fields fresh with spring green. Weathered farm buildings were scattered here and there, and we passed cattle grazing near our path. After hiking in the woods for most of our first five hundred miles, we felt a new sense of freedom in the open pastures.

We rounded a hilltop and saw I-81 in the distance, with a cluster of buildings huddling along its outline. We were nearing Atkins, Virginia, and our guidebook promised a country-style restaurant ahead. Back and forth we wound, across the rolling pasture land, through a grove of apple trees, descending the easy hillsides until we bottomed out at railroad tracks. A white blaze painted on the side of the rail assured us we were on the right track. We left the trail and headed up Highway 11 to The Barn Restaurant, where I sampled the salad bar—delicious, but lacking flowers.

Leaving the restaurant, I took a few steps down a small grassy incline and felt a muscle pop in the back of my leg. After all those steep, rocky climbs, my first injury came from just one small misstep.

As we walked back along Rt. 11, we met a lone hiker. My first meeting with Einstein was brief, but I knew I wanted to meet him again, somewhere, sometime. About my age and obviously a deep thinker, he seemed the embodiment of a Southern gentleman. Einstein was headed to the restaurant we had just left, and we went back to looking for our white blazes to get back on the trail.

The afternoon flew by, with ideal hiking weather and easy walking through fields and an occasional wooded area.

As afternoon faded to evening, we hiked a narrow corridor of the trail, surrounded by private property. We had long ago passed all available campsites, and the properties here were posted with signs prohibiting camping. But the evening light was quickly ebbing away and we had only two choices, both undesirable: either hike in the dark or find an illegal stealth campsite.

Being the fine, upstanding citizens we were, we opted to camp illegally. Both daylight and options were limited, so we scrambled down a bank and set up our tents beside a small stream at the edge of a meadow. The consistency of the cow patties told us cattle had recently passed through and probably used the stream as a watering hole. We would be sure to leave early in the morning, before they returned.

I cooked a gourmet dinner that night, dried beef stew enhanced by morel mushrooms. That afternoon, while hiking down Little Brushy Mountain, I had found several along the path. I could resist no longer; I dropped my pack and searched the surrounding area. Finding a patch of those succulent spring morsels, I triumphantly packed them away for dinner. I may have been encircled by cow patties, but I was king of my castle, dining on delicacies on my thirty-seventh night on the trail.

Randall Lee Smith was a troubled young man who lived near Pearisburg, Virginia. In May of 1981, he murdered two AT hikers at the Wapiti Shelter, not far from the home he shared with his mother. Smith pled guilty to second degree murder and was given thirty years in prison. After serving only fifteen years, he was released with ten years of probation. According to reports, during his incarceration he had only one visitor, one time. His mother visited him once in fifteen years, and it seemed there was no other friend or family who cared about him.

Released in 1996, he went back to live with his mother until she died in 2000. Then Randall Smith lived alone in a small shanty near the Appalachian Trail in Pearisburg. Law officials and several local residents tried to keep watchful eyes on him, but in April of 2008 Smith went missing. His mail had last been picked up in March, and no one had seen the man since. Some theorized he was camping in the woods, but he could not be located, so a missing persons report was filed.

On the evening we were stealth camping among cow patties, two fishermen were camped near Dismal Creek, one day's hike ahead of us. While they were eating supper, Randall Smith walked into their campsite. They extended hospitality, feeding him a meal of fresh trout and beans, and chatting over supper. When Smith rose to leave, he said, "Guys, I got to get out of here." And as thanks for their kindness, he shot them both. Fortunately, both men survived and were able to get help.

Smith stole the fishermen's truck, and the hunt for him ended when he crashed the vehicle while being chased by the police. He was admitted to the Roanoke Memorial Hospital for several nights, then released to police custody and jailed.

For the next few days, officials were on the trail with posters of Randall Smith, talking with hikers, trying to piece together his behavior during the last month. Had we seen him? Had we hiked or talked with him? I didn't wish to insult anyone, but I noted that Randall Smith, age fifty-four, with a grubby appearance, did look a lot like someone I'd hiked with: both Marathon Man and Sailor. Come to think of it, he looked a lot like me, with my unkempt hair and scruffy beard. The reality was that we never truly knew *who* we were hiking with. Although that was an unnerving thought, I never felt threatened by anyone I met on my hike.

Since law officials were everywhere on the trail, trying to investigate the movements of Randall Smith, the AT was closed just past Bland, Virginia. Shuttles transported hikers around the closed section to a point twenty miles farther up the trail. Some hikers were happy to ride those twenty miles instead of walking them, but many others chose to wait until the trail opened again.

Sailor and I both had mail drops waiting at the post office in Bland, so we decided to hitchhike into town and get a room at the Big Walker Motel, just off I-77. The trail brought us onto U.S. Rt. 21/52, directly across from the Mountain

Top Holiness Church, whose sign welcomed us to Bland. We were soon in the bed of a pickup, traveling the two and a half miles into town.

The Big Walker Motel sat on a hillside overlooking I-77. We had quite a hiker gathering that afternoon as many other hikers came in off the trail. We learned the trail would reopen in the morning, so Sailor and I planned to rise early and hike as long as possible the next day to make up for lost time. We had hiked only eleven miles that day; our goal was to reach Pearisburg, forty-three miles north, in just two days.

The next morning on our way out of Bland, we stopped at a small restaurant at the back of the local CITGO station and downed a delicious breakfast and plenty of coffee. We were soon on the road again, with our thumbs in the air.

Since the shooting, locals were reluctant to pick up hikers. We'd just resigned ourselves to walking the two miles back to the trail, when a lady graciously stopped and gave us a ride. She refused to be deterred by recent events; she enjoyed meeting hikers and kept a log of everyone she picked up.

The previous day had been short, we were rested, and we'd consumed large quantities of food in town, so we felt strong and the miles passed swiftly. The terrain varied little all day, with only a gentle climb up log steps to another Brushy Mountain. Virginia has nine Brushy Mountains and four mountains named Brush.

The trail led under a series of power lines that hissed and crackled. Although I always felt a bit uneasy standing under such power, the open area surrounding these lines usually gave us great views. Many of the lines went over the mountaintops, and from those heights the snaking lines of cable following cleared pathways over the ridges looked like an undulating highway leading to some distant town.

Steps formed of rocks and logs took us down to Kimberling Creek where a dramatic suspension bridge crossed the water. Wildflowers bloomed in profusion, and the rhododendron was just starting to show its color. Walking through a thicket of the large bushes, I questioned the sanity of sampling the huge blooms. Buds were beginning to open, but my appetite was not quite large enough to taste rhododendron that day.

Toward evening, we met hikers headed south. From them we learned that the Wapiti Shelter, site of the 1981 murders, was just ahead. We'd heard other hikers emphatically refuse to stay at that shelter, and now Sailor and I were faced with the choice ourselves. We had hiked over twenty-six miles and were ready to call it a day. And even though a sense of the macabre surrounded Wapiti, the shooter was now in jail. Another bonus: we would probably have the place to ourselves.

I don't believe in hauntings and ghosts, but the place did have an eerie atmosphere. The building was actually a new structure; the old shelter had been torn down after the murders. Still, I could not escape thoughts about what had happened on this site. One act had caused so much pain, and its consequences still trickled down to strangers just passing through more than twenty-five years later.

Sailor and I ate our meal in the shelter, but refused to sleep inside. We pitched our tents a little distance to one side of the building. No one else showed up that night. Although logic argued I was safe, I will admit that I found a good-sized rock and kept it within reach in the vestibule of my tent . . . just in case.

Morning arrived, and we were still alive.

The day started with an eight-hundred-foot climb and a fantastic view of Pearis Mountain from a rock outcropping. The forest floor was carpeted with ferns, and as we crossed Pearis, we walked through God's wild gardens, thick with blooming azaleas.

Descending the mountain, we headed to Pearisburg and checked in at the Plaza Motel. The weather forecast for the following day warned of an 80 percent chance of high winds, rain, and cold. We considered taking a zero day, but only briefly. Even though we'd left the business world, both of us were still very goal-oriented.

The next day was Mother's Day, May 11. Many hikers in the surrounding hostels and motels heeded the ominous warnings and stayed indoors, but Sailor and I again bet on the 20 percent chance that the weatherman was wrong.

If our mothers could have had any inkling of what lay ahead for their two sons, they surely would have wept.

At six in the morning, we stopped at Hardee's for a quick breakfast. Another hiker told us Randall Lee Smith had died in his cell the night before. Some thought he took his own life, but later reports said he died of natural causes, perhaps from his injuries in the car crash. Whatever the case, most people we met seemed relieved; they were rid of a longtime local embarrassment.

We hiked a mile on Rt. 100 to get back to the trail, and we were soon on Highway 460, searching for a white blaze. Settling into our stride, we climbed uphill for six miles. Then the wind picked up and the temperature began dropping dramatically. Coming out onto Rice Field, we had a panoramic view of Pearisburg and the community we had just left—and imminent trouble. Stretching across the entire horizon, a low, menacing cloud formation hung over the landscape. It had 80 percent written all over its dark face. Rice Field Shelter was in our sights, a wire fence separating it from the meadow. We climbed the fence and hustled for the protection of the shelter.

But the cold wind stormed after us, through the open front of the building. There was no refuge, and we concluded that we might stay warmer if we kept on hiking. Back over the fence we went, now heading into gale-force winds.

We hurried up the trail, knowing we couldn't outrun the storm, but moving as quickly as we could to keep warm. We passed under a power line as the wind whipped the lines back and forth with a force that broke off sections of the ceramic insulators. We skirted around the falling pieces. A cold mist settled over the landscape as the storm raged in and swallowed us.

The next several hours were misery as I'd never known misery. Misery and fear. Sleet and high winds pummeled us. My hands were so cold I could no longer feel the hiking poles I held. At Symms Gap Meadow, the thunder roared and lightning flashed as we hiked through the open field. Behind me, I heard Sailor yell the obvious, "We shouldn't be out here, you know."

"Right," I yelled back, "but our options are limited." There were no trees large enough to shelter us, but I was certain we wouldn't want to stand under a tree anyway with lightning striking everywhere around us. "Just stay as low as you can, and maybe the lightning will miss us." Across the cold, mist-shrouded meadow we hiked, bent as low as possible.

We must have looked like camels, our backpacks like humps as we hurried along.

Crack! Sizzle! A lightning bolt streaked several hundred feet ahead of us. I was sure there were targets on our packs, and that storm was determined to zap us. Another earthshaking boom, and another explosion of lightning on our path.

"Dear God, Your aim's not very good," I mumbled. Several frightful moments later, my prayer changed. *Dear God, go ahead and hit me if You want. I'm cold and wet and miserable, and a well-placed lightning bolt would at least warm me up.*

The only reply was the howling of the wind, and when no bolt hit, I heard my own adrenaline-laced shouting.

"If You're not going to zap me, here are my demands. I came out here on this trail because You assured me You'd meet me here. Never did You mention conditions this horrible. I want this storm to end! And not only do I want it to end, I want sunshine—and I want it NOW!"

Yes, I admit, I threw a fit, and although some folks might think we mortals should not talk to the Creator of the universe in this way, I believe He rather appreciated my forthrightness.

Thirty minutes later, we were walking in sunshine.

I'm not suggesting God gave in to His child's temper tantrum. But perhaps He does understand our anger, and maybe He listens to our frustrations. Maybe He is not put off when we get a little emotional.

Sailor and I congratulated each other on being alive and began the process of drying out. The next shelter was seven miles away, but we hoped to reach it before another deluge hit us. The sun dried and warmed us for several hours, but as we came in sight of the Pine Swamp Branch Shelter, rain began falling again.

We hurried to the shelter, but again found no refuge. A previous storm had toppled a tree onto the building, collapsing most of the roof, and only a shell remained. Sailor quickly erected his tent and disappeared into his safe harbor. I, on the other hand, was busy being brilliant.

On both sides of the shelter, a few feet of roof remained, covering what was at one time the interior wooden platform. Could I possibly squeeze my tent under those few feet for more protection from the downpour? I erected my tent on the picnic table outside the shelter, then picked up Big Agnes and shoved her sideways under the protruding roof. Half of the tent was now under the remnants of roof, but since Big Agnes sat on the wooden floor, I could not properly extend the rain fly. There was no way to stake the fly, as I would have on the forest floor, so I just threw the rain fly over the top of the tent, hoping the water would run off and drain away from my campsite.

I dashed across the trail to a stream and filtered water for my meal, with raindrops pelting me relentlessly. But then another problem presented itself. Inside shelters, we normally hung food bags from the ceiling to keep the contents out of reach of resident rodents. There was no roof and no place to hang my food for safekeeping. The night was probably too miserable for even mice to be out and about, but just in case, I sacrificed.

I still had several packs of Little Debbies with me, and I placed one pack outside my tent on the wooden floor as a peace offering to any nibbling night creature that might be hungry. Hopefully, the offering would prevent any mouse from chewing a hole in my tent while in quest of the bigger food bag within.

At last the cold, frightening, miserable day was over. I relaxed, climbing into my sleeping bag, smug about my tent location and mouse offering. However, my brilliant tent setup was not working brilliantly. Water leaked into the front of the tent, soaking the top of my sleeping bag. I sopped up all the water I could with my shirt, and once again crawled out and tried to reposition my tent. Then I scrunched myself and the sleeping bag into the only corner that was still dry.

The good ship Big Agnes stayed afloat, although she took on quite a bit of water. I spent most of the night bailing and listening to the wind moaning through the splintered edges of the roof and creating haunting sounds as if the shelter were mourning its loss.

13

It Is What It Is

When morning light finally signaled the end of the night's torment, I stuffed my wet and lumpy sleeping bag into its sack and unzipped my tent to check on the Little Debbies. The delicacy had not been touched. I knew that the package contained over two hundred calories, fuel I could not ignore. The cakes were my own breakfast.

Not wishing a repeat of yesterday's misery, I donned my GORE-TEX rainsuit, then quickly dismantled my tent. This day was also rainy, windy, and cold, but never matched the terrible conditions of the previous day. We hiked eighteen and a half miles and called it a day when we reached Laurel Creek Shelter. This shelter did have a roof and faced away from the wind. We dropped our packs with relief; at least there was a possibility of a good night's sleep here.

I pulled my sleeping bag from its stuff sack, and it dropped to the floor with a thud. Still damp from the previous night, the bag carried the stench of wet feathers. I could not sleep wrapped in the foul smell, so at the least I would need to dry the area where I would lay my head. Brilliance struck again. I crawled inside the sleeping bag with my cookstove. Tenting the bag over my head, I lit the stove and began the drying process. The smell was horrible, but the tactic actually worked—the dampness warmed and evaporated.

Just when I was congratulating myself on my ingenuity, a new aroma permeated my little cocoon—burning feathers. I had burned a hole in the bag, and feathers were escaping, landing on the stove and bursting into a display of fireworks. Alarmed, I threw back the sleeping bag, and a cloud of feathers puffed into the air around me, drifting gently to the floor.

Duct tape patched the burned hole, but at least I had a dry place to lay my head that night. Granted, I also had a splitting headache from the fumes I'd inhaled, but I willingly paid that price for a good night's sleep. I scooped up some of the feathers on the floor and stuffed them down a small gap in the shelter floor. Mice might reject my Little Debbies, but surely they would appreciate this gift.

My efforts did produce rest that night, and morning brought the gift of sunshine. It's incredible how sunshine can improve one's disposition. A sunny day also gave us an opportunity to dry out all our gear. At noon, we stopped at the Niday Shelter and, under the midday sun, spread tents, sleeping bags, and all our wet clothes over any and every bush. In an hour, we again had dry equipment and our packs were several pounds lighter.

As I had planned this hike and counted the miles and days I would be on the trail, I questioned whether I might become bored hiking through the woods day after day.

I never did. Every twist and turn brought new wonder.

I remembered a quote from Benton MacKaye, the originator of the AT. He said the ultimate purpose of the Appalachian Trail would be "to walk; to see and to see what you see."[1] How often we witness a scene of great beauty but don't comprehend what we see. A beautiful sunset, a bright full moon, brilliant stars on a cloudless night. We are too busy to see. The stresses of life blind us. Our eyes behold, but we do not grasp the greatness of what God placed here for our enjoyment.

Several weeks before, walking along a lovely stretch of trail where flowers splashed their colors everywhere and trees towered above me, I remarked to God that He had done a particularly good job on that section of the trail. I heard Him reply, *You are my son, and I made it for you.*

The Creator of everything I saw had named me as a son. I was an heir. How wonderful is that? If we could actually grasp the significance of that father-child relationship, then perhaps we could also begin to see what we see—and maybe even know what we know.

Sailor and I hiked in twenty-one miles of sunshine that thirteenth day of May. By evening, we were crossing Rt. 620, a small country road that follows Trout Creek. We weren't too far from the next shelter, but it was half a mile off the trail and we did not want an additional mile of hiking. Hiking wisdom recommends camping away from highways, but this was a small country road and we were ready to call it a day. Our tents went up, in sight of both the creek and the road.

Most of our clothes and equipment had dried in the sunshine during our noonday break, but my shoes had been

1. Jim Schmid, ed., "Trail Quotations part 3," *American Trails*, http://www.americantrails.org/quotes2.html.

damp for most of the day. Now, as we stopped for the night, I realized that even my shoes were dry; everything had finally recovered from the downpours of the last two days.

I took my water filter to the knee-deep Trout Creek, running clear and cold just across from our campsite. Perched on a rounded rock, I filtered a liter of water and then jumped back to the creek bank. And slipped. My dry shoes were once again waterlogged.

We were on the trail early the next morning. Morning sun slanted through the trees and the beauty of a Virginia spring throbbed around us. We crossed Trout Creek on a footbridge, and immediately the trail turned upward. Our challenge of the day would be Cove Mountain, with rock formations along its spine. The most prominent formation, Dragon's Tooth, jutted upward another thirty-five feet from the mountain. Our descent proved every bit as difficult as the climb. The trail downward was a series of rock steps and switchbacks; u-shaped iron rods had been inserted in the cliff walls, handholds to assist hikers navigating the steep path.

Eight miles brought us to Rt. 624. A small grocery down the road promised hot breakfasts, pizza, sandwiches, and supplies. The lure of food was irresistible. And when we arrived, we found real luxury: restrooms.

We ate. And ate. We sat on the concrete outside the store and feasted.

I checked my phone and found I had not only service but also a message. My youngest daughter had been busy herself the previous day. While I was laboring over the Virginia mountains, she was laboring to give birth to a son named Isaac.

159

"I'm a grandfather!" I yelled to Sailor.

"Congratulations!"

I'm an absentee grandfather, I thought to myself. Should I have been with my daughter instead of trekking through the mountains? Her mother never would have missed this event. I called my daughter and she was very clear: yes, she wanted me at home.

By the next evening, Sailor and I would be in Daleville, Virginia, where my friend Ina would meet me and drive me back to Damascus for Trail Days. I had scheduled two zero days to attend the event; Ina would then bring me back to Daleville, and I would continue my hike. But after talking with my daughter, I considered riding back home with my friend, spending several days there, and then coming back to the trail.

A big question mark was written on that plan: If I took a break now, would I ever get back to the hike? My imagination put me at home with my family, relaxing on my front porch. The picture was so enticing that I knew if I left the trail, I would probably never come back. And yet—I had a new grandson to hold and a daughter who wanted me to come home. I still had a few days to mull it over.

I dangled at the edge of the cliff, peering cautiously over the edge. McAfee Knob, one of the most photographed spots on the AT, juts out over a long valley; and from my perch I could see tomorrow's challenge, Tinker Cliffs.

On my hikes in the Grand Canyon, I'd developed my own system to rate "survivability levels" of falls from precarious perches. The scale of danger ran from broken bones to hospital stays to extended hospital stays to certain death. McAfee Knob registered somewhere between "extended hospital stay" and "certain death." Trees below might snag a plummeting hiker and prevent instant death, but death might be the more favorable ending. Still, I couldn't resist the photo op, standing at the tip of the rock with nothing but sky behind me, and then sitting, reclining casually with my legs dangling over the edge.

As I lounged at the edge of the high rock, I was still mulling over my dilemma. This spot was seven hundred miles into my hike, almost one-third of the distance to that sign on Mt. Katahdin. Every mile brought new people and experiences into my life. I was leaving behind the old and becoming new. And I *liked* what I was becoming. What adventure and transformations lay ahead? What might I miss if I went home now? What things did God still want to show me?

Another ending. This was my last night in Sailor's company. Tomorrow we would arrive in Daleville. From there, I would head back to Trail Days in Damascus and Sailor and his son would continue the hike together.

We stopped at Campbell Shelter for the night. Situated on a slight incline set back from the trail, it was a peaceful spot. Deer ventured close to the shelter throughout the evening, unalarmed by our presence. The quiet spring evening in the woods was a perfect ending to a perfect day.

Tinker Cliffs were beautiful . . . and challenging. The trail threaded through, around, and over massive boulders, and we scrambled over formations with unusual names like Snack Bar Rock, Lunch Box Rock, and Hay Rock.

I could not ignore the stabbing pains in my left leg. I'd altered my hiking gait after pulling a muscle on that incline outside the restaurant, and the change had possibly put more strain on my left leg. Or maybe, after seven hundred miles, my legs just decided they were tired. I limped toward Daleville, and the only thing that kept me walking was the promise that once I reached town, I would have two zero days to recover.

We left the woods abruptly. Emerging from the safety of the forest and finding ourselves at the edge of a major highway always astounded us. We stood on Rt. 220, where thousands of cars passing daily probably never noticed the small path through the trees, leading 717 miles south to Springer Mountain, Georgia.

A short walk down the highway brought us to a Howard Johnson, where Sailor would stay for the night and meet his son in the morning. I had a four-hour wait for my trail boss Ina to arrive and take me back to Trail Days. Hikers on many roads in all directions were finding their way to the reunion. During the time I waited, several cars pulled into the parking lot, and the occupants rolled down windows and asked if anyone needed a ride to Trail Days.

Ina arrived at six o'clock. Seeing me for the first time since Springer Mountain, she burst into tears. Turns out, though, these were not tears of joy at seeing me again; rather, she was shocked by the pathetic figure I presented. I could barely walk, had lost almost forty pounds, and was undernourished and undergroomed.

For the next two days, Ina pumped me full of anti-inflammatory drugs and huge quantities of high-calorie foods. In retrospect, my trail boss probably saved my hike.

Trail Days, begun in 1987 as part of the Appalachian Trail's 50th anniversary, is a gathering and reunion, a chance for hikers to share stories and knowledge, to meet old trail friends, and to take a few days of rest. Vendors set up booths hawking equipment and food, and music and activities fill two days. A city of tents springs up, and everything quirky and timeless about the trail permeates this celebration of the AT family.

In my pre-hike life, my judgmental spirit would have stifled any enjoyment of this event. I would have looked askance at this odd assortment of humanity. Now I was a part of it. I had lived on the trail for almost two months, and I knew the character of many of these hikers. In Damascus, I looked at the crowds and knew these were some of the most genuine and honest folks I would ever meet. Time and again, I had witnessed hikers young and old come to the aid of another. It seems like the less a person has, the more willing he is to give it away.

Two days passed quickly, and I was still in considerable pain. My leg ached and my decision to continue my hike also left an ache; I knew my choice was selfish and this hike was taking priority over my family. Ever since I'd heard the news of my grandson's birth, I had been arguing with myself. If I went home to see him now, the risk was great that I would never return and finish the hike. Little Isaac would not even know Grandpa had been missing, but I knew I was disappointing my daughter.

Her sad "I need you here" lingered in my mind when Ina dropped me off back in Daleville. I limped across Rt. 220 to the trail, a pathetic figure who had just put his own agenda above his family. For the first time since my first hours on the trail, I was hiking alone, and thoughts of family and home intensified my loneliness.

Dear God, I hope You're out here today, because I haven't felt this alone in a long time.

For eleven miles I struggled to keep moving; every step sent sharp pains through my shin. At Wilson Creek Shelter, I found six other hikers already settled in. I set up my tent outside, both to avoid the snores and to have my own space while I felt sorry for myself. I had disappointed my daughter. I was homesick. My body ached. And I realized I was starting over—I recognized no one inside the shelter. A rainy night matched my mood, but the morning brought sunshine, and I started a new day.

The trail crossed the Blue Ridge Parkway several times in the twenty miles I hiked that day. Those twenty miles were made possible by more drugs than I take in most years. Twelve Advil taken throughout the morning did nothing to curb the pain. In the afternoon, while on a break at Cove Mountain Shelter, I met Cheech, a hiker who had also been at the Wilson Creek Shelter the previous night. Cheech had just returned to the trail after a hiking injury and subsequent emergency surgery. He carried prescription pain pills and generously shared them with me. After taking the big blue wonder pill, I went floating over the blue ridges, which soon became the Blur Ridge Mountains. I no longer felt pain in my leg; I didn't feel much of anything. All I was aware of, on that dreamy afternoon, was a little stomach discomfort from my pharmaceutical diet.

At the Bryant Ridge Shelter that night, I reflected on my two solitary days. I'd been worried about the prospect of hiking alone, but I realized the loneliness I felt at times was now superseded by another feeling: confidence. I was confident hiking alone. I was going to be all right out here, after all. I had survived losing my wife, I had survived leaving my job, and now I was passing another test. I could survive by myself. *I am on the adventure of a lifetime, and I will enjoy what each day brings, whether I'm alone or in the company of others.*

Cheech also stopped at Bryant Ridge, and I thanked him for sharing his painkillers. He reached into his medicine bag and gave me four more for the next day. Trail magic!

I needed those painkillers for several big climbs. Apple Orchard Mountain loomed ahead. But I never saw Apple Orchard. A thick fog bank parked on the mountain and refused to move. Bare tree limbs reached out of the fog as I passed, and trail signs were barely visible until I stood in front of them. The fog and blue pill combined to make my memories of that morning vague and dreamlike.

Later in the day, visibility improved and I hiked along a ridge where the elements were gearing up for battle. On one side of the ridge the sun shone brilliantly; on the other side storm clouds threatened. I hoped the sun would prevail.

I smiled a lot that day too, and I'm fairly certain that was not an effect of the drugs. It was impossible to look at spring wildflowers and not smile. Those bursts of color that I had rushed past and never seen in my old life now brought little surges of joy. On that day, pink and white azaleas bloomed in profusion along my path, an absolute gift from God.

My solitary plod ended at seven that evening; I had hiked 22.7 miles. Arriving at Matts Creek Shelter, I found it empty.

Tents were pitched within sight of the building, but the shelter itself was unoccupied. I dropped my pack inside and anticipated a quiet night, having the shelter to myself.

Before unpacking, I checked the register to read the daily trail news. There was a reason I had the building to myself. Recent entries complained of an infestation of fleas. Hikers recorded horror stories about waking up at night to find bites all over their bodies, and so I camped outside that night along with everyone else.

As I signed my entry in the register, another name caught my eye. For weeks, I had followed Sir Enity and his journal posts. His entries always spoke about peace and love and often ended with "If you can't carry it in your heart or on your back, you probably don't need it." Since I marched to the beat of a faster drummer, I often caught up with hikers ahead of me. And the entry tonight told me I had finally caught up with Sir Enity.

There were others whom I hoped to overtake on the trail too. A priest on sabbatical was on a pilgrimage somewhere ahead of me. A young man was hiking along the AT as part of a trek around the world. I hoped to meet them and hear their stories.

I set up Big Agnes and went to the creek to filter water. A lone figure emerged from a tent at the edge of the creek and joined me. Sir Enity had entered my world. We introduced ourselves, and in the ensuing conversation I found that his wife had also passed away, after a short illness just eight months before. He told me his story.

"After she passed away, I took a good look at my situation, took stock of what was important to me, and decided I didn't need anything that I couldn't carry in my heart or on my back. I gave away 90 percent of my accumulated stuff and came to the trail."

His wife's body had been cremated, and Sir Enity carried a vial of her ashes with him to scatter at the base of the Mt. Katahdin sign. "I cannot tell you how much I miss her," he said. He didn't have to try; I already knew.

"You know, Apostle, there just isn't any way to make sense of it. It is what it is," he added sadly.

Of all the moving words that have been written about loss, this phrase puts it most succinctly. I lay in my tent that night and kept returning to his words and the image of a man carrying a vial of his wife's ashes with him on the long, hard path to Maine. His grief was so familiar to me.

It is what it is.

14

Chasing Dreams

On the trail, I was shedding not only the stresses of my business life, but also all the distractions that had kept me from truly seeing myself, others, and this hike we call Life. I was learning to see what I saw. God had said He would meet me on the trail. Experiences and people that in my everyday world would have passed unnoticed now carried messages I was able to hear. I finally had time to listen and learn.

Take the footbridge over the James River, for example. For many years, hikers had only one route across this river, a narrow two-lane highway that made the crossing dangerous. A local man's vision and determination changed that for me and for every other hiker on the trail today.

Bill and Laurie were a local couple who thru-hiked the Appalachian Trail and found themselves transformed into believers in the mission and vision of the AT. They became active in the Appalachian Trail Conservancy and worked as trail maintainers with their local club. Their stretch of trail included that bridge crossing the James River, and for over a decade Bill single-mindedly pursued the dream of a separate hiker bridge spanning the waters. Many times throughout those years, the new bridge seemed an impossibility. But today it reaches 625 feet across the river, a testament to Bill's hard work and a series of serendipitous events.

Bill saw possibilities in five railroad piers in the river, no longer in use, owned by a local businessman. He visited the owner and explained his dream. The owner agreed to sell. Not only did he agree to sell, the asking price was only $1.00. Bill had the solid beginnings of his bridge.

Nine years of clearing obstacles, both financial and legal, finally resulted in the dedication of the James River Foot Bridge in 2000. The dedication of the bridge was also a memorial to Bill, who had died of cancer just months before and never walked across his own dream.

I stood by the bridge and read the memorial plaque: "Bill pursued his passions, honored his dreams, and cherished those around him." This man had not just raced thoughtlessly through his life. I compared my own life. Did I even know what my passions were? Had I let my dreams die? Would I cherish the people in my life and appreciate what they brought to me?

I climbed all morning, arriving at the top of Bluff Mountain just before noon. It was my highest elevation of the day. The view was grand, but the company was even grander: at the peak, I found Sailor and his son also enjoying the view.

That afternoon I walked a section of the trail where rhododendron blossoms drifted down and lined the path with pink petals. I felt like royalty parading along a path of homage, or a bride floating down a petal-strewn aisle. Either notion seemed a bit ridiculous. I was just a solitary hiker wandering down God's trail through His great outdoor cathedral.

Euphoria cranked up my courage. Now was the time to sample rhododendron. I plucked a nice specimen and hesitated only a few seconds before popping it into my mouth. *They sure look a lot better than they taste*, I thought as I chewed and chewed and chewed.

A twenty-two-mile jaunt through the mountains ended at Brown Mountain Creek Shelter where I stopped for the night, happy to see that Sailor and his son were also there. Sir Enity, though, was low on food and needed to resupply. He hiked two more miles to U.S. 60, where he hoped to hitch a ride into Buena Vista. There he would find a motel, buy food, and head back to the trail in the morning.

The next day, I arrived at U.S. 60 just as a truck dropped off Sir Enity, who brought an extra Burger King breakfast sandwich he had decided to gift to the first hiker he met. And luckily, that was me.

It was a good beginning to another hard day of climbing. Bald Knob and Cold Mountain both demanded strenuous effort from legs and lungs. I thought back to the day Sailor, Marathon Man, and I had entered Virginia. We had anticipated easier hiking. And the springtime Blue Ridge Mountains were easier than the frozen, snow-covered Smokies, but this entire hike was far more difficult than I had ever imagined.

Sir Enity and I set our sights on Rockfish Gap, which we hoped to reach in two days. The Gap marks the entrance to Shenandoah National Park and is only a short distance from Waynesboro, Virginia, where we planned to make a town stop. On the top of Cold Mountain, I had cell service and called ahead to make a motel reservation.

Toward evening, we crossed the small, rutted Crabtree Farm Road that cuts through the forest. A four-wheel drive vehicle was parked near the trail, and a young couple had spread a private picnic. Sir Enity hesitated to crash their party, but I insisted that we at least attempt to mooch some food. It was one of the best trail magic moments of my entire trek. The couple offered bananas, carrots, tortilla chips, drinks, bread, and a complete Mountain House meal that I stashed away for later consumption. The young picnickers had already given us most of their supplies, but they asked if we needed anything more.

"How about Aleve? Would you have any of those?" I asked. My shin splints were almost gone, but so was my Vitamin I.

"Sure do," the young man replied, and he poured out a handful for me.

The trail magic energized us for the last climb of the day, Priest Mountain. Several hundred feet below the summit, we stopped at the Priest Shelter. A church group had commandeered the building, so Sir Enity and I set up our tents nearby. We found entertaining reading material that night; hikers were using the Priest register as a confessional. Records of transgressions filled the pages; the most frequent sin reported was the theft of toilet paper. During town stops, hikers often unroll a liberal amount of toilet paper to take with them for later use.

Sir Enity and I crossed Priest Mountain in the early morning light. The day was difficult but rewarding; twenty-four miles took us to heights and depths. From 4,063-foot Priest Mountain, we dropped to just 997 feet at the banks of the Tye River, where we wobbled across a wooden suspension bridge that swayed like a pendulum. Then it was back uphill as we headed into the Three Ridges Wilderness area to a height of over 4,000 feet that gave us splendid views over the valleys and mountain ranges. White mountain laurel bloomed around us, and purple and white flowers flaunted their wild beauty along the path. Several graceful waterfalls coursed over rocky drops.

We finally stopped on top of Hanging Rock and took a moment to imbibe the sweetness of the day. Below us lay farms and fields of the beautiful Shenandoah Valley. At our backs, honeysuckle blossoms sent out their sweet aroma. I felt fortunate, one of the privileged few who would ever sit on this spot and savor such a moment.

Sir Enity finally convinced me to stop sniffing the flowers and get moving. The rest of our day was filled with stream crossings, log steps up and down inclines, and mountaintop experiences in the sky. We had no particular goal except to get as close to Waynesboro as possible.

The sun was dropping in the sky when we reached Humpback Mountain, still eleven miles from Waynesboro. We were not stopped by darkness or our physical condition. We were halted by our surroundings. Near the crest of Humpback, the trail led over rocky outcroppings at the breathtaking edge of the mountain, with views reaching for miles over the Shenandoah Valley. Sir Enity voiced my thoughts: it would be fantastic to camp here and watch the day disappear over the valley.

We searched for a camping area and found a grassy spot perfect for our two tents, just a few yards back from the jutting stone ledge. I set up Big Agnes and within minutes had water boiling for a hot meal. Hidden somewhere in the rocks, Sir Enity called my name. "Apostle, get over here! You've gotta see this!"

I grabbed my food and headlamp and followed the direction of his voice. He was perched on the rocks with the world stretched out far below. I found my own seat in the grandstand, an indentation in the stone that fit my body and still held lingering warmth from the day's sunshine. We sat and watched the sunset in silence, two wanderers on a lonely trail, both on our own quest for peace. Among the billions of humans on earth that night, only we two had these front row seats as earth moved from day to night.

The sun disappeared, and now, across the expansive valley, twilight slowly ebbed away and darkness descended. Smaller lights flickered on, as folks in distant buildings lit their little worlds against the darkness; lights were going on in my much larger world too, as the stars grew brighter. Soon there was no horizon; sky and valley melded into one, and the entire world was blackness with tiny dots of shimmering light. The God of the universe had just ended another day in the Shenandoah Valley, moving the light on its journey westward, on to other beginnings and endings.

We sat in awed silence long after darkness had arrived, and then stumbled back to our tents. During the night, the local deer snorted their disapproval of the two invaders of their grassy spot, but we slept and rested well at the edge of the world.

God had allowed two rock dwellers to sit ringside while He worked His majesty. I am astounded that some folks think this all started with one big bang.

The morning light glowed softly as it fell on the mountain and returned to the valley after its overnight journey. We had only eleven miles to Rockfish Gap, almost all downhill. The trail down Humpback Mountain was rocky but scenic, crossing streams and winding through the forest.

The woods ended at the bottom of a highway embankment. We'd arrived at Rockfish Gap, where I-64 and U.S. 250 intersect. Here too the Blue Ridge Parkway transitions into Skyline Drive. We crossed the road to an information center and found a list of people willing to drive hikers into Waynesboro. We chose a name, made the call, and were picked up by a lively and informative lady of eighty-four years, who drove us to the Quality Inn where we had made reservations.

Arriving in town at noon is almost like a day off. Food, laundry, and resupply were the order of the afternoon. At the laundromat, I washed every article of my clothing. Yes, even what I was wearing at the time. I stepped behind a bank of washers—to avoid causing a distraction and possible arrest—shed my clothes, and donned my rain gear.

Across from me, a hiker emptied a food box on the floor. His big, floppy straw hat and a flute lying nearby told me I had at last caught up with Padre the priest. I introduced myself. He was staying that night at a local church hostel. I wanted more time to talk with this man and hoped our paths would cross again.

We ate and rested—important activities during town stops.

The next morning during breakfast at the Quality Inn, a hiker walked in, topped with a mop of brown hair I immediately recognized. Back at the Barn Restaurant in Atkins, Sailor and I had been headed back to the trail when we had met this hair and the mind underneath.

I reminded Einstein of our meeting and we chatted. "With a name like that, you must be a deep thinker," I joked. But he was, indeed, a solemnly reflective person. "I'm just out here contemplating everything I've ever been taught," he told us.

Contrary to Sir Enity and me, Einstein had a wonderful wife who was fully alive and supportive of his quest to hike the 2,200-mile think tank. We invited him to hike with us, and now our group not only had heart and courage—we had a brain.

We three joined others gathering at the entrance to Shenandoah National Park and went through the formality of filling out permits admitting us to the park.

The Appalachian Trail and Skyline Drive both wander through Shenandoah National Park. The trail crosses the famous highway several times. Other times, walking high on a mountain, we would see the scenic blacktop route snaking along below us.

The second day in the park, we stopped for an impromptu ceremony on Baldface Mountain. We had just completed mile nine hundred. Sir Enity scrawled "900 Miles" on a dead tree by the trail. We admired his handiwork and signed our names, knowing the act violated the "leave no trace" principle of hiking, but wanting to leave a point of celebration and encouragement for fellow hikers.

The park has a series of waysides, businesses located along the highway for travelers to eat, fuel, and shop. We stopped at Big Meadows Wayside for lunch, where I was shocked to see gas prices had risen to over $4.00 a gallon. I predicted that more folks would soon be walking.

Sir Enity was meeting his brother at Big Meadows, and they planned to hike together for several days. Einstein and I went on together, but he would meet his wife in Front Royal and then I would again be hiking alone. The three of us made plans to meet again in Harpers Ferry a week later.

That evening as Einstein and I approached Skyland Road, I could not resist the temptation of a soft bed and a good meal. Skyland Lodge and Restaurant was just down the road, so I headed there and Einstein planned to camp just a short distance down the trail. I would catch up with him the next day. I know I paid too much for those comforts that night, but the prime rib and blackberry cobbler sure hit the spot.

The next morning, I ate breakfast with a hiker who was attempting a thru-hike for the third time. The previous year he had made it to Connecticut, but then fell ill and had to leave the trail. And now this year, in Virginia, he confided to me that this was his last day. He was going to quit. "I am just so tired and lonely," he told me. He had called home, and his wife told him he could come home only if he promised not to make another attempt the next year. "I wanted to do it so badly, but I miss home too much." I thought again of those words: *unless it's the most important thing in your life at the time, you probably won't finish.*

Nearing Elkwallow Gap, I began to look for Einstein's campsite. I had not caught a glimpse of him all day, but in the event I didn't catch him, we had agreed to camp here at the end of the day.

The area was not suitable for tenting, though; it was full of dense bushes and undergrowth. I guessed Einstein had kept on hiking, looking for a good site.

The trail crossed the highway just one-tenth of a mile from Elkwallow Wayside and more food. I was detoured by the thought of a hot dog and an ice cream bar. The treat was delicious, but the day was slipping away and I still had not found Einstein. I hurried back to the trail.

Less than a mile from the Gap, a trail leads off the AT to Range View Cabin. At this intersection, just a few feet off the trail, Einstein had set up camp. I never saw his tent and kept on hiking.

Several hours and several more Skyline Drive crossings later, I was still looking for Einstein's camp. I hiked over four peaks on Hogback Mountain in the fading twilight, and I picked up my pace. The light was starting to play tricks on me.

At this point in the Shenandoah Mountains, most hikers had already reported seeing bears. I had not seen any. Two days before, I was hiking a short distance ahead of Sir Enity and Einstein; at a road crossing, they called for me to stop. When they caught up with me, they told me I had walked right by a large bear, less than fifteen feet from the trail. I had never seen the animal, but they had even photographed it.

In broad daylight, I had been unable to see a bear, but now in the fading light I was seeing bears everywhere. Tree trunks became shaggy threats, and several times I stopped in my tracks, heart pounding, as I waited for the distant tree-trunk bears to move away from my path. And it was not just bears that lurked in the darkening evening; I saw dogs, cats, and wolves, as the faint light conspired with rocks and stumps and bushes to give me the heebie-jeebies.

Finally, a trail sign. With relief, I read that Gravel Springs Hut was two-tenths of a mile to the right. Surely Einstein would be there. I found my way to the shelter in the near-darkness, filling my water bottle at a spring along the trail. At the front of the shelter, I peered through the shadows at hikers already in sleeping bags.

"Hey, is Einstein in there?"

"Not in here," came the reply.

Several hundred feet past the shelter and behind the privy, a few tent sites sat vacant in the dark. No one else was here. I set up my tent and cooked my food, wondering what had happened to Einstein.

A bear pole had been erected to hang food bags. It reminded me of a maypole, about fifteen feet tall with hooks protruding from the top to suspend bags high in the air. Nearby, I found a metal pole with one hooked end. I placed the heavy food bag on this hook, then lifted it unsteadily toward the hangers at the top of the maypole. It was a difficult balancing act, made even more difficult by darkness. My headlamp shone into the heavens as I waved the long pole skyward and tried to hang the dangling food bag above any bear's reach. I swayed and teetered around the pole, working to make the connection, feeling like a May dancer weaving in the May night. I imagined bears watching from the woods, laughing heartily at my antics.

I awoke several times during the night, hearing loud crashing in the undergrowth around my solitary camp. I shone my light through the tent and yelled at whatever was out there.

Morning arrived at last, and the shadowy bears had eaten neither me nor my food.

That last day in Shenandoah National Park, I saw five bears. It was no wonder, then, that a noise crashing through the woods behind me made me jump and whirl around.

Einstein came blasting up the trail. His unique hiking style had only one speed—the same velocity, uphill or down. I struggled up difficult hills, but he never slowed. On this afternoon, I was sure that he had cranked up the speed one more notch; it was the day he was meeting his wife in Front Royal.

The trail crossed U.S. 522 at Chester Gap. Sailor and his son were also at this road crossing, trying to get a hitch into Front Royal, four miles away. I still had fifty-three miles to hike in two days to reach Harpers Ferry, West Virginia, so I wanted to keep moving. "See you guys in a few days," I yelled to Einstein as I headed up the trail.

The trail followed the southern boundary of the National Zoo. Chain fencing encircled several thousand acres, and my guidebook said that many rare and endangered animals were behind those fences. I didn't see any animals, but I did see holes in the fence that would have allowed large animals to escape. Perhaps they were all on my side of the fence by now.

At five o'clock I arrived at the Jim and Molly Denton Shelter. This comfortable shelter boasts a front deck and inviting deck chairs. I could go no farther. I settled in with the intention of getting an early start the next morning. I was the only person there, so I set up Big Agnes inside the shelter. A brother and sister team doing a section hike arrived later that night, but they set up their tents nearby.

A good night's sleep prepared me for my longest hiking day yet.

The day started with great promise. I was on the trail soon after five thirty; the sun came up, and I was feeling good.

The first twist of the day came in a field where weeds growing to my shoulders crowded the path. As I pushed my way through, with only my head above the weeds, dust and pollen flew everywhere. When I came out at the end of the long field, I was coated with a layer of white dust.

Half a mile later, I lost the trail in a rocky area where the white blazes seemed to have evaporated. I stumbled in circles for quite a while before finally spotting one of those small white rectangles. Once back on the trail, I could hardly believe my bad luck—I was forced into yet another field filled with those tall weeds. A second dust storm ensued as I pushed my way through the maze.

At the other end of the field, I met the brother and sister who had camped at the shelter the night before. They seemed surprised to see me. "Apostle, why are you headed back to the shelter?"

I had made one too many turns around that rock pile, looking for blazes, and I was hiking the wrong direction, retracing my steps of the morning. Now I had to navigate the dusty weed patch a third time.

Twelve miles into my day, a trail cut off to the right, leading to Sky Meadows State Park. At this intersection in the woods, someone had placed a wooden park bench, a perfect spot to take a break.

I heard the warning thunder and quickly pulled my rain cover over my pack. But the day was warm, and I decided not to wear my rain gear. I would just take the shower, and hopefully the sun would soon return and dry me out. The plan worked . . . sort of.

The rain soon turned into a downpour. I tried to find shelter under a tree, but I was soaked through in fifteen minutes. The sun did return and I was almost dry in less than an hour. But then another downpour soaked me. Three times I went through this wash and dry cycle. The third time the sun appeared, I was in the woods walking a downhill path, hunched against the rain striking my shoulders, when the sun sent dazzling beams of light through the trees, meeting the shimmering mist rising from the ground. The sudden brilliance lit up the woods, and I took it as a promise from God that He was finished blasting me with storms . . . for this day, at least.

In the middle of the afternoon, I stood in front of a sign welcoming me to the Roller Coaster. This section of the trail covers nine miles of steep ups and downs. Before I started this hike, I read about this series of hills and imagined the fun of flying up and down these rollers on the way to Harpers Ferry. But now I noted that the welcome sign also bore this message:

HAVE A GREAT RIDE AND WE WILL
SEE YOU AT THE BLACKBURN TRAIL
CENTER (IF YOU SURVIVE)

So I was finally here, and it wasn't fun. None of the hills were extremely tall, but the cumulative elevation gain and loss rivaled many of the biggest mountain climbs on the trail. Steep upward scrambles were followed by immediate and dramatic drops. No switchbacks allowed.

The Roller Coaster is notoriously difficult, but it's still a popular area for day hikers; I met others enjoying a spring day in the Virginia woods. I shared the trail for a time with a woman walking with two dogs, and every now and then I caught sight of a Boy Scout troop. But most of these folks were only doing sections of the rollers or were crossing the AT while following other trails of their own. I was single-minded, climbing and dropping, climbing and dropping, pushing myself to survive to the end and claim my reward.

If I could finish this stretch, my day would cover twenty-eight miles. But even better, my reward would be the hiker special waiting at the Bears Den Hostel. For just twenty-five dollars, I could have a bed, do my laundry, and enjoy an entire pizza, a pint of Ben & Jerry's, and a can of Coke. That promise kept this weary hiker climbing and descending. It's amazing what a human being will do in pursuit of a goal.

At eight thirty that evening, I stumbled into the Bears Den Hostel. I had hiked 28.2 miles, my biggest day thus far on the trail. I'd been completely turned around and had hiked the wrong way; I'd hiked all the killer rollers. But I was still smiling. I had achieved my day's goal.

I also had a pizza, two cans of soda, and a pint of Ben & Jerry's in front of me.

I went to bed, exhausted, clean, and full. The next day, I would finish Virginia, the longest state on the AT, and enter West Virginia, the shortest state. In Harpers Ferry, I wanted to visit the little church beside the trail where I had prayed for our family. But the most satisfying thought was that tomorrow I would fulfill a promise I had made to myself that day over five years ago while standing on the trail outside Harpers Ferry.

15

The Storm

The Bears Den Hostel was one of the most comfortable and elegant on my entire hike. The building is a Tudor-style stone mansion, built in 1933 by local stonemasons, and formerly the home of a Washington, DC, doctor and his opera singer wife. Now the mansion-turned-hostel offers accommodations for twenty-six wayfarers. I left reluctantly in the morning.

Back on the trail, I hiked slowly, enjoying the views along Bears Den Rocks. Half a mile later, I was walking the shoulder of Virginia Rt. 7 in the deliciously named Snickers Gap. Then into the woods again, off on a twenty-mile stroll on a delightful Sunday in June.

White mountain laurel bloomed brilliantly in the morning sunshine. The blossoms of these bushes are small and cuplike, as though offering a deep drink of their beauty. A photographer had set up his tripod along the trail and was busy snapping photos. I stopped to chat and found that he photographed the wildflowers of the Appalachian Trail as a hobby and had some of his work published in several prominent magazines. My obvious interest in the wildflowers of the trail encouraged him to explain the similarities and differences of mountain laurel, azaleas, and rhododendron. "All three are poisonous," he cautioned. I didn't tell him about my eating habits, but I decided it might be wise to discontinue my wildflower sampling.

The blossoming everywhere distracted me; I had my nose stuck in every flower I passed. My usual attention to the trail floated away on the sweet scents of the morning, and I never saw the root that trapped the tip of my hiking pole while my body and pack continued moving forward. The pole was strapped to my wrist, and the tip was lodged firmly under the root. Something had to give, and it wasn't the root or the pole. My body did an about-face, and before I had a chance to react, I was on the ground.

My pole now resembled the letter C. I tried straightening it over my knee and used a little more persuasion from a rock, but then it looked like a lightning bolt. Hopefully I could find an outfitter in Harpers Ferry who would supply me with a vise to further straighten the pole.

At Crescent Rock, I paused on the high rock formation and enjoyed my final view over the vast and beautiful Shenandoah Valley.

Shortly before noon, I took a break at the David Lesser Memorial Shelter. My body was demanding nourishment, and the shelter was conveniently close to the trail. I relaxed, my feet propped up, and reflected on the milestones I'd reached. I had left Virginia that morning and entered West

Virginia, my fifth state. I had also just passed the thousand-mile point. Two months ago at Springer Mountain, a thousand miles seemed an impossible dream; yet by getting up each morning and stubbornly hiking north one step at a time, I had walked that dream into reality. And here I was, with over a thousand miles behind me. Yes, I will admit it—it felt good.

The day was hot and humid, and I needed more water. My guidebook showed a spring another two-tenths of a mile down a steep grade, but there was also a gas station with a deli at Keys Gap, three miles farther down the trail. I would get food and water there.

Walking up Rt. 9 in Keys Gap, I saw the dark cloud moving in from the east. The skies opened just as I reached the store, and I took shelter under the awning over the gas pumps as hail and rain pounded above and around me. Things were looking up. I had finally managed to avoid a downpour. One of the greatest pleasures on my hike was being safe and dry in a shelter during a storm. I had been unfortunate thus far; I was usually on the trail when storms hit, and I absolutely despised being drenched by the rain.

On September 10, 2002, shortly after we received the verdict on Mary's cancer, I had visited Harpers Ferry while she spent time with our youngest daughter. Now, almost six years later, I was remembering those days as I hiked toward the little mountain town. I had chosen to come here then because it offered something to think about other than our sadness. I had visited the historic St. Peter's Catholic Church, where I'd knelt in prayer for our family.

As I crossed the ridge at Loudoun Heights on this June Sunday, Harpers Ferry opened up before me and my dream had come to pass. I remembered that day in 2002, when I had looked up into these hills and promised myself that someday I would come hiking out of the woods, cross the bridge over the river, and walk into town on my own AT hike. I had no inkling of the enormity of my wish, nor did I have any idea what circumstances would bring me back. But I was there now, about to realize my goal of walking into Harpers Ferry knowing exactly what lay between Springer Mountain and this town.

From the ridge, a steep descent on switchbacks brought me ever closer to the bridge over the Shenandoah. The path went through a ravine filled with wild, purple periwinkle, and I emerged from the woods.

I stopped before crossing the bridge. In my mind, I saw a man standing on the other side, looking wistfully up into the hills. He resembled me, except that his hair was combed and he had no beard. He was forty pounds heavier, although with my backpack included, we weighed about the same.

I crossed the Shenandoah River and felt like I was coming home. Part of that feeling was because I knew I'd fulfilled a dream. But for weeks now, my mind had linked Harpers Ferry with home for several reasons. In this town, I was just a little over five hours from my home in Ohio, and it was as close to home as I would ever be during my trek to Maine. Ina, my trail boss, planned to meet me here in Harpers Ferry for a day, and it would be the last time I would see anyone from home until I finished my journey two months from now.

Every step beyond Harpers Ferry would take me farther away from home. Thinking about leaving the town and continuing northward, I felt a sadness. I was ready to go home. *Even if I quit here*, one part of my brain argued, *it will still be an accomplishment. Not many people hike a thousand miles.* I toyed with the idea of going home for just one week, to rest and visit my children and grandchildren. *You won't come back*, said another part of my brain.

This trail had opened my world. I had hoped for new experiences, new people, new ideas, and a new conversation with God. The first thousand miles had already exceeded my expectations. And as I debated going onward, I wondered, *What more is there? What else could there possibly be that God wants to show me?*

The stubborn part of my brain echoed my dad's voice, repeating words he had often quoted to his children: *whatever you do, do with your might. Things done by half are never done right.*

The journey was only half done. I must continue. No matter how much home tugged, I knew I had to finish this hike.

Crossing the river, I nodded a perfunctory howdy to my imaginary past self at the end of the bridge. Then I headed up the trail toward Jefferson Rock and St. Peter's Church. For a long time, I had pictured myself going back into that church. On the spot where I had begged God's help, I planned to thank Him for allowing Mary to be with us four more years after her diagnosis.

I went up the steps, through the stone arches, and, ignoring the "CLOSED" sign standing guard, I pulled at the carved wooden door. It was locked. Dropping my pack, I knelt right there by the front door and prayed.

Top left, Skyline Drive below the trail; *center left*, half gallon ice cream challenge; *bottom left*, view of Duncannon; *above*, ladder climb; *below*, Lehigh Gap

The Appalachian Trail Conservancy headquarters is just a short walk up High Street. At the headquarters, thru-hikers take their photographs for publication in a book documenting that year's class of hikers, much like a school yearbook. I posed for the picture and filled out brief personal information. I was hiker number 191. Back at Springer Mountain, I had been hiker number 391 heading north. Somewhere along those thousand miles I had passed two hundred of my fellow sojourners.

On High Street, I passed an outfitting store. I asked inside if they could help with my crippled hiking pole, but found that my Leki hiking poles were under warranty for life. A helpful clerk replaced the bent sections with two new sections at no cost. I congratulated myself on paying a little extra for quality hiking gear.

Later, in my room, I went through every article in my backpack. I would send home all my winter gear. Anything that I did not need every day would go home with Ina, including my hat, gloves, fleece, and my five-degree sleeping bag. I had purchased a much lighter forty-five-degree sleeping bag at the outfitter. I even briefly considered sending home my rain gear. But I decided to keep it and stuffed it into the bottom of my pack. When all was said and done, I had relieved my pack of six pounds and would head north feeling much lighter.

Einstein left me a phone message that Sir Enity was sick and would take several days off the trail, and that he himself would not be in town for another day. We three had planned to meet in Harpers Ferry, but I decided not to wait for my friends. I had already taken one zero day here, and they could catch up with me later.

As I maneuvered my way through Harpers Ferry, back again on the trail northward, I was assaulted with mixed feelings. As much as I wanted to go home for a break, I had decided to finish the hike and not take the chance of never returning. I also knew there was no more debating. One thousand miles before, Mt. Katahdin had seemed almost impossible. But now there was no going back.

I walked down Shenandoah Street, made a right at the edge of town, and passed under a trestle to a path that led to the Potomac River. A footbridge crossed the river, and then the trail turned onto the Chesapeake & Ohio Towpath. For several miles, I walked along the old towpath, the Potomac on my right and the abandoned canal on my left. Dozens of turtles sunned themselves on logs jutting out of the murky canal waters.

I felt like a new hiker. I carried a noticeably lighter pack, my pole was straight, and I had new tires. A second pair of New Balance shoes were on my feet, and I dodged last night's puddles, attempting to keep my new shoes dry. I was hiking with a new state of mind and in a new state of the union.

The Potomac River marks the border between Maryland and West Virginia. I had spent one month crossing Virginia, but only one day hiking West Virginia. Maryland has the second shortest section of trail, only forty miles, which meant I would cross Maryland and enter Pennsylvania in only a few days. Entering a new state was always my most encouraging measure of progress. Even though measurement by mileage was much more realistic, I felt a sense of accomplishment when I left one state and moved on to the next. Now, in less than a week, I would progress from state number four to state number seven.

The morning was heavy and humid as I left the C&O Towpath and started my climb toward Weverton Cliffs. Many switchbacks later, I enjoyed a view of the Potomac River flowing through a gorge far in the distance.

Just before noon, the trail led into Gathland State Park. I stopped at a fifty-foot stone memorial dedicated to Civil War journalists, sat on a nearby park bench, and kicked off my shoes. Back in Harpers Ferry, I had bought a huge sandwich, and this seemed a good spot for a leisurely lunch break. I admit I was influenced somewhat by the nearby Coke machine. A cold Coke and a turkey sandwich on a park bench. You call this hiking?

I inserted my money and pressed the button and a fruit drink dropped out. Disgusted, I tried again, and another cherry drink clunked down. Two disappointing fruit drinks and a turkey sandwich later, I lazily gathered my stuff and started back down the trail.

I had no warning that I was about to be swallowed up by the worst storm I have ever seen.

Nearing Fox Gap, I heard distant rumbling. I had walked through so many showers that I'd often forgo rain gear and let the rain soak me, hoping to dry out later in sunshine. But for some odd reason, this day's rumbling compelled me to dig out my gear as well as put the protective cover over my backpack.

In a small clearing in Fox Gap, a monument honors Major General Jesse Reno, killed nearby in the Battle of South Mountain during the Civil War. I stopped to read the plaque on the memorial, and without warning a blast of wind nearly knocked me off my feet.

I ran across the clearing to the trail leading into the woods, thinking that under the tree canopy I might find some cover from a downpour. But in seconds, shrieking winds drove rain and hail through the woods so violently that there was no shelter anywhere. I could barely see the trail through the whiteout of rain and ice. Trees bent and twisted in the wind, and I knew I must get away from the trail and those writhing trees.

I ran to a small incline off to the right, topped by a fencerow along an open field. Fighting my way up the bank, I looked for protection, some shield to break the ferocity of the storm. A cluster of prickly bushes seemed thick enough to shelter me, and I crouched in them, covering my head. But the winds blasted through the bushes, and a white sheet of rain and hail pummeled my body. I heard trees crashing to the ground; a branch hurtled through the air, striking my head. There was no refuge, and I knew I was in deep trouble.

The woods were not safe, but where to go? In the open field, branches and leaves and other debris swirled in crazy hysteria, as the wind snatched up and flung away anything it could grab. A lone maple stood in the center of the field. Its branches were twisting and tossing, but the tree seemed young and supple enough to withstand the violence of the wind. I remembered the giant trees uprooted by a storm in the Smoky Mountains. They had looked so large and indestructible, yet they were too rigid and could not bend enough to withstand a huge wind. Their roots had been set in rocks, not reaching deep enough to hold firm. This maple in the middle of the field should have a good root system, I reasoned.

I bent low and ran through ankle deep water to the tree. The wind was almost a physical being, charging against me, pushing me back. When I reached the tree, I grabbed the trunk and held on, wrapping both arms tightly around it. The monster storm howled around me; the wind whipped through the field and both lightning and thunder crashed simultaneously and constantly.

It was just a matter of time until the tree blew over or I could no longer hold on and was blown away. I slid slowly to my knees, hugging the trunk, and begged God to save my life. I knew there was a very good chance I would die right there in that field. I was terrified of the storm, but I was not terrified of dying. I actually felt at peace with the possibility. I clung to the tree, on my knees in streaming water, wind tearing at my body, rain and hail pounding me. I hung on. I knew God was there. And I knew that even if this storm killed me, all would be well.

The winds slowly quieted. I was not going to die or be blown away. When I thought it was safe to return to the trail, I splashed back into the woods and was stunned by the damage. Splintered trees lay across the trail, sometimes hiding it completely. Branches littered the path, and at times I could find no guiding white blazes. More than once, I crawled through the branches of downed trees or walked the bridge of a downed tree trunk to find my way along the trail.

If I had stayed in the woods, I would not have escaped being hit or even crushed by flying and falling timber. Even the low spring undergrowth looked beaten and weary.

Less than a mile later, I stumbled into the Dahlgren Backpack Campground, a small campground that had a block building with showers and restrooms. I had been that close to shelter!

Two hikers had taken refuge from the storm inside the block building. When I walked in, I could see incredulity on their faces. "You were out in *that*?" they exclaimed.

"Yes. And it was the most terrifying experience I've ever had." I sat down, thankful for human company and a place to rest, trying to regain my calm before I continued my hike.

For the next several miles, I walked through a path of destruction. From Turner's Gap to Washington Monument State Park, the trail was often buried under fallen branches and trees. As I picked my way over, under, and around, I wondered if there were other hikers who had been without refuge in the storm.

In Washington Monument State Park, I climbed a thirty-foot stone tower and had a view over Boonsboro, Maryland. I heard sirens in the distance, emergency vehicles dealing with the storm's aftermath.

Climbing over one final fallen tree, I was suddenly past the storm's devastation. White mountain laurel blossoms graced the path, and the trail was clear.

I will forever question every choice I made that morning. What if I had waited for my friends in Harpers Ferry? What if I had left town one hour earlier? What if I had not stopped for a lunch break at the war memorial? I might have avoided being caught in the middle of that storm.

But perhaps I was exactly where God wanted me to be.

I saw the enclosed footbridge and heard the traffic. The caged path led over I-70, where no one in the ceaseless flow of cars had an inkling of the destruction in the forest.

One and a half miles later, my day ended at Pine Knob Shelter. I had hiked twenty-four miles, even with the storm trying to stop me. And for some reason, that new pair of shoes I had so carefully protected from puddles only that morning were now soaked.

Two other hikers were staying at the shelter. They had heard the storm in the distance but were fortunate enough to be ahead of it. I described what they had missed. Hanging my rain gear on a wooden peg at the front of the shelter, I discovered a hole torn in the pants by the prickly bushes where I'd tried to take refuge.

A good spring flowed near the shelter, and I filtered my water and cooked a meal. It was already dark when I finally unrolled my new sleeping bag for the first time. It wasn't much more than a blanket, and I was happy for the pair of Patagonia long johns I had decided to keep. I was warm and safe. What more could a person want?

The following day, a hiker told me of news reports of 70 mph winds and tornado sightings, and I told him, yes, I was aware that there had been a storm.

This day too was hot and humid, and by the middle of the afternoon when I arrived at Pen Mar Park, a pleasant tree-filled area with picnic tables and a pavilion, I was happy to stop for a rest. The park straddles the Maryland-Pennsylvania border, and views from the pavilion look out over a plain of farmland, stretching for miles. I met an old caretaker who was roaming the grounds on a golf cart, and he offered to get me two soft drinks.

With drinks in hand, I spotted a swing and sat down, kicked off my shoes, and swung away some time. The sound of thunder interrupted my rest, and I headed for the pavilion. From there, I watched the lightning flash over the vast plain; rain poured down, and I thought about the vagaries of our choices and the sometimes disproportionate consequences. My lazy swing ride here had delayed my journey long enough that I was now under a roof safe and dry, avoiding this latest storm.

While waiting out the storm, I consulted my guidebook, wondering where I could camp that night. Five miles ahead were two shelters, side by side, named Deer Lick Shelters; that would be my goal.

My eye caught an interesting fact in the guidebook. A thru-hiker will climb and descend a total of ninety-one miles on his hike from Georgia to Maine. That's an elevation gain and loss the equivalent of climbing Mt. Everest almost seventeen times. No wonder I huffed and puffed and my legs ached.

Thinking about climbing Everest seventeen times, I left Pen Mar Park and soon arrived in William Penn's territory: my seventh state, Pennsylvania.

That night at camp, I overheard a hiker describing to several others what a terrible storm he had walked through the day before. "Were you in Washington Park during that storm?" I asked.

"I was caught in the middle of it, and I wish I had pictures to prove what I went through," he replied. "I thought I was going to die."

"I can prove it for you." I brought out my camera and showed them pictures of the storm's destruction. While we had endured the violent weather, hikers just a few miles north were completely unaware of the storm.

By noon the following day, I had already hiked thirteen miles. When the trail crossed U.S. 30, a colorful page tacked to a tree caught my attention, and I was immediately led astray by the pictures. Beautiful images of Italian food, all kinds of alluring delicacies for which I had no resistance. I headed down Rt. 30 quicker than you can say spaghetti.

Taormina's Italian Restaurant did not disappoint, and I soon had salad, garlic bread, and a steaming bowl of spaghetti in front of me. It sure beat the peanut butter and pita bread I had planned to eat. Loaded with calories, I went back to the trail and hiked longer and stronger than ever. I knew that if I didn't slow down, Einstein and Sir Enity would never catch up with me.

A day later, several miles outside of Pine Grove Furnace State Park, I reached a major milestone in my trek. I officially passed the halfway point. Springer Mountain was 1,088.4 miles behind me; Katahdin was 1,087.8 miles ahead.

That milestone called for a celebration. At noon, I walked into Pine Grove Furnace State Park and stopped at a small general store for a thru-hiker tradition, the half-gallon ice cream challenge. Anyone who finishes the challenge is awarded a little wooden spoon. For me, the word *challenge* is as irresistible as the word *food*. Just being able to accomplish anything labeled a challenge is reward enough. Entries in the journal inside the store, though, indicated that completion of this task was not always a pleasant experience.

My choice was a half-gallon of Hershey's chocolate ice cream. I would have liked chocolate syrup with it, but the store had none. I washed down the ice cream with sixteen ounces of Mountain Dew. All went surprisingly well. I enjoyed all but the last ten bites, and in thirty-eight minutes, the ice cream was gone. Surprisingly, I was still hungry, so I followed the ice cream and Mountain Dew with a cheeseburger.

I did not feel much like hiking that afternoon, so I checked in at the Ironmaster's Mansion and then joined several other hikers for a swim in nearby Fuller Lake. This area was the site of the Pine Grove Furnace years ago. Fuller Lake was a former iron ore quarry that eventually filled with groundwater.

In the evening, the proprietor of the Ironmaster's Mansion Hostel gave us a tour. The mansion had been a stop on the Underground Railroad moving slaves north to freedom. We dropped through a small trapdoor in a closet, and stood in subterrestrial rooms where fugitives had often gone into hiding.

A Girl Scout troop was also staying at the hostel; the girls and their sponsors joined us on the tour and afterward prepared themselves a Mexican feast. The aromas drove us hikers crazy; we kept drifting by their table, looking as sad and undernourished as we possibly could. (Yes, I *did* have a cheeseburger, a soda, and a half-gallon of ice cream still rattling around my digestive system.) Finally the invitation came. "Hey, you hikers. We have lots of leftover food. Do you want any?" We were in that kitchen until every morsel had disappeared.

That night, as I slowly lowered myself into my bunk, my stomach made strange rumbling noises. Appropriately, I was in the middle of an area with a long history of making cast-iron products, and those rumblings were just the normal noises of a cast-iron stomach.

16

Pilgrim's Progress

Another muggy morning dawned. I left the Ironmaster's Mansion at six, but soon found the trail barricaded by red fencing. A construction project adjacent to Fuller Lake had temporarily rerouted the AT. I had not read or heard about this rerouting, and being a rigid purist by now, I had no choice but to scurry over the fence and pick my way through the construction area. It was Sunday, so no workers were on-site to deter me.

As I hiked, my thoughts drifted home. Back in that life, for all of that life, I had attended church on Sunday morning. It was more of a habit and way of life than a spiritual event; sadly and unfortunately, I'd been bored many times in church services. My boredom was not the fault of the church or pastors; I'd had some of the best pastoral care.

My disinterest wasn't God's fault, either. It was my own doing—or rather, my lack of doing. I had never taken much

time to communicate with God, never really w
tried to find out who He truly was. I had grown
long list of dos and don'ts as my religion, and in
if heaven was going to be an extension of the religi‹
here on earth, then I was going to be bored for eternity.

In the last five years, though, I had been asking God, *Who
are You? What connection does my life have to You?* I wanted
to know God, and I wanted answers from Him.

As I hiked that Sunday morning, I had my own church. It
was not a religious experience at all. As a matter of fact, I
was losing my religion out here. And what I lost in religion,
I gained in spirituality.

Just the two of us walked together that Sunday—the Creator of the universe and me, worshiping in His grand cathedral. I didn't enjoy God's choice of music that morning; all
around me, cicadas were screaming.

But in spite of the cicadas' noise, I hiked with the clarity
of thought that was a gift of the trail. Alone and without
distractions, I knew without a doubt that I had done the right
thing in leaving my job. I knew I was where I was supposed
to be. I knew my life was in God's hands and I could trust
Him completely. And I knew He was walking with me.

One of the things God was showing me more clearly was
how available He is to every man and woman alive, and I also
saw how many obstacles we put between ourselves and Him.
Some of you, my readers, may never have considered God ap-
proachable, and you may be convinced I've taken leave of my
senses when I tell you of conversations with Him. I assure you,
I'm not crazy. (I know, I know. I quit my job and decided to walk
2,200 miles; perhaps you do have a right to question my sanity.)

When I started my AT hike and planned to write a book about the experience, that was all I intended to write: the walk, the adventure, a few observations about life. I never had any intention of writing a "spiritual" book; but then, I also had no idea that I would lose my religion and become spiritual. I tell you this—dialogue with God is available to you, to anyone. And furthermore, God actually desires conversation with us.

On the trek north from Springer, I settled the question of whether or not God was in control of events in my life. Although I still often asked why He took Mary from our lives, I no longer doubted that there was a reason. God sees the big picture, and perhaps I will not have my "why" answered until my next life.

The day when God so vividly revealed to me that He had adopted me as a son and therefore I was heir to everything I walked through, I had boldly (and perhaps foolishly) asked, "God, I have another question. Why do You allow young and innocent children to be harmed? If You are in control, why does that happen?"

His reply was, *Son, if you knew the answer to that, then you would be God.* So many things in life are a mystery; so many things I cannot possibly understand. I decided to just let God be God, and accept whatever He chose to reveal to me. What I could not comprehend, I did not need to know.

The day was uncomfortably hot and humid. I left the cicada choir behind and a new sound filled the woods, the soft sound of raindrops hitting leaves and falling to the ground. It was the most unusual rain I had ever heard. And I wasn't getting wet. I had walked into a Gypsy moth rain.

Sometime around 1868, a French scientist brought Gypsy moth eggs to America, hoping to produce a silk-spinning caterpillar that was immune to disease. Some moth escapees in the Boston area found the trees and foliage of Massachusetts much to their liking, and they thrived and reproduced unhindered. Attempts to eradicate the moths have been largely unsuccessful, and now each year this little pest defoliates one million acres as it chews its way across America.

A colony had settled here and was munching its way northward. The sound of rain in the woods this morning came from the caterpillars' excrement falling through the few leaves on the trees. Bits of leaves floated down and covered the forest floor with a layer of chopped green, and small poop pellets bounced off my head as I hiked. In many areas, posted signs warned that pesticides had been applied, but I hiked through without incurring any noticeable harm. The Gypsy moth colony didn't seem to be suffering much harm either.

The Appalachian Trail winds through Pennsylvania for about 230 miles, and I'd heard many horror stories about the rocks of the Pennsylvania AT. I had imagined fighting rocks all across the state, but I was enjoying the landscape very much. The miles of continuous rocks would come in the upper portion of the state's AT. Now I was passing through woods and farmland that reminded me of home.

Resting on a rock by a spring, I ate my lunch and watched families driving by, going home from church. Many of them were Mennonites, recognizable by their dress. They paid scant attention to the unkempt hiker sitting just a few feet from their passing vehicles. Had they known I was a fellow member of their sect, many would likely have stopped and chatted, and within minutes we would have discovered mutual friends and relatives and experiences. I had interesting stories to tell, and I would have welcomed the comfort of a good conversation. But since I didn't pass the sight test, no one stopped or even acknowledged me.

The miles through this landscape were some of my most memorable. I crossed fields where aromatic fresh-cut hay lay waiting to be raked and baled. In cornfields, tender stalks were just beginning to grow; I disturbed several deer munching the succulent sprouts. Large houses and barns and silos anchored neat farms. I glimpsed clusters of buildings from a distance as I walked alone through the quiet fields. It was Sunday afternoon, and I imagined all those families happily enjoying Sunday together. I knew that my sisters and parents were planning a family gathering for that evening, and I longed to be there with them.

In midafternoon I walked into Boiling Springs, where the trail followed a spring-fed lake and several B&Bs invited me to stay. Despite the extreme heat, I still felt good enough to continue hiking. My guidebook told me that Harrisburg Pike, U.S. 11, was eight miles ahead, and there I'd find a motel and a diner just half a mile west of the trail. If I continued, my day would cover twenty-seven miles and I would also be positioned to make Duncannon the following day. I was trying to plot a course that would give me a soft bed three nights in a row.

I bought and ate a sandwich at a store in Boiling Springs, then attacked my eight-mile challenge. Those miles led through more farm fields and crossed many roads. At U.S. 11, a pedestrian bridge took me over the traffic; I skidded down the embankment and headed up the highway toward the motel.

The room at the Super 8 was inexpensive, but the shower was hot and the bed was soft. At the Middlesex Diner across the road, good food and friendly service lifted my spirits. Back in my room, I finished the day with a call home and talked with my parents and sisters for the first time since leaving for my hike. After typing an entry into my phone for the Trail Journals site, I collapsed onto the soft bed.

The next morning, a trip across U.S. 11 to the diner started my day off right with a delicious breakfast, good conversation, and plenty of coffee. I wanted to make eighteen miles that day.

My goal was Duncannon and the Doyle Hotel, a must-stop for most hikers. In the early 1900s, Anheuser-Busch built a number of upscale hotels, all featuring bars where the company sold their products. Then Prohibition came along, and the hotels were sold. The Doyle was one of those hotels, named after a family who owned it for many years. In the early days of the Appalachian Trail, most of the pioneer hikers stayed at the Doyle, and quite a bit of folklore grew up around the old hotel. I looked forward to experiencing the storied building for myself.

I was not alone in the fields this morning. Farmers were out on their tractors, raking hay in preparation for baling. Few aromas in nature surpass the sweetness of freshly cut hay.

Occasionally a post bearing the familiar white blaze reminded me I was still on the trail, even though I was in the middle of hay fields. But as it always does, the trail eventually led me back into the woods, where a raised wooden walkway crossed a marshy area.

At Hawk Rock on Cove Mountain, I stopped to rest and take in the terrific view of Duncannon and the beautiful Susquehanna River far below. From my vantage point, I studied the layout of the town. I needed this introduction to Duncannon, since I'd heard the entrance into town was not well-marked.

I eventually found North Market Street and then the large, red brick building that is the Doyle Hotel. Both Duncannon and the Doyle had seen better days, and reminded me of a beauty queen whose glamour has faded with age. But as in many other towns, I would find that my lasting memories of Duncannon did not center on buildings but on people.

With temperatures in the upper 90s and oppressive humidity, all I wanted was to check into a room and cool off. My room on the fourth floor was twenty-five dollars and had the same air-conditioning system it had had over one hundred years ago—windows. A small sign gave instructions: "Open at your own risk." Someone had taken the risk, because the window in my room was wide open, framing views of dilapidated roofs.

Each floor had one small room offering a washer, a dryer, a shower, and a commode to be shared by the entire floor. I jumped into the shower with my clothes still on. During the day, I had stopped often to wring the sweat from my shirt, and I hoped a good shower now might precondition my clothes for the washer.

The stifling heat drove everyone to congregate in the bar, where it was cool in more ways than temperature. The food was excellent and a serene ambiance filled the place. But more than anything, I enjoyed the people I met there.

Somehow Sailor had passed me on the trail and arrived at the Doyle hours before me. In a few days, his second son would be meeting him in Port Clinton. Sitting at a table in the cool bar, Sailor and I reminisced about our earlier hiking days, and my friend introduced me to Pilgrim, a minister of the gospel, who had been hiking with him. Pilgrim did not appear to be a thru-hiker; he was clean-shaven and his white hair was closely cropped. Both men were taking a zero on the following day; Sailor was still fighting blisters and Pilgrim's feet were just plain tired.

I'd have gladly paid double to sleep on the floor in the coolness of the bar, but that was not permitted, so I walked up three flights of stairs to my hot room. It was a long night. I put a fan on a chair in front of the window and tucked back the curtains so they wouldn't obstruct the air flow. That didn't help much, since I was just moving 90-degree air. My window overlooked railroad tracks, and several trains blasted through town during the night. I'd drift off to sleep, only to be jerked fully awake by a passing iron horse.

In the early morning, I heard voices across the street and remembered that I'd seen a restaurant that was open for breakfast. I needed no persuading and I certainly needed coffee. Perched on a barstool at the end of the counter at Goodies, I downed several cups of brew. I debated taking a zero here in Duncannon to avoid the heat, but finally decided against it.

A familiar figure walked in and headed toward me. I greeted Pilgrim; he ordered coffee to go, and we chatted. I was explaining my reasons for being on the trail, and I could see that he was getting more excited by the minute.

I soon finished my story, saying, "Pilgrim, I cannot describe the things God has been revealing to me on this trail. I never knew God to be this real before." By now, Pilgrim could no longer contain his excitement.

"You know, Apostle, I'm taking the day off today, and I've got no reason to be awake this early except that I felt God telling me to get myself up and go across the street and see someone. And now, I've no doubt that you are the person He wanted me to see. Let me tell you a true story.

"I was a minister for many years in several prominent churches. I also had a ministry trying to reach young teenagers, wanting to teach them the gospel and trying to get them off drugs, but I was discouraged because I wasn't seeing any results for my efforts.

"Then one day God told me to grow my hair long. 'You want me to do what?' I asked. 'Grow your hair long,' was the reply. Well, then I had to make a choice. Either continue ministering with my hair short and appear normal, or risk embarrassment and ostracism from my community. I decided to listen to God and grow my hair. And not only did I let it grow—almost all the way down my back—but I also braided it into dreadlocks.

"A most amazing thing happened. The longer my hair grew, the more connection I had with the kids. I preached the gospel boldly and was never ashamed of it. Kids were being saved and delivered from sin and drugs."

I sat dumbfounded, listening in a mix of awe and contrition. In awe, because God knew I needed encouragement that day and had sent Pilgrim across the street to meet me. But I also felt nudges of shame, admitting that just three months ago, back in Religiousville, Ohio, I would have emphatically pronounced this man crazy. For most of my life, I would never have responded to such a request from God because I was too worried about what other people would say. I have no doubt now that God has spoken to and perhaps made unusual requests of many people in our big pile of Christianity, but because we are so concerned with our image, we're afraid to break free. We care more about what other people think than about what God wants.

My family's area of Ohio has over four million tourists visiting every year, seeking what they perceive we have, what makes our community unique and attractive. The most precious thing we have, we keep hidden away so we don't risk embarrassing ourselves. We'll gladly take visitors' money in exchange for all else our community offers, but we seldom offer up the best thing we could possibly give them: the path to hope and peace with God.

So just between you and me, has God spoken to you? If He did, would you recognize and listen to Him? Do you have the courage to follow His wishes, even if what He asks seems totally irrational? I know this: He does speak, He will speak, He is speaking. If you want a life of real freedom, then listen to what God is telling you.

Back at the Doyle, I gathered my gear and prepared to leave, stopping down the hallway at the laundry/shower/restroom cubicle to fill my water bottle. There I met Pilgrim again as he arrived to use the laundry.

"Apostle, I'm going to pray for you," he said. When Anheuser-Busch built that hotel over one hundred years ago, I'm sure they never envisioned a prayer meeting taking place in that dingy little room. Pilgrim's loud prayer reverberated throughout the building. He prayed blessings, safety, and wisdom on my journey.

With those supplications still ringing in my ears, I left the Doyle. I've stayed at some beautiful resorts with upscale amenities; but never have I had accommodations so minimal, sleep so impossible, and yet enjoyment so great as my stay at that old hotel.

I walked up Cumberland Street and turned onto High, following it out of town. High Street was filled with churches and residential buildings. One man was spraying weeds along his driveway, and he greeted me. "I was worried about your town for a while," I said. "All I could see from my hotel were bars and only one church. But now I see all the churches are on High Street."

He grinned. "We have seven bars and seven churches," he said. "We're a well-balanced town."

The trail leaves Duncannon over the Susquehanna River via a sidewalk on the four-lane Clarks Ferry Bridge. I was crossing the river when an oncoming plumbing supply truck stopped in the middle of the bridge.

"Hey, are you hiking to Maine?" the driver shouted, across two lanes of traffic and the concrete barrier. I assured him I was headed to Katahdin. "God bless you, brother," he yelled. With his long ponytail bouncing about and our conversation shouted over traffic, he declared his longing to hike the trail. Cars and trucks lined up behind him and zipped between us as he reminded me how fortunate I was to be doing this hike. I invited him to come with me and for a moment thought he might actually leave his truck right there in the middle of the bridge and start walking north.

"Don't let the dream die," I yelled before he finally drove off. "Do it someday. It'll change your life."

The heat and humidity of the day made a difficult thousand-foot climb even more draining. Eleven miles from Duncannon, I stopped at the Peters Mountain Shelter. It was only the middle of the afternoon, but I was hot, tired, and sleepy, and the next shelter was still a long distance away. Distant thunder made the decision for me.

The shelter was mine alone until later in the evening when Franklin arrived. I'd been reading his journal entries, but our paths had not crossed until this night. I slept well, and when I was ready for the trail at five the next morning, Franklin was also packed to leave. For the next week, we hiked together. Our styles were similar: get up early and hike late.

We were finally in the dreaded Pennsylvania rocks. The trail was strewn with a rubble of large stones; at times, the path completely disappeared as the white blazes went up over huge rock piles and forced us to follow. We could not establish a hiking pace, since every step required caution. Our perspiring bodies became quite an attraction for the local black fly population. They swarmed around, greeting us as honored guests to their rocky domain.

Just across Pennsylvania Rt. 501 is the aptly named 501 Shelter. Franklin and I took refuge from the heat and discovered a solar shower. It was a breathtaking affair for us and a temporary setback for the flies.

Inside the shelter, we found a notice announcing a hiker feed at the pavilion in Port Clinton, two days ahead of us. A group of Mennonite boys from the area had done a thru-hike several years before and now did a yearly hiker feed in appreciation of the trail magic they had received on the AT. The group even offered to pick up hikers at road crossings and transport them to the feed. Our timing was perfect; if the rocks allowed it, we expected to arrive in Port Clinton the night before the event.

Two days later, two weary hikers did reach Port Clinton, their bruised feet aching from the rocky trail. We desperately needed a break, and what luck that folks here wanted to feed us! Escorted by our swarm of flies, we crossed the Schuylkill River and entered the town.

Our destination was the Port Clinton Hotel, an 1800s stage-coach stop. Over the years, the stagecoach road had been broadened and paved, and now cars and trucks rushed past on Rt. 61, only five feet from the front porch. The tempera-ture was at 100 degrees when we walked into the bar, where air-conditioning and a large bowl of spaghetti brought me back to life. We booked two rooms upstairs in the old build-ing, and small air-conditioning units in each room promised a restful stay.

The hiker feed began with breakfast on Saturday morn-ing and continued through lunch and into the afternoon. As we approached the pavilion in the morning, I could tell that the group responsible for this good deed was from the Conservative Mennonite tradition of my own upbringing. I greeted them in Pennsylvania Dutch, and they looked as if an alien had just landed among them. Once their initial surprise passed, we quickly found common ground and com-mon acquaintances. And just as quickly, I belonged. I even had an invitation to stay that night at the Brubakers' farm.

That day turned into a zero day for Franklin and me. We ate and socialized through breakfast and lunch. Sailor arrived. Padre the priest was there. Rhino, a German hiker, and his dog joined the group. Many other hikers that I'd met briefly on the trail stopped for the event. It was a trail family gathering.

Toward evening, three hikers loaded up their packs and headed into the countryside to the Brubakers' dairy farm. Franklin, Padre, and I would be staying in a Mennonite home that night. Padre had grown up on a farm and was curious about farming here in Pennsylvania, and we simply could not turn down the offer of an air-conditioned, fully furnished basement with a shower.

That evening, while visiting with Mr. Brubaker, I remarked that this beautiful farm country reminded me of home. As we talked, I realized that I was, indeed, home.

We were in Berks County, site of the first Amish settlement in America. My own history was tied to this place. I recalled a story my grandfather and other relatives had often told, the saga of the Hochstetler Massacre. My family's story intertwined with that of the Hochstetlers in Berks County.

William Penn had generously granted land first to the Quakers and then also to the Amish and Mennonites, and folks were immigrating to Berks County from Switzerland and Germany. The first immigrant in our family, Johan Jacob Stutzman, arrived in America in Philadelphia, Pennsylvania, on October 2, 1727. He had traveled on the ship *The Adventurer*, but his personal adventure did not end happily. His wife and most of his family died on the long voyage; only he and two sons survived. Once in Pennsylvania, he was homesick and wanted only to return to his homeland. So to raise the fare for his trip home, he farmed out his two boys to Amish farmers in Berks County. His sons eventually raised families of their own in America.

One of Johan Stutzman's grandsons, Christian, married Barbara, daughter of the Hochstetler family living just east of Northkill Creek. In September 1757, Christian Stutzman and Barbara Hochstetler were already married and living near her parents when Indians attacked her parents' home during the night. The Hochstetler family took refuge in the basement, and the Indians set fire to the house. As fire threatened the basement door, the family doused flames with cider and beat back the fire throughout the night. In the morning hours, thinking the Indians had finally gone, the family emerged from the basement through a small window. But one young warrior had lingered behind—some accounts say he had stopped to eat a peach from a tree—and catching sight of the family, he alerted his cohorts. A renewed attack ended with the killing of Mrs. Hochstetler and two of the children; two other sons and Mr. Hochstetler were taken captive by the Indians.

The massacre is a well-known story of the Amish settlement in Berks County. I'd heard it many times, not only because it was part of the history of the first Amish in America, but also because my family descended from Christian and Barbara Hochstetler Stutzman.

I explained my lineage to my host. "The site of the massacre is only a few miles from the trail you're hiking," he told me. "Tomorrow, when I take you back to the trail, I'll show you where it happened. And in all likelihood, you've been hiking through land your ancestors lived on centuries ago."

The next morning, Mrs. Brubaker prepared us a delicious breakfast and then her husband took Franklin and me back to Port Clinton. Padre stayed behind; it was Sunday morning, and he wanted to attend Mennonite services with the family.

Beside old Rt. 22 and behind the tourist attraction housing Roadside America (an extensive miniature village and railway), a historical marker tells of the Northkill Amish, the first Amish Mennonite settlement in America, and the Hochstetler massacre. The Northkill settlement dissolved after this attack; my ancestors moved first to Somerset County and then on to Holmes County, Ohio, where they were joined by other Amish families. Holmes County is now the largest Amish settlement in the world, visited by crowds of tourists drawn to the area by the peace and tranquility they believe this community has found.

Into this mix of history and religion, the hiker Apostle was born and raised, left his home in search of peace and tranquility, and trekked unknowingly back to his own roots. Whether from Europe to America, from Berks County to Holmes County, or on a trail from Georgia to Maine, every generation has its own reasons for pilgrimage.

17

Summer Solstice

Franklin and I followed the Schuylkill River for a short distance, then headed into the woods and started climbing.

Eight miles later and one thousand feet higher, we stood on Pulpit Rock and looked over the farms and villages of Berks County. The perimeter of our cathedral that Sunday morning was the distant horizon, and the ceiling reached to the sky, where scattered puffs of white drifted against a blue background. An artist greater than Michelangelo had painted the ceiling of this chapel. The birds chorused in worship, and I stood amazed at the scene before me. The homily that morning was brief and heartfelt: "Oh great God, how marvelous is Your creation. Amen!"

The trail was littered with rocks of all sizes, and we picked our way carefully over them, always watching for the white blazes. Wildflowers found little space to grow here, but we discovered an even more edible plant. Wild blueberries were just starting to ripen, and they were much sweeter than the blossoms I had sampled.

Conventional hiker wisdom predicts that hikers make fewer miles in this rocky stretch of Pennsylvania, but Franklin and I developed the agility of mountain goats as we bounded from rock to rock and clambered over twenty-two stony miles that day.

We stopped for the night at the Allentown Hiking Club Shelter, arriving in time to see Rhino coming out of the woods carrying a dead tree—not just a portion of the tree, but the entire trunk and branches. Rhino loved fires, and he wasn't satisfied with a small campfire; he wanted an inferno.

This was Rhino's second thru-hike. A German television crew was documenting his journey and met him at designated points along the trail to do updates for the program. We had all assumed he took the name Rhino because of his size and strength, but his trail name was simply a shortened version of his last name, Reinhold.

Rhino built a huge pile of dead trees and lit his bonfire. The colossal blaze kept every mosquito at bay that night. Franklin and I set up camp several hundred feet from the heat and smoke of the conflagration; even so, the glow lit our tents all night. When we left at five the next morning, a huge pile of embers still burned brightly. For the next few nights, hikers would have fire waiting for them when they arrived.

Six miles into another rock-strewn day, I lamented that I needed a coffee break. Franklin surprised me with an offer; he had little bags of coffee, but no stove. He'd sent his stove home to save weight. For the only time on my entire trek, I stopped and brewed coffee. We were high on Blue Mountain on a ridge trail called The Cliffs, and we sipped our coffee as we sat on an outcropping of rocks overlooking fantastic views. I've had better coffee, but the blend of nature and good conversation made this a special brew.

Franklin and I both enjoyed bicycling, and we reminisced about our favorite rides. He recalled a bike ride originating in Asheville, North Carolina, near his hometown. It was a naked bike ride protesting energy consumption and all other kinds of overconsumption. (In my mind, folks wanting to bicycle naked had issues far greater than anything they might be protesting.) The local law officials' only participation in the ride was to arrest those who were actually overexposed to the sun.

The story of the naked bike ride reminded me that the first day of summer was five days away. On the trail, that day is traditionally naked hiker day. Hikers do actually hike without clothes. (I assumed, though, that they surely must wear shoes.)

"Franklin, what are your plans for naked hiker day?"

"If I rode a bike naked—and I certainly did—then I'll have no problem hiking naked. What about you, Apostle? You going to hike naked?"

"No . . . probably not." Every admonition about modesty and decency taught by my parents and preached from the pulpit was shouting reminders of sin and evil. "There's no way I could ever hike naked, even in the woods."

But what about tradition? That first night, back in my tent in Horse Gap, I had promised myself that I'd live the life of the Appalachian Trail and that I'd meet new ideas openly. *Oh, well. I still have five days to consider the possibilities*, I told myself.

We finished our coffee and continued across Blue Mountain, while eight hundred feet below us, traffic burrowed through the mountain in a tunnel on the Pennsylvania Turnpike.

At Lehigh Gap, we crossed the Lehigh River and the white blazes went up over the face of rocky cliffs. This was not a stroll down a pleasant woodland path, but a precarious climb that required careful placement of feet and hands as we pulled ourselves upward slowly and cautiously.

At the top, we walked through the landscape of another world. All vegetation had died; dead trees lay everywhere. A zinc plant had mined the area for over eighty years, and sulfur dioxide emissions resulted in the deforestation of the mountain. We found tiny bits of life; blueberries were making a comeback among the rubble. Franklin and I assumed they were toxic, but we ate them anyway.

The absence of trees gave us a great view, but a large black cloud hung ominously over that view. The wind picked up, and Franklin suggested setting up our tents and taking refuge from the storm. During all those weeks of walking in the rain—why had I never thought of that simple plan? We pitched our tents beside the trail in record time and waited inside while the storm raged several miles away. But it never arrived, missing us completely.

Water was limited in this area, but our guidebooks showed a spring called "Metallica." We were unable to locate it, but we did find a sign posted by a trail angel, telling us that he had stashed bottled water for hikers at the Little Gap road crossing. We were too late; by the time we arrived at the crossing, all the water was gone.

Our only choice seemed to be a quick dash into town. Danielsville, Pennsylvania, was down the road 1.5 miles, but hitchhiking failed us again and we started walking. Thunder rumbled in the distance. We'd gone half a mile when I stopped; I thought I heard running water. Franklin was ahead of me, and I called him back. Searching the roadside weeds, we found a strong spring. Feeling like explorers making an important discovery, we promptly dubbed it the Franklin Apostle Spring.

We filtered a supply of water and hustled back to Little Gap as the storm moved closer. Our tents went up on stealth campsites, and we finished just as the rain hit.

In a few days, Franklin would meet his wife at Delaware Water Gap and would take two days off the trail. I would again lose a hiking partner. But less than a day ahead of me was Fargo, and I was hoping to meet him. He was a cheesehead from Green Bay, Wisconsin, with a Norwegian dialect that sounded as if he had just walked off the *Fargo* movie set. I'd seen Fargo's journal entries for several months and knew I was slowly gaining on him. My register entries were usually brief, but Fargo's were the shortest I've ever seen. He entered only his name. Franklin had hiked with Fargo previously and thought I would enjoy this character. He asked me to give his regards to Fargo if I did catch up with him.

Shortly after crossing Fox Gap, we arrived at Kirkridge Shelter. Franklin and I had the shelter to ourselves, so I set up my tent inside, hoping to isolate myself from all bugs. A large, yellow moon rose and lit up the shelter. I unzipped my tent and stepped outside, watching the moon's soft glow illuminate the entire mountainside.

We were no longer alone; a couple had walked up the trail earlier. She was limping painfully and he tried to encourage her onward. The limp was undoubtedly caused by the high heels she wore. Those heels and her clean dress and overnight bag told us she was not a serious hiker. We watched them in amusement. The male had some hiking skills and apparently wanted his girlfriend to share the experience of the trail. From the snippets of conversation that drifted into my tent that night, I didn't think this hiking-togetherness would last much longer.

"I told you not to wear heels," said he.

"But you didn't tell me about the rocks and roots," said she.

"Just go to sleep."

"I can't. The floor's too hard."

I slept soundly, assured we were well-protected from any marauding bears as her high heels lay within easy reach, at the foot of her sleeping bag.

We walked the six miles to Delaware Water Gap before breakfast. As usual, the first order of business was food, so we crossed town to the Water Gap Diner, one of those small-town eateries where the food is excellent and the atmosphere friendly.

While Franklin and I ate breakfast in a booth by the window, a familiar figure strode by. The homemade flute sticking out from the backpack and the floppy straw hat told us Padre the priest was in town. I rapped on the window and motioned for him to join us. Our conversation that morning confirmed to me that God answers prayer, in His own way and His own time.

I spoke about what had brought me to the trail, the heartache of losing my wife, and the grief of my children. I'd found healing on this trail, and God was revealing much to me. "What mountaintop experiences I've had out here!"

"This hike reminds me of the paschal mystery," Padre replied.

What's the paschal mystery?" both Franklin and I wanted to know.

Padre explained. "It refers to the suffering, death, and resurrection of Jesus Christ and the promise of life that gives us. I walk through the low valleys on this trail and see dead trees and decaying matter, and I'm reminded of the death of Jesus. But I continue on to higher elevations and see new growth and new life that reminds me of His resurrection.

"That's the rhythm of our spiritual lives too. We walk through valleys, we lose loved ones, we suffer, we struggle, we experience many kinds of deaths. We travel on and we reach a higher plane, where we pause to enjoy the views, look back to remember where we came from, and look forward to mysteries still ahead of us.

"But we do not stay on the exhilarating mountaintop. If we sat there and never moved on, the views would no longer be enjoyable. And so we go on, just as we do on the trail.

"After valleys and struggles and even deaths, we always have the hope of new life. Someday we'll pass through the last valley and finally reach the last mountaintop, and we'll never be bored by the glorious view that awaits us there."

Padre was putting words to what I had been discovering as I walked this path. This trail mirrored my spiritual journey. I was finding that gift of hope and new life. I knew I was on a mountaintop at that table in the Water Gap Diner. Even Franklin, who had admittedly soured on Christianity, felt the sacredness of the moment.

We spoke of salvation, the blood of Christ, and the cross. I was both amazed and delighted. Padre and I agreed on fundamental issues of salvation—a Mennonite and a Catholic priest! Perhaps I wouldn't have to get Padre "saved" after all.

Heaven had expanded its borders, and I wouldn't be spending eternity talking only with other Mennonites!

"But what about all those rituals you have?" I asked Padre.

"In the Mennonite church, we don't have or believe in rituals."

When Padre finished laughing, he reminded me that he had just been in a Mennonite service the previous Sunday, and yes, the service was filled with ritual. I wondered if God had a reason for putting me on the trail with a Catholic priest.

The Presbyterian Church of the Mountains faces Main Street, not far from the Appalachian Trail. A hostel located in the basement is available only to long-distance hikers. Franklin and I stayed there, along with Padre and Rhino—and Rhino's dog, Ronja. Dogs sometimes became nuisances on the trail, but this dog was the smartest and best-behaved dog I've ever met. I picked out a bunk next to Rhino and Ronja, hoping Ronja would protect me from any church mice that might attack during the night.

Rhino and I both stopped at the post office to pick up scheduled mail drops, but neither of our packages were there. Rhino decided to stay in town another day, waiting for his mail, but I didn't want to waste time, so I asked the post office to return mine to sender once it arrived. Missing that food box wasn't a crucial issue, since I was moving into New Jersey and New York, where delis and roadside groceries are plentiful.

Leaving town, I walked along I-80 and crossed the bridge over the Delaware River as cars and trucks whizzed by at dizzying speeds. Crossing the river meant I was entering New Jersey, my eighth state. I happily left the busy interstate and climbed. Five miles later, I had my first surprising views out over this new state. I'd expected towns and industrial sites and congested highways, but all I saw now were trees, hills, and a few houses dotting the countryside.

I might have moved to a new state, but I had not left the rocks behind. It would be several days until the rocks finally became fewer and I could concentrate on anything other than where to place my next step. When most of the rocks disappeared from the path, New Jersey became a delight.

I could hear and almost feel a mysterious sound throbbing through the forest, starting staccato and building into a loud vibration, like a chest of drawers being pushed across a floor. I'd read about the territorial drumming of a Ruffed Grouse, but as I walked through the woods of New Jersey and listened to the amazing sound, it was hard to imagine it was only a bird beating his wings.

Once the rocks had almost disappeared, the trail improved, and my hiking became more aggressive. Two days and fifty miles later, I found a "secret" shelter. Jim Murray had thruhiked himself, and he then built a shelter on his private property available only to fellow thru-hikers. Earlier that afternoon, I'd sought shelter from a rainstorm by squeezing under a low rock overhang. I shared the tight space with a hundred Gypsy moth caterpillars also attempting to stay dry. Jim Murray's small and rustic cabin was a welcome refuge for the night.

The cabin sat under scattered trees at the edge of a mowed, green field. It was late when I walked up to the door. The cabin could sleep four people, and two had already settled in. One of the hikers lay in the loft above; on the main floor, another hiker stood in the small cooking area, brewing a pot of tea.

224

"You look like you could use some hot tea," he offered, as I took in the long brown beard and hair that reached halfway down his back. I gladly accepted his offer and inquired if they had room for one more.

"Yes, we do. And there's a solar shower outside, if you want to use it." That sounded good to me, since some of those caterpillars had crawled on me while I was counting them, and I wished to wash away that memory.

I started the introductions. "Where are you from?"

"We just met here tonight. I'm Dave. I suppose you might say I'm from Colorado." I suspected there must be a story, since he wasn't sure exactly where home was, but I didn't question further.

A large hand extended down from the loft, and a man's voice welcomed me. I couldn't understand his name, but he said he was from Scansin.

"Where?" I asked. And I got the same reply, Scansin.

"Never heard of it."

"Oh, it's up nort dere, where da Packers play in Green Bay. Scansin."

Dave, from possibly Colorado, interrupted to translate for me. Scansin was actually Wisconsin.

"Let me guess. You're Fargo, aren't you?" I directed to the loft.

"Yah, sure, you betcha," came back down.

"Franklin sends his regards."

"Dat's my buddy! Youse been hikin' wit him too?"

Dave had gone outside, and while I sipped my tea, Fargo informed me that Dave was known on the trail as Drifter Dave and his home was actually the trail itself. He had no money, and lived from hiker box to hiker box. The tea I was drinking had come from the last box he had raided. He ate what he could yogi or find in nature, and he was just recovering from being violently sick from poisonous mushrooms he had eaten.

While we talked, several mice ran through the room. The door to the cabin stood open, and watching the mice, I strategically placed a hiking pole over the threshold of the door. In one moment of perfect timing and sheer good luck, I flipped the pole just as one mouse ran over it. The little fella made a high, arcing flight through the open door and landed right at Dave's feet. I cringed inwardly as I waited for Dave to put his literal stamp of approval on my work with his boot.

Instead, he reached down and picked up the mouse, cupping it in his hands. "What should I do with it? It'll die if I leave it out here," he said. He walked around the back of the cabin to find sanctuary for his new friend. I suspect he may have even brought it back into the cabin later. Fargo told me there were hikers who were uncomfortable with Drifter Dave, but watching his gentleness with the mouse and thinking of his sharing the little tea he had, I was convinced I had nothing to fear from the man.

The next day, Dave planned to go into Unionville, New York, to visit the mayor and see if he could "score some tobacco." We were in New Jersey, but the trail followed the state line, so the New York town of Unionville was just half a mile off the New Jersey AT. The mayor welcomed hikers to his home, inviting them to stay, feeding them, and providing transportation around town. Fargo and I went to Unionville for breakfast, but it was far too early to stop and see the mayor.

Dave stayed behind at the shelter that morning. The hiker box was locked in another small building, and he intended to wait in hopes that someone would show up and give him access to the box. He would visit the mayor later.

Weeks later, I had a conversation with a hiker who'd been at the mayor's house when Dave arrived. "Did he score any tobacco?" I asked. Turns out Dave got his tobacco and several good meals, and was being driven around town in the mayor's Cadillac.

Fargo was a retired pharmacist and had come to the trail several weeks before I did. While I knew a little about a lot, Fargo knew a lot about a lot and was always willing to share his knowledge. He loved hunting, fishing, and the Green Bay Packers. He was a good family man, and his wife missed him. Well, I'm not sure if she missed him or just wanted him to come home. Their house in Green Bay was for sale, and if it sold, Fargo would leave the trail to go home and move. The real estate agent had things under control, but Fargo's wife still wanted him to come home, just in case they found a buyer.

"Why are you out here, then?" I wondered.

He had retired at fifty-six, and he had dreamed of the trail for a long time. "Da missus dropped me off down souse, never figgering I'd last. I luf it out here, but every time I call da house she wonders when I'm comin' home."

"Have you thought about not calling home?" I offered.

"Da missus wud skin me alive, you betcha."

As we hiked along after breakfast, I realized it was the first day of summer. That meant it was also naked hiker day. So what was I going to do?

It's tradition.

No, I couldn't. A Christian could never do anything like that.

Why can't a Christian do that?

Isn't immodesty a sin? Back home, I would be embarrassed to be seen without a shirt, and now I was considering hiking without any clothes at all. But I wanted the satisfaction of knowing that I had done something that scared me. It would certainly be a foolish thing, but would it be sin? I believe that thoughts can be just as sinful as actions, so if anyone caught sight of me and went down wicked thought paths, that would be sin. And I'd be guilty of causing sin.

Okay, be realistic, Apostle. The only reaction there's going to be is laughter. Furthermore, aren't Christians free from legalistic dos and don'ts?

There was the dilemma I'd faced all my life. "I can't do it because I'm a Christian," or "Because I'm a Christian, I have the freedom to do this." Which one applied? Which one was the truth?

I heard myself say, "Hey, Fargo, how about some naked hiking today?"

"I'd forgotten about dat. Believe you me, no one wants to see dis here figger. I'll be in deep doggy doo if da missus finds out."

Fargo didn't debate as long as I had, though. "But, hey den, let's do it anyhow. You go down da trail dere, tree or four hunnert feet, and I'll stay back 'ere, den I'll catch up wit ya layder." Sounded like a good plan to me.

With my heart threatening to pound its way out of my chest, I rounded the next bend and cautiously surveyed the area for any other human presence. I wanted to do this, but desperately did not want to get caught. Many hikers will say that if no one sees you hiking in the bare essentials, it "doesn't count," but in my case, I would be the only one who knew and I was the only one who mattered. I remembered Franklin's naked bike ride protest. I needed a protest.

I know! I'll protest sin! That's what forced us into wearing clothes in the first place.

"Sin, I doth protest thee," I mumbled while slipping out of my hiking gear.

I'd lost so much weight that my birthday suit hung from my ribs in waves of wrinkles. I left my backpack unbuckled and slung my clothes over the top. Feeling like a naughty boy, I cautiously moved along. Two senses were on high alert; my ears strained to hear any sound of humans, and my eyes darted everywhere to watch for poison ivy.

My naked hiker day was only naked hiker minutes. It was over in several hundred feet. It was exciting and exhilarating. It was foolish, and I was relieved when it was finished.

I dressed quickly and waited for Fargo. He was grinning. "Dat felt grayt. I went at leest five hunnert feet, don'tcha know."

As we exited our Garden of Eden and walked down Oil City Road toward the Wallkill River, we laughed and giggled like little kids. We had only known each other a few hours and had already hiked naked; go figure.

We were nearing Vernon, New Jersey, when the trail cut through a swampy area. A raised wooden walk wove through the cattails and swamp grasses. I met a young lady on the walkway who was snapping photographs. Something stopped me, and instead of just saying hello, I took time to chat with her.

During our conversation, I sensed that God wanted me to tell her about my journey. As I told her about losing my wife, she started to cry. She'd lost her best friend to a drunk driver, and as she struggled with her loss and grief, something had drawn her to this spot. God had placed her in my path that day, and I shared with her the only thing I knew that could match the pain of such a loss: God knew how she felt, and even though it might be hard to believe, God loved her and would comfort her.

I wondered how often God had placed people in my daily path with needs that I never sensed . . . because I was always too busy.

18

The Pharmacy Shelter

Here were the rocks again. The trail became more difficult, the ridges covered with large, rounded rocks. On one of the rocks, we found a painted line designating the state line between New Jersey and New York.

I was in my ninth state, but state eight still held my thoughts. New Jersey had been completely different than I'd imagined. I'd seen three bears in the last two days, not counting the two that had crept through the woods without their clothes.

My thoughts were interrupted by loud thunder, and Fargo and I hustled to the nearby Wildcat Shelter. We thought we'd wait out the storm and then continue, since it was only two thirty (one thirty in Scansin). But we settled in when we realized the next shelter was still fourteen miles away. We'd already done seventeen miles that day, and we decided to take some time to study our guidebooks and plan our miles for the next few days.

Several days ahead was the RPH Shelter. Fargo pounced on this name. As a former pharmacist, he knew RPH stood for "Registered Pharmacist," and he was convinced that the shelter had something to do with the pharmaceutical industry. Perhaps a group of pharmacists had built the shelter. We started referring to it as "the pharmacy shelter," and Fargo could hardly contain his excitement at the thought of staying at this potential monument to his retired peers.

The first morning in New York, we arrived at a road crossing where a notice posted on a tree announced the opening of a new deli. I couldn't resist the thought of coffee and several fresh sandwiches. Fargo wanted to keep on walking, so we agreed to meet at the William Brien Memorial Shelter that evening. I went for coffee and sandwiches, and Fargo went on down the trail.

Several miles later, back on the trail, I crossed over the New York State Thruway and entered Harriman State Park. This park has over 46,000 acres, thirty-one lakes, and more than two hundred miles of trails, including 18.8 miles of the AT. It was difficult to believe that New York City with its eight million plus people was only thirty-five miles south of me while I hiked through the park, completely alone.

The trail passed between two rock walls called "The Lemon Squeezer." The space between the two rocks narrowed as I walked through, both sides of my backpack rubbing the rocks on either side. At the end, I either had to remove my backpack or raise myself on tiptoe for the final squeeze through. I managed the squeeze, but I wondered how Fargo, who was a larger man than I, was going to maneuver this little stretch of the trail. Fortunately, there was an alternate route, a blue-blazed path around the obstacle, marked for lemons larger than myself.

Once through the squeeze, I was faced with a six-foot rock wall. Removing my backpack, I tossed it to the top of the rock formation and then found finger- and footholds to inch my way to the top.

The William Brien Memorial Shelter stood empty when I arrived in the late afternoon. Fargo was nowhere to be found. I guessed that he had moved on, since this structure was dilapidated and in need of repair. The graffiti covering the walls inside suggested visitors other than hikers. Most shelters have hiker graffiti, but most of that is carved with a knife or drawn with a marker. Not many thru-hikers carry spray paint.

Believing Fargo was ahead of me, I went on. Several miles later, I reached the top of Black Mountain. From that height, I was certain I'd see New York City in the distance, but cloud cover hid the view.

I went down the mountain, and the trail crossed the Palisades Interstate Parkway, a four-lane highway carrying traffic to and from New York City. A road sign told me I was thirty-four miles from the city. I carefully cleared the first two lanes with their busy traffic and reached the wooded median. In this buffer zone, I found a trail register. Fargo had not signed it; he was still behind me somewhere. I quickly scribbled my name, and dodged the speeding cars to cross the other two lanes.

I was back in the woods immediately. A small footbridge led over Beechy Bottom Brook. I knew the next shelter did not have a water supply, so I uncoiled my filter, dangled it into the brook, and filtered two liters of water. A difficult fifty-foot rock scramble took me to the top of West Mountain.

The West Mountain Shelter was more than half a mile off the trail and the day was fading away. I decided to stop for the night and stealth camp in a small grassy spot right next to the trail. My campsite had a grand view out over the Palisades Parkway and toward the cloud-enshrouded city of New York. Earlier in the week, I'd found two bags of tea someone had left at a shelter; I sat on the rocks, enjoying the view and sipping a cup of tea.

Throughout the night, stomping and snorting and loud crashing let me know the local animal population was upset at my intrusion. The area was covered with blueberry bushes that supplied my breakfast the next morning as I crossed West Mountain and headed to Bear Mountain.

Atop Bear Mountain, a forty-foot stone tower honored George W. Perkins, a business partner of financier J. P. Morgan. George Perkins had been chairman of the Palisades Interstate Park Commission and was instrumental in saving the west bank of the Hudson River (known as the Palisades) from quarry operators. He was also involved in the Appalachian Trail Conference and helped establish many trails in the area. The first miles of the AT opened here on October 7, 1923, and went from Bear Mountain through Harriman State Park.

I paused to rest at the base of Bear Mountain and, shielded by a tree, watched an amazing scene. Twenty feet from me, a newborn fawn wobbled toward its mother. I stood in awe and watched as it suckled, its white spots clearly visible.

After several minutes, I quietly slipped away, headed toward more wildlife encounters. The AT dipped to the lowest elevation of the entire trail, 124 feet. And there, I came face-to-face with two black bears. No cause for alarm, though, as the bears were part of a zoo. The trail passes through the Trailside Museum and Zoo, and thru-hikers are granted free passage.

On the other side of the zoo, I came out to the Hudson River and Bear Mountain Bridge. Here again, thru-hikers are given a free pass over the toll bridge. But before I crossed the Hudson, food again called. I walked to the nearby town of Fort Montgomery in search of lunch and found a wonderful deli. The lunch break cost me several hours, but it did reconnect me with Fargo. Coming back to the bridge, I caught sight of him strolling out of the zoo.

"Fargo!" I yelled, glad to see him again. "Get away from that zoo quick, before they realize you're missing!"

On the other side of the highway, I spied a Pepsi machine beside the toll house. A three-foot concrete barrier separated the sidewalk from the roadway. I couldn't resist a cold drink, so I dropped my backpack, dodged the traffic, and claimed my Pepsi. Returning, I intended to impress Fargo with my athletic skills by leaping gracefully over that barrier. I was feeling light on my feet without my backpack, and with Pepsi in hand, I dodged two lanes of traffic and launched over the concrete barrier. That is, my mind and half of my body launched. The other half somehow didn't get the message. I landed, quite ungracefully, straddling the barrier, half of me on the bridge, and half on the sidewalk.

"Dat's gotta hurt bad," sympathized Fargo.

"Where have you been? Where did I miss you?" I asked in a high-pitched voice. Might as well change the subject.

Fargo was drawn to water like black flies are drawn to thru-hikers. He'd gone swimming. Two miles before the shelter where we'd planned to meet, he had discovered Lake Tiorati and stopped for an hour to swim and cool off, while I walked by unknowingly. For the rest of our time together, Fargo was in whatever water we met, whether a puddle or a lake. Crossing the Hudson, I made certain he didn't jump off the bridge.

The Graymoor Spiritual Life Center is home to a group of Catholic men called the Franciscan Friars of the Atonement. Located on four hundred acres overlooking the Hudson River valley, the Center's mission is to discover what lies inside each individual and to foster unity between God and man and unity between all people. In times past, hikers were welcome to eat with the Friars, but that was no longer a policy. I was deeply disappointed, since I had hoped to interact with these men.

We were, however, permitted to sleep in a pavilion on the grounds. Fargo and I spread out our gear and were soon joined by a newcomer. Garmin had started his hike on February 17, almost six weeks before I arrived at Springer Mountain. By the time he finished, Garmin probably had walked more miles than any other 2008 thru-hiker. He covered many AT miles three times—his sense of direction was horrible, and other hikers often met him hiking the wrong way. We welcomed him into our merry little band and promised to keep him headed north if he stayed with us.

Saint Gertrude and Stretch, two hikers I had not met, set up their tents outside the pavilion. I would hike with Gerty later in my journey, but Stretch would soon be off the trail. Fargo told everyone about the Pharmacy Shelter just one day ahead of us. Tomorrow night, he would be staying at the shrine he was certain was dedicated to fellow hardworking pharmacists.

From a friary tower on the hill above us, a bell announced the arrival of every new hour throughout the night. I woke at every toll, so we got an early start toward the RPH Shelter. I didn't need to worry about Fargo disappearing again; I knew exactly where he'd be that night.

It was a nineteen-mile hike to RPH, and since the bell had tolled for me all night, I was tired and happy to see the nondescript block building, resembling a one-car garage. Since it had become Fargo's shrine, Garmin and I allowed him to enter first. Several bunks lined the walls, and the only contents were a desk and a chair. A concrete patio with a picnic table graced the back of the shelter. We saw no pharmacy paraphernalia anywhere, except for a half-empty bottle of Tylenol on the small desk.

"Your museum is kind of empty," said Garmin, as we surveyed the room. Although Garmin was directionally challenged, he was never at a loss for words. "If this is the tribute shelter for pharmacists, I can't wait to see the lawyer shelter."

We found a pizza shop menu on the desk, so we ordered delivery of three large pizzas. Gerty and Stretch arrived, but it was still early, so after stopping in to tour the RPH, they headed for the next shelter.

While we waited for our pizza, the call of nature took me to the privy, newer than the shelter and also built of blocks. Seated inside, I noticed a small plaque on the wall dedicating this block outhouse to Ralph's Peak Hikers, a local hiking club. The shelter was also named for the club; "RPH" was "Ralph's Peak Hikers." As best as I could, considering I was laughing so much, I finished my task and went in search of Garmin and Fargo. "Hey, Garmin, you need to go to the privy, don't you? Okay, what I meant was—you really must go to the privy. Be sure to read the dedication on the wall before Fargo sees it."

Soon, another round of hearty laughter came from the block throne room. "Hey dere, you gots to tell me what youse guys are laughing at out dere."

"Just wait . . . Garmin is reading the history of the Pharmacy Shelter."

Fargo's subsequent dejection was soothed somewhat by the delivery of our pizza, and while the three of us sat at the table concentrating only on food, a figure approached from the nearby road. A man who looked to be in his midsixties sat down at our table, greeted us, and asked if we needed anything. Steve lived in a neighboring town, and although he was not a hiker himself, he enjoyed stopping by the shelter occasionally and talking with those passing through. He offered to take us into town if we needed supplies, and we decided to make a quick trip to Wal-Mart. A new Lincoln SUV waited by the roadside, and Steve seemed to have no objections to three dirty thru-hikers riding in his spotless vehicle. Boxes were piled high in the back of the SUV, and I asked Steve what he did for a living. "I'm a pharmacist," he said. "I own seven pharmacies in the surrounding villages."

Fargo was astounded. I looked at Garmin, and we both shook our heads in disbelief.

"Believe you me, I told youse guys dat was a pharmacy shelter."

The coincidence was almost too bizarre to be true. But anything can happen on the trail. That's another gift of the trail: incidents so unexpected and inexplicable and whimsical that I could only shake my head in amazement. The morning before had held just such surprises.

Very early in the morning, we spotted a circle of plastic pink flamingoes in the woods. Garmin and I stood in their midst and took our picture. Who would have taken the time to carry pink flamingoes out here? (Later, we talked with a hiker who claimed the circle marked the home of a rattlesnake family. I doubted the story, but I admit it did send shivers down my spine.)

A little farther down the trail, we stood under the Dover Oak, proudly claiming to be the largest tree on the AT. Back in Virginia, the Keffer Oak makes the same claim.

Soon after, we walked through a field where round bales of hay lay in the morning mist, then crossed a marshy area on bog bridges, and suddenly arrived at a train stop. The railroad tracks were empty as we crossed, but next to them, here in almost-the-middle of nowhere, a blue bench perched on a raised platform. Apparently, trains did stop here several times a day, for anyone wishing to hop a ride to New York City.

We crossed Rt. 22. A short walk down the road brought us to a nursery and landscaping center that was just opening for the day. I spotted an employee on the porch, called good morning to him, and jokingly asked if there was coffee available. We were invited in and the owner himself brewed us a pot of coffee while he and Fargo talked hunting and fishing. We sat on the front porch, drinking coffee and distracting his workers from their morning routines.

On the trail again, we walked through a field where someone

had painstakingly built a shell around an old water tower, transforming it into a rocket ship poised for takeoff.

It was barely seven in the morning and we'd only walked three miles.

One of the biggest surprises the trail held for me was just that—the surprises.

19

Kindness and Courage

On June 27, another hot and muggy day, we entered Connecticut. Ten miles ahead was the town of Kent. We needed a break, so we called ahead to book a room. No price would be too great for a shower.

I was wrong; $120 did seem too much to pay for a shower. Kent was an upscale town, a playground for rich folks from New York City. Antique shops, B&Bs, expensive chocolate stores, and other attractions made Kent inviting, but too pricey for hikers interested only in a shower and rest.

Garmin called the owner of Backcountry Outfitters to inquire about getting a ride to nearby Wingdale, in hopes of finding a cheaper room. The owner agreed to pick us up at the road crossing, take us to our motel, and pick us up again in the morning to return to Kent, where we all had scheduled food drops. Fargo, who thoroughly enjoyed staying in shelters, would stay behind in the woods.

We came to the road crossing where we would meet our ride and a BMW convertible was waiting for us. The ride was exhilarating and the motel was indeed cheaper—only $60 for our shower. What we had not considered, though, was the price of gas. The next morning when our BMW taxi dropped us off in Kent, we paid another $60 for the ride. Our shower had cost us $120, after all.

I walked the streets of Kent, admiring antique stores and art galleries. Garmin was meeting a former school friend at a road crossing several miles up the trail, so he was already gone by the time I stuck out my thumb for a ride back to the trail.

As I rode back to the trail in a beat-up Volvo, I spotted a floppy hat and a flute and knew that Padre would probably be catching up with me soon.

Seven miles later, I found Fargo relaxing at the Stewart Hollow Brook Lean-to. I convinced him break time was over, and he joined me again. I wanted to keep on schedule for my "Connecticut Plan." The truth was, I longed for more comforts. I would probably be in Connecticut for three nights, and if all went according to plan, I would spend all three nights in a soft bed. I'd had my fill of shelters and stealth camping for now.

We followed the Housatonic River for several miles; the path was level, with the best trail conditions we had seen in days. A familiar figure was walking toward us, headed south. We greeted him.

"Hey, Garmin, enjoy your trip back to Georgia."

His internal compass had failed him again, and we turned him around and headed him north to meet his friend.

My plan was working to perfection. The second night I had a soft bed in Cornwall Bridge and a great six o'clock breakfast at Baird's General Store.

The third leg of Connecticut took me 21.6 miles to Salisbury. From the top of Prospect Mountain, I called Maria McCabe. Maria was an eighty-year-old lady in Salisbury who opened her home to thru-hikers. I made my call in the evening and interrupted Maria's card game with her brother-in-law.

"Hey, Maria, there's two good-looking middle-aged men wanting to stay at your house tonight. How does that suit you?"

"I'm taking quarters from my brother-in-law right now, and he's still got a few left that I want," she replied. "But if you're at Lower Cobble Road at seven o'clock, we'll pick you up."

As we approached Lower Cobble Road later that evening, an elderly lady appeared at the trailhead and yelled up to us, "Where are those good-looking men I was promised?"

"Just wait till we get showered and into fresh clothes. You'll be impressed."

Going to Maria McCabe's was like going to grandmother's house. She welcomed us as if we were family. We learned she had outlived two husbands and several boyfriends and took in hikers to supplement her Social Security income. I'm not certain how much the hiker boarding helped her budget, since she didn't charge much and allowed us to raid her refrigerator. I believe she thrived, instead, on the hiker conversation.

She brought out a notebook where guests had written notes of thanks for her hospitality. In the cold of winter, she told us, when she was lonely or sad, she would take out this hiker journal and read all of the nice things people had said about her.

As we retired, Maria told us that she never moved any body parts before eight in the morning, but we were welcome to cook our own breakfast. Fargo and I were in the kitchen by six, and I cooked eggs and bacon for us both. Before we left the McCabe house, we wrote nice things in the journal for Maria to read on some dark and cold winter day.

We navigated our way out of Salisbury, following directions Maria had given us the night before. The early morning was already hot and muggy, and we were sweating long before we started our last Connecticut climb, Bear Mountain.

Back in 1885, a local man was convinced that the highest point in the state was atop Bear Mountain, so he hired a mason to construct a tower on the summit that would be visible to the surrounding countryside. Somehow the mason managed to haul 350 tons of rock to the mountaintop and designed a rock pile in the shape of a pyramid without using any mortar whatsoever. Turns out the mountain wasn't the highest point in Connecticut after all, even though a plaque embedded in the rocks still makes the claim. The pyramid eventually collapsed, and although several attempts were made to rebuild it, maintenance became too troublesome over time. The pile was stabilized and the plaque inserted into the side of the rubble.

Fargo suggested I scamper to the top and have my picture taken on this so-called highest point. The view was splendid. To the south lay the Berkshire Mountains; to the west, the Catskill Mountains; to the east, the Housatonic Valley unfolded; and to the north, Mt. Greylock boasted its summit as the highest point in Massachusetts.

All along my journey, I was intrigued by the importance folks put on the highest point in any state. The only state that bragged on its low point was New York, where I'd walked through the zoo.

A mile later, we were in beautiful Sages Ravine. The trail followed a brook whose waters cascaded over rocks and gathered in lovely, inviting pools. Large trees sheltered us as the scenic stretch of trail led out of Connecticut and into Massachusetts. On one tree, a sign fastened above a white blaze welcomed us to my eleventh state. Just a few days earlier, entering Connecticut had given me a psychological lift; I was finally in New England. The southern states were done; the middle states were finished; I just had to finish these New England states—and then I could go home.

Our destination for that day was a rustic New England inn in South Egremont, twelve miles ahead. The inn offered a hikers' discount during the week if rooms were available. We would be celebrating that day. We expected to pass the 1500-mile mark that afternoon, and tomorrow was Fargo's 57th birthday.

Before the celebrations, we had to conquer Mt. Everett. Its summit was covered with blueberries, and we bounded left and right off the trail, eating the delicious morsels. But the descent from Everett was tricky; the trail was slick, the rocks were slippery, and sitting and sliding was often the best way down. At breakfast in town the next day, we talked with a paramedic who told us they had been called out to Mt. Everett many times to rescue fallen hikers.

Once I had skidded to the bottom of Everett, I'd passed the 1500-mile mark of my hike. We had made it down the mountain with no serious mishaps, and we hitched a ride into South Egremont.

The Egremont Inn has welcomed guests for over 225 years, and was built first as a tavern in 1780. Six years later, the final battle of Shay's Rebellion was fought and lost only one mile from the tavern. The rebellion was led by a group of farmers, angry at high taxes imposed by the state. In many cases, the state confiscated properties of those unable to pay. The farmers rebelled and, in effective protests, shut down local courts, prohibiting judges from enforcing the debt collections. In return, the government assembled a four-thousand-man militia to show the farmers who was in charge. At the battle near South Egremont, four farmers were killed and the rest fled north. Shay's Rebellion was over.

During the Revolutionary and Civil Wars, the South Egremont Inn was used as a hospital. At different times in its history, it also housed a store, a school, a post office, a temperance house, and a hotel. Today it is a charming twenty-room inn. History creaked from the long flights of wooden steps leading to my hot shower and soft bed.

I was in danger of becoming soft myself. My hike was turning into a town-to-town trek. I found myself scheduling my days around towns, not shelters. Something was changing. I acknowledged that it wasn't the soft beds that lured me into town; I could sleep just as well on a hard shelter floor or on the ground in the forest. I came to town for the people. I craved interaction with more folks than just my few fellow hikers.

Leaving town after breakfast at Mom's Country Cafe, we passed the field where a tilting stone obelisk marked the battle of Shay's Rebellion. The farmers' last stand against the government had taken place here. Where are those brave farmers today when we need them? There are so few people still willing to take a stand against injustice.

The next two Massachusetts days were filled with river fordings, railroad crossings, and bog bridges across marshy lowlands. At mile 1,537, the trail crossed I-90 over an enclosed footbridge. The traffic whizzed beneath us as we walked over the Massachusetts Turnpike. Six weeks later, I would be rushing through here at 70 mph, but today I was still traveling between 2 and 3 mph.

Our goal was to be in Dalton, Massachusetts, for Fourth of July weekend. For several weeks, the trail grapevine had been telling us about the Bird Cage Hostel in Dalton; it was not listed in our guidebook, but our curiosity was roused and we hoped to celebrate the holiday there.

Early one morning, I set forth from the shelter by myself; Fargo would get a later start, but I was on a mission. I left the trail when it crossed Pittsfield Road. Just a short way down this road lived a lady I wished to meet, the famous cookie lady.

Marilyn and her husband run a small blueberry farm; hikers have been stopping here for many years, enjoying her home-baked cookies. No one was stirring at the shingled house when I arrived. I walked around the yard, admired potted plants, and dawdled on the front porch, signing a note board on the wall and making no attempt at quiet, hoping the household would soon wake up. Rufus finally realized a visitor had arrived, and he barked Marilyn awake.

The two chocolate chip cookies were good, but far more satisfying was my conversation with Marilyn Wiley, a real trail angel. I had woken her for two cookies, but the hospitality and warmth she gave in return brightened my day.

Sometimes it takes only a few kind words to transform someone's day. How can we be too busy to tell the people we most cherish what they mean to us? I remembered Maria McCabe's notebook, where total strangers had written "nice things" that warmed her in lonely times.

Maria McCabe knew the secret: seeds of kindness sown into others' lives can return and encourage us in our own winters of loneliness.

Fargo was just arriving at the Pittsfield Road crossing as I came back to the trail after my chocolate chip detour. I kindly described for him the cookies I had eaten.

Shortly after noon, we followed the AT into Dalton. At first glance, the small town seems quintessential Americana, but it's a real money town, built on money by money for money. Dalton's largest employer is Crane & Company, producing all the paper used for Federal Reserve notes in America. Every piece of paper money in your wallet right now came from Dalton, Massachusetts.

But it wasn't the money made here that warmed my spirits. What made my stay in Dalton a favorite memory was something of real value: families. Front porches and lawns were filled with family activities on this holiday weekend.

We'd found the Bird Cage Hostel, marked not by a sign but by a bird cage on the lawn, and my own hiker family was gathering there. Fargo, Padre, Rhino and Ronja, myself, and others celebrated the Fourth in Dalton. Another hostel in town invited the Bird Cage guests to a hiker feed, and we sat down to corn on the cob, baked beans, and an all-American picnic.

In this town that produces the money that often brings out the worst in people, I saw and felt what life is truly about: families, togetherness, unity, acceptance, respect, and love for God. Those ingredients build strong spines and foster the courage to do what's right in any situation.

That's something all the money in Dalton can never buy.

20

The Path to Freedom

"ey, Padre, who goes to heaven and who goes to hell?"
Apostle and the priest enjoyed Independence Day,
strolling through small town America. Padre had shattered so many of my stereotypes about the Catholic Church. Here was a man who fasted and prayed and sought God's will for his life. I confess, though, I did think maybe I'd trip him up with this question. I expected one of those predictably vague answers, such as, "No one can know who will get to heaven," or "No one's sure if hell exists." But I should have known that Padre would never give me a pat answer.

"Many years ago, St. Catherine of Siena said, 'All the way to heaven is heaven because Christ is the way.' In my faith, we now say, 'Heaven all the way to heaven; hell all the way to hell.' The path you're on today will lead you to your eternal destiny. If Christ is your guide, He will lead you to heaven.

There are two guides and two paths, and you choose which you will follow."

I also believe in two paths for our lives. And our choice of path has life-and-death consequences. Both paths take us to a chasm at the end of this life, but one of those paths has a cross that spans the chasm and leads to another life.

The pathways to our eternities also reminded me of the trail I hiked every day. The Appalachian Trail had a destination. As long as I followed the white blazes and studied my guidebook diligently, the path would lead me to Mt. Katahdin. Countless other paths led away from the AT and away from my goal. My life was like this trail. I had already taken many of those side paths, but God always welcomed me back.

I enjoyed hiking with my new trail friends, but times of solitude on the trail gave birth to new growth within me. Conversations with Padre had given me much to think about, and for the next several days I would have plenty of time to ponder. I would be alone on the trail over the next mountain.

Fargo worried about everything, and now he worried about the difficulty of Mt. Greylock looming ahead of us. The hostel owner offered to take hikers twenty miles ahead, to the other side of the mountain and a higher elevation, from which hikers would have a much easier hike back to Dalton. While Padre and I walked the streets of Dalton and talked paths to eternity, Fargo was slackpacking those twenty miles back to town. He'd join us for the festivities that evening, and then the next morning he'd get a ride back to the other side of Mt. Greylock and continue north, a full day ahead of me.

Padre and Rhino would meet the TV crew tomorrow for an update on Rhino's hike, so I would be alone for the next few days. I planned to hike several big days to catch up with Fargo. Without me to coax him into longer days, he liked to stop early in the afternoon, so I felt confident I would catch him again.

Mt. Greylock lived up to its reputation as a difficult climb for purists heading north. As I neared the summit, rain and fog obscured the War Memorial Tower with its plaque declaring this the highest point in Massachusetts and telling me to "Take a deep breath and enjoy the views." I took deep breaths, but the shroud of fog hid the views. Even the white blazes were difficult to spot, and I moved cautiously, careful not to lose my path. Six miles of slippery trails going down the mountain made the descent as exhausting as the climb. Rainy Mt. Greylock was everything Fargo had feared.

Late in the afternoon, the trail intersected Rt. 2. I was tired, wet, and hungry, so I trudged three-tenths of a mile west to a motel and grocery. Being warm and dry was such a relief and pleasure, I did not care that I paid far too much for the motel room. My feet were dry when I crossed the road to the grocery; the motel room hair dryer had overheated several times during the hour it took to dry my shoes.

I went wild in the grocery store. If you've ever gone grocery shopping when you're extremely hungry, you know what happened. The bags I lugged back across the road cost me over fifty dollars, but what a feast I had that night: a whole chicken, a container of mashed potatoes, an apple pie, bananas, a bag of chips, a can of Coke, and a pint of chocolate ice cream.

Sunday, July 6. This well-fed hiker was on the road at five in the morning, heading down Rt. 2. I crossed the Hoosic

River, followed Massachusetts Avenue, and turned into a residential driveway. White blazes painted on the blacktop led me between the house and a flower garden and back into the woods.

Nature worshiped that morning. The brook's song often broke into choruses of waterfalls, and rounding a bend, I caught sight of a tree rejoicing. The leaves on one branch were shaking and dancing while the rest of the tree remained silent and still. I'd seen this once before on my hike; it was probably caused by the patterns of breezes, but I remembered Psalm 96 talking about the trees singing for joy and Isaiah 55 speaking of the mountains and hills bursting into song and clapping their hands. This tree was clapping its hands and singing for joy that morning, surely one charismatic tree.

Climbing toward Eph's Lookout, I encountered God through an emotional conversation that left me weeping facedown on the ground and changed my life's journey.

But first, I want to tell you a story.

I was a seeker. I wanted to know who God was. For most of my life, I knew I wanted to follow the right path, but it always seemed so difficult—almost impossible. I'd been taught the rights and wrongs of living, but I knew little about the heart of God. Now I wanted to know Him, and I wanted to know if He was involved in my life here on earth. If His divine hand was in events, what was His plan?

I had three uncles who were ministers at three local churches. The church I attended as a young boy was led by one uncle. Ours was the most conservative of the three churches. We looked askance at the second uncle's church, where more liberal dress and smaller head coverings were permitted. Both these churches watched in horror as the even more liberal Mennonite church of my third uncle permitted far more insidious evils, such as television and the disappearing head covering.

But what interested me was the peace that all three of these men carried about themselves. While I had all kinds of doubts, fears, and confusion, my uncles seemed to have no questions about their faith. I watched them, and wondered.

I discovered their secret on December 31, 2002, during the funeral service for the uncle who had led the most liberal Mennonite church. Apparently, he had fallen in love and spent his life reading love letters. He passed away at ninety-three, and he was in love with God, a real, genuine love. The love letters came from the Bible, God's letters to us. My uncle was committed to reading his Bible daily, and in the last eight years of his life he had read the Book cover to cover ten times. When he lost his sight toward the end of his life, another uncle would drive to his house and read the Scriptures to him.

The moment of insight at his funeral hit me like a physical force, and I slumped down in the pew. How could I know God if I didn't read what He had written to me? When I was dating Mary, she had sometimes sent me a love letter, and I couldn't wait to rip it open and read what her heart was feeling. That was what I wanted now. I desperately wanted to know the heart of God.

As soon as the burial service was over, I drove to the local bookstore and purchased a new Bible, determined to read it with a new mindset. If my uncle could read this Book ten times from age eighty-five to ninety-three, then I certainly could read it through too. On January 1, 2003, I started my journey. I begged God to reveal Himself to me in His Word.

By June 1, I had read it through. I read it again and again, ten times over the next five years. I kept myself on a daily reading schedule, and I took my Bible with me everywhere. Before that year, I would have been embarrassed to be seen carrying my Bible anywhere except church. Now I no longer cared who saw me. In airports, hotel lobbies, hospital waiting rooms, or traffic jams, I was never without my book of love letters.

Little by little, the heart of God came into focus. His patience and mercy amazed me as I read of His love toward so many flawed individuals in the Bible. King David stumbled and sinned many times, yet he was a man "after God's own heart." Story after story about weak people God used in mighty ways gave me hope. I wondered at the courage of those who obeyed when God asked them to do seemingly ridiculous tasks. Noah could have protested, "Dear God, You want me to build a large boat and You're going to destroy the world with a flood? I don't get it."

I was encouraged by John 14, where Jesus promises to go to heaven to prepare a place for us and then return and take us there. In the last chapter of the Bible, Revelation 22, Jesus tells us twice, *Behold, I am coming soon.* The verses reminded me of that pulpit-pounding minister who had scared me so badly over forty years ago.

As I hiked that July morning, I thought back to all the doctors' offices and hospital rooms where I'd read my Bible during Mary's four-year battle with cancer. When the first bottle of chemotherapy chemicals dripped into her body, our family gathered around her bed and prayed. I opened

Above, bog walk in New Jersey; *below*, Shay's Rebellion obelisk; *top right*, atop Moose Mountain; *center right*, bog crossing; *bottom right*, Saddleback Mountain

my Bible at random and read Psalm 91. In this psalm, God promises to be our refuge and our fortress if we trust in Him. Mary took this chapter to heart and read it every day for the next four years.

On the day I left Springer Mountain, I opened my Bible and saw that Psalm 91 was the next chapter in my reading regimen. I remembered how Mary cherished that psalm, but now it spoke new meaning to me as I read God's promise that if I made Him my dwelling place, He would command His angels to guard me. As I started my hike, God's Word told me *no disaster shall come near my tent* and that the angels would protect me from striking my foot against a stone. An encouraging message for someone getting ready to hike the AT! I knew I was not alone in that horrible storm.

I didn't hike alone this Sunday morning either. As I had done countless times before, I asked God why He had taken Mary. "Do you realize the loneliness, the grief, the hurt we've endured without her?"

A soft voice spoke in my spirit. *Paul, I'm coming soon.*

"What? What are You saying?" I asked in bewilderment.

I am coming soon.

"You're coming soon," I repeated. "Yes, I've read that in the Bible and many people have said that for many years, and nothing has happened." My tears started. "Did You take my wife away from me and ask me to give up my job so You and I could meet on this mountaintop and You could tell me this?"

If that were true, then God truly was in control of my life. He had been there all the time during Mary's sickness.

"But why are You giving me this message? Scriptures say no human can know the actual time You'll be returning, and Your 'soon' in Scriptures has already been several thousand years. Why are You telling me this now?"

Paul, I want you to take this message to others: I am coming soon.

"Oh no, not me, God! You've got the wrong man. That's not for me to do—that's a message for ministers to deliver," I argued. "I'm a scoundrel. Don't You remember that silly naked hike?"

But you're My scoundrel. You'll reach people that ministers will never reach.

"How's that going to work? How am I going to reach anyone?"

You're writing a book, aren't you? Put this message in your book.

"Oh my goodness, God, now You're messing with my book too."

I'll get it into the hands of people who need to hear My message.

"But everyone will think I'm completely crazy," I sputtered.

Yet I could not ignore everything God had been teaching me on this hike. Did I really believe the things I said I believed? Did I believe God told Pilgrim to let his hair grow long? Wasn't I telling folks that God would speak? Hadn't I admired the bravery of those farmers in Shay's Rebellion? What about *my* courage? In the face of probable ridicule, would I sink into cowardice?

So I was a scoundrel; I might as well also be a fool for God.

Our conversation had brought me to the top of Eph's

Lookout. I dropped my pack and fell facedown on the rocks, weeping.

"God, if that's the message You want delivered, I'll do it."

I stood up, picked up my pack, and took in the surrounding views. Four little words brought me freedom, like new life breathed into me.

I am coming soon.

It is a message from God that assures me He is in control. There's so much anger and hatred everywhere, and greed and corruption are out of control. But nothing that happens is a surprise to God; He is right on schedule—His schedule.

To everyone who wonders what this world is coming to, God says, *I am coming soon.*

God is not telling us to sit around and waste our time waiting. He doesn't operate on our timetable. *I am coming soon* is a message to live, a message of healing and a message of peace. When all around you is despair and chaos, God is in control and will be your refuge and fortress if you trust Him.

I am coming soon. That message gave me new hope. When I was a teenager, those words struck me with fear and despair whenever I heard them; now they filled me with comfort and peace. I knew I was free at last from my guilty bondage to dos and don'ts. I knew Mary was okay, and I knew I was going to be okay. It was almost as though I heard her say, "Paul, live!"

As I hiked away from Eph's Lookout, the rocks and trees and hills were rejoicing. This trail had become a path to freedom. God was in control, my life was in His hands, and I was free to live. And if my book never sold—well, I'd remind God that this addition to the book was *His* idea.

Who does God want to encourage with this message? I may never know. He's the one who will place this book exactly where He wants it.

21

Golden Days

One mile after making my promise to God atop Eph's Lookout, I claimed Vermont as my twelfth state.

In the Green Mountain State, the AT follows the Long Trail, the first long-distance trail ever constructed, running the length of Vermont from the Massachusetts border on the south to the Canadian border on the north. The AT and the LT run together for a hundred miles, over many of the summits and high ridges of the Green Mountains. Near Killington, the two trails split. The Appalachian Trail heads east to New Hampshire and the Long Trail continues north to Canada.

The day was hot, but trail conditions were not too difficult. Eighteen miles into the new state, the trail crossed Rt. 9 and I met my first Vermont trail magic. At a parking area, two former hikers invited me to raid a cooler filled with soft drinks. Two cans of pop and three bags of snacks propelled me forward with a new burst of energy.

One of my goals on this trek was to hike one day of thirty miles or more. This seemed like a good day to do it.

At seven in the evening, I arrived at Goddard Shelter, in a lovely setting close to the summit of Glastenbury Mountain. Towering pines surrounded the shelter, and a crystal clear spring flowed only a few feet away. I'd already hiked 28.5 miles and the next shelter was four miles away. Those four miles would put my day well over my thirty-mile goal.

At Goddard, three section hikers had set up their tents outside the shelter and generously told me I could set up mine inside if I wished. I debated. How important was that goal of thirty miles?

One of the hikers talked proudly of the long and hard eighteen miles he'd done that day. "How far did you hike today?" he asked me. I paused for dramatic effect and then tried to answer nonchalantly.

"Twenty-eight and a half miles."

"Wow! Are you a thru-hiker?"

"Yes, I am. I've just passed the 1600-mile mark today."

"Hey, guys!" he yelled to his buddies. "Get over here! This guy hiked over twenty-eight miles today and 1,600 on the trail." I was a celebrity. The importance of making those thirty miles receded as the three hikers gathered around and listened to my stories. That morning I'd asked God to send interesting people into my life that day, and now here they were, even if they were only interested in what I'd done.

The simple pleasures of the evening—good conversation, a cold and clear spring, a shelter nestled in the pines—convinced me that I was done hiking for the day. With the evening light slanting through the trees, I set up my tent inside Goddard Shelter and cooked my meal. The soft sounds of swaying pines lulled me to sleep. I never achieved my goal of thirty miles, and I have no regrets.

The section hikers never stirred as I left Goddard Shelter at the first hint of morning light.

I managed only nineteen tiring miles that day. In the Green Mountain National Forest, I trudged up Stratton Mountain. On the summit, I climbed even farther, scrambling to the top of a fire tower to take in the stunning vista of mountains dotted with ski slopes. That night, I stood on the shore of Stratton Pond and soaked up the peaceful mood created by placid waters reflecting the surrounding mountains.

Stratton Pond Shelter was a newer A-frame construction with an extended roof that protected several benches and a picnic table. For several hours I had the shelter to myself; at dusk, another hiker showed up. The young man's mother had recently passed away, and our conversation reminded me of the pain of my children's loss.

Our shared sadness and reminiscing was interrupted by a new member of the hiking community, who came running at full speed toward the shelter. He carried no food or water. As he approached the few steps leading to the front of the shelter and prepared to leap inside, the young man and I both yelled, "STOP!"

The German shepherd obediently stopped. We expected a hiker to arrive and claim him, but no one else appeared. The dog wore a collar with no tags. We took compassion on this traveler and fed him, but never allowed him inside the shelter. He was obviously well-trained and obeyed our commands to stay outside. At least, he obeyed until we were asleep. When I awoke the next morning, the dog was lying beside my bunk. Perhaps I had needed a guardian that night.

My next hiking partner would be a German shepherd. The young hiker left the shelter shortly before I did in the morning, and I encouraged the dog to follow him. No luck. He was obviously waiting for me. I did not wish to be responsible for a dog on the trail; the shepherd, however, seemed to think he was responsible for me.

All morning he stayed with me, leading the way. Occasionally he'd glance back to make certain I was keeping up. Several times, I darted down a side trail in hopes of losing him, but that dog turned back and found me again every time. I stopped to filter water from a stream; he drank too, and then plopped down in the water just upstream from me. That put an end to my filtering; I still had a small supply of water left and didn't relish the thought of drinking dog-flavored water.

Early in the afternoon, the trail crossed Vermont Rt. 11/30 and cut through a parking area before entering the woods again. The summer day had heated up; I was hot and thirsty and needed to find more water soon. But I spotted relief. A half-full (or half-empty, depending on your point of view) two-liter bottle of Diet Coke lay in a ditch alongside the parking area. I sniffed the contents briefly and then, much to my own disbelief, quickly guzzled down the warm liquid.

A partial sheet of plywood lay along the roadside, probably blown off a passing truck. I pulled it from the weeds and stretched out on it for a short break. My trusty canine companion rested nearby. We lounged contentedly, only half-conscious. A car door slammed and a well-known voice roused me. "Hey dere, Apostle, dat's a good-lookin' partner wit you dere, don'tcha know. Und where did you get da soda?"

Fargo! He had taken a quick hitch into Manchester Center, several miles west, to resupply and was now returning to the trail.

"If I knew I was meeting you here, I'd have saved some Diet Coke for you. This dog showed up at the shelter last night, and now I can't get him to leave my side."

Fargo's ride had not yet left the parking area, so we convinced him to take the German shepherd back into town. We coaxed it into the backseat, and it pressed a sad face to the rear window, watching me walk away with Fargo. But when the driver opened his door to enter the car, the dog jumped out and soon caught up with us. Once again we returned to the parking area, happy to find the driver waiting. This time, both dog and driver stayed in the car as we made our escape.

If that dog had stayed with me for several days, I probably couldn't have sent him away. I'd already been thinking of names for him. I was glad that his life did improve as a result of meeting me. Another hiker told me later that he had been at the local outfitter when the driver brought the dog to town, and someone at the store had offered to adopt him. Back in Manchester Center, Vermont, someone has a very loyal dog who was my protector for a day.

It was good to have another human to talk with again. We covered just about every subject you could imagine on our stroll through the woods. There were a few hours every afternoon, though, when Fargo was silent. Those were the hours he spent with his headphones on, listening to National Public Radio. During those hours, I had the woods and my thoughts to myself. If anything important happened in the world, Fargo gave me an update.

I had ample warning of the thunderstorm rolling over White Rock Mountain, but I foolishly kept walking instead of donning rain gear. The downpour soon pummeled me. I squeezed myself under a small spruce, but it gave little shelter. By the time we arrived at White Rocks Cliff, I was cold and shivering. I called a hostel in Rutland and made reservations to be warm and dry.

The Back Home Again Hostel in downtown Rutland is run by the Twelve Tribes Community, a religious group living a communal lifestyle. The Twelve Tribes attempt to replicate the early church as it is described in the New Testament book of Acts.

In the early 1970s, Elbert Spriggs and his wife had a ministry in Chattanooga, Tennessee, working with several different denominations. One Sunday evening, he arrived at church and was dismayed to find it canceled due to the Super Bowl. His solution was to form his own church, calling it the Vine Community Church and meeting in a local park. Later, that church evolved into the Twelve Tribes, the Commonwealth of Israel. The members of the community take on Hebrew names, and all resources are pooled and distributed as needed. The women dress plainly and the men wear beards. Except for the ponytails on many of the men, these people look very much like the plain folks of my community.

From White Rocks Cliff, I also called Abner and Virginia, old acquaintances of our family who now live near Rutland. They knew of my hike and had offered to treat me to a meal whenever I passed through. I took them up on the offer and we ate at a nearby café, also run by the Twelve Tribes. Abner and Virginia were amazed at my appetite, and I'm sure the

Twelve Tribes appreciated the large bill my friends cheerfully paid at the end of the evening.

Some consider the Twelve Tribes a cult, but their hostel offered us warm beds, hot showers, and friendly hospitality. One of the community members also gave me another nugget to ponder. "When we stopped going to church and started being the church," he told me, "something wonderful happened."

A community member drove us back to the trail in the morning. Good food and warm beds had rejuvenated us, and we were ready for whatever surprises Vermont had waiting up the trail.

The first surprise was more trail magic. The night before, I'd had a craving for Mountain Dew. I walked the short distance from downtown Rutland to a Wal-Mart, where I'd spotted a pop machine outside. The machine took my money but refused to give up the can of soda. Wal-Mart was already closed, so I had no choice but to go back to my room with my craving unsatisfied. Soon after getting back on the trail the next morning, we found a cooler and a box of snacks waiting in a clearing in the woods. A white plastic chair was provided for any weary hiker needing a break. I opened the cooler, and there was a block of ice surrounded by cans of Mountain Dew and Pepsi.

I may have overdone it just a little. After several Hostess Twinkies and three cans of soda, on top of the morning's coffee, I had twenty-seven teaspoons of sugar in my system. I was a rocket, fueled for takeoff. I burned through my sugar buzz and nineteen miles in record time and left Fargo far behind, but we had planned our stop for the night, and we'd meet at the end of the day.

At one time, the Appalachian Trail passed through Killington just across from the Inn at Long Trail. This inn caters to skiers and hikers and is a must-stop for many because of its authentic Irish Pub and dining room. The dining room is actually built around a large boulder that juts into one side of the room. Where you expect to see a wall, you're faced with a huge stone outcropping.

The AT was rerouted when a ski resort purchased the land the trail crossed. Now the trail passes Killington west of town. When I came to U.S. 4, I took the short walk to the inn, wanting to make this well-known stop. I walked in and admired the hardwood floors, the fieldstone fireplace, and the rustic interior. And at the bar, a familiar face sat grinning at me.

"Hey dere, Apostle. Where ya been?" The last I'd seen Fargo, he was disappearing in my sugar buzz dust.

"Fargo! How did you beat me here?"

"I took dat udder trail up dere, da one dat goes tru da ski resort."

"You blue-blazing cheesehead!" Fargo had found the old AT and gone across the ski resort property to cut off several miles. "Fargo, when you summit Mt. Katahdin—assuming you do before da missus calls you home—you'll be thinking about all these miles of AT you missed."

"Believe you me, Apostle, dat was da traditional route I hiked to get here. Und when I'm on dat Mt. Katahdin, I'll just be glad dat I finally got dere!"

The inn's French onion soup and shepherd's pie were just as delicious as the hiker grapevine had promised, and we spent an enjoyable evening lounging about the inn. Fargo rummaged through the hiker box and found a sixteen-ounce can of SPAM. He didn't want to carry an extra pound of weight, so he offered the can to me. I accepted, thinking it might make a unique meal the next evening.

But let me tell you, folks—just as wading through lots of spam and junk email on your computer can be unpleasant, so is trying to eat a whole pound of SPAM at one meal. The next night at the Winturri Shelter, I finished my usual hot meal and then unveiled my can of SPAM, much to the amusement of other shelter guests. My little folding camp knife sliced the chunk of mystery meat. Then I dropped each slice back into the bottom of the can and fried it on the stove, piece by piece. The first slice was delicious; the second slice was good; the third slice was tolerable; and the fourth slice was forced down.

I had eaten only half of the meat.

"Hey, Fargo, you want the rest?" He eagerly accepted, and then I saw his little plot. I'm sure he realized back at the inn that no one could eat that much SPAM at one sitting, and now he thanked me for carrying it all day for him.

The next night would be our last in Vermont, and as Fargo and I neared Happy Hill Shelter, a wonderful aroma drifted through the trees. A group of section hikers were grilling hamburgers over a fire. We didn't even attempt subtlety. "Hey, guys, you have any extra hamburgers for two tired and hungry thru-hikers?" A fair exchange was arranged. Several fat and juicy hamburgers were traded for several hours of trail stories.

The next morning we hiked six easy miles, passed under I-91 near Norwich, and crossed the Connecticut River. Halfway across the concrete bridge, an embedded marker declared that we had entered our thirteenth state, New Hampshire.

West Wheelock Street led us toward downtown Hanover and Dartmouth College. Dartmouth was founded in 1769 by a Puritan minister for the purpose of evangelizing Native Americans and then sending them out as missionaries. I doubted that many missionaries were still being produced at this elite Ivy League school. Every year over sixteen thousand students apply for admission and about one thousand are accepted. Becoming a missionary is more difficult than it used to be. Many had called, but few were chosen.

The hiker rate at the local inn was a mere $250 per night, so we flagged a taxi and headed out of town to a more reasonable roadhouse.

Fargo had a mail drop arriving in the morning, and while he waited for the post office to open, I ran across the street to a pharmacy. I had decided to buy a little radio and headphones. Why get my news filtered through Fargo when I could hear it firsthand?

For the next several days, I hiked with my new companion. Instead of conversing with the Boy Scout troop and their sponsors at Moose Mountain Shelter, I lay in my tent, connected with the outside world. I was a well-informed hiker, traversing those first mountains in New Hampshire. I conquered Moose Mountain, Smarts Mountain, Mt. Cube, and Mt. Mist, all while enduring information overload.

But something was wrong. Out here in the woods, this toy was destroying my newfound freedom. I no longer heard my footsteps on the pine needles or the birds singing or the wind rustling through the trees. Sure, the golden oldies station was playing my kind of music. Bob Dylan and Crosby, Stills

& Nash reminded me of my past, but somehow I was being robbed of the present. I had traded the joy of nature and conversing with God for a little radio clipped to my backpack.

The radio had to go. I stashed the radio at the bottom of my pack, and returned to living. If the world fell apart, Fargo would surely let me know.

I heard the ribbons of birdsong in the forest and the snap of a small branch under my foot. My music, my distraction, was the clicking of my poles and the sighing of the wind.

Thank You, God, for Your beautiful creation.

Welcome back, Apostle.

22

The White Mountains

Fargo and I sat at the Hikers Welcome Hostel and listened to southbound hikers complain of brutal trail conditions in Maine and New Hampshire's White Mountains. These hikers had started on Mt. Katahdin just a month ago and had only several hundred miles under their boots. We, on the other hand, had hiked over 1,800 miles and had already seen all kinds of trail conditions and weather. Fargo and I were certain the complaints came only because these southbounders were not yet in hiking shape. After everything I'd endured in the last one hundred days, I was certain I had seen everything the trail could possibly throw at me.

Then again, how many times had the Appalachian Trail already surprised me?

We'd left the trail and stopped at the hostel in the tiny village of Glencliff, New Hampshire, nestled in a high mountain valley at the edge of the White Mountain National Forest.

Tomorrow Fargo and I would enter those White Mountains. We studied our guidebooks, charting our course for the next several days. Camping rules are very stringent in the Whites and tenting sites are limited; hikers are rightfully concerned about the trek across these mountains.

Scattered across the White Mountains are eight huts maintained by the Appalachian Mountain Club in New Hampshire. These rustic mountain lodges are popular tourist destinations and a stay is quite costly. Most of the huts allow a limited number of thru-hikers to stay in exchange for work, usually sweeping or doing dishes in return for the privilege of sleeping on the floor and eating leftovers after the paying guests are finished with a meal. Fargo and I hoped to do several of these work-for-stays as we traversed the Whites.

Padre and Rhino also stopped at Hikers Welcome Hostel. Padre had a habit of losing things, and he'd just lost his third set of hiking poles. Hikers occasionally leave their poles in vehicles when hitching a ride, but losing three pair had to be some kind of record. I was certain Padre would need poles to conquer the mountains ahead of us.

I was tired, but I knew I only had a few more weeks on the trail. Just these mountains in New Hampshire and then beautiful Maine.

My Trail Journal entry that night:

The climbs are either getting tougher or I'm getting weaker. I am 63 miles from Mt. Washington. . . . I don't know how I'll feel when I'm closer to done with this hike, but right now I'm so ready to be done. I am just completely worn out right now. Some good news, though, only 398.5 miles left. Just a little walk in the park.

Early the next morning, Fargo and I labored up Mt. Moosilauke, the first time we climbed above tree level in New Hampshire. Close to the summit, trees were short and stubby, and a sign warned that we were walking through fragile alpine vegetation and requested that we stay on the marked trails. How can anything that survives these harsh mountaintop conditions be considered fragile?

Trail signs disappeared, and the path was marked instead by rock cairns, small directional piles of rocks. We finally stood at the top of our first White mountain and took in the incredible view; waves of blue and purple peaks stretched to the horizon.

A gusting and chilly wind reminded us to keep moving, and we picked our way down the rocky descent alongside a tumble of waterfalls. We maneuvered down the mountain, finding only small blocks of wood fastened to the rock faces for footholds. We'd conquered the first mountain of the 117 miles of trail that cross the White Mountains. Moosilauke, it turned out, was also one of the easiest climbs.

The sun made a short appearance. The small brook we followed was too inviting; Fargo jumped in for a swim, as was his habit. Rather than hiking on, I waited for him, lying on my back on the trail and soaking up the welcome sunshine.

I heard the clomping and clicking before Padre came into view. He was moving fast, and I saw he'd been outfitted with another set of hiking poles; he explained that he'd found them back at the hostel. I admired the pink poles with purple baskets, obviously a girl's set of ski poles.

"Wow, Padre, that's quite a fashion statement you're making. Too bad not many people will have a chance to admire them, since you'll probably lose those too."

Padre had decided to make a big push for the finish, and he thought this would be the last time we'd see each other. We exchanged addresses and said our good-byes, and my friend and his pink poles were gone.

Trail Journal, July 19, at the Galehead Hut:
I hiked the 10.4 hardest miles of my life. I never imagined how difficult the trail would be in NH.

The stories were true. Hiking conditions here were brutal. Every mountain climb was an exhausting experience. Rain, wind, and sleet battled us as we struggled up and down steep trails crossing Mt. Lincoln, Mt. Lafayette, and Mt. Garfield.

We had hiked only ten miles on the day we arrived at Galehead Hut early in the afternoon. Wet and shivering, Fargo and I inquired about doing a work-for-stay and were told that those spots were usually not given out until at least four o'clock. The next hut was still eight miles away, and we had no intention of hiking one mile farther that day. We stayed at the desk and informed the woman that we intended to be the first four o'clock hikers she would see; we were not going to stray far from that spot. Only one other hiker showed up that afternoon, and all three of us were hired.

The huts in the White Mountains are staffed primarily by college kids, each hut having its own group of workers who are referred to as "the croo." Summer jobs at these mountain lodges are prized gigs, but there's hard work involved too. No roads lead to the huts; all food and supplies have to be carried or helicoptered in. Thru-hikers are usually welcomed, since they not only help with the work, but also assist in disposing of leftover food.

The third hiker that day was St. Gertrude. I'd first met Gerty and Stretch back at the pavilion at the Graymoor Spiritual Life Center, and later they had stopped for a visit at the Pharmacy Shelter. Now Gerty arrived at Galehead Hut alone.

"What happened to Stretch?" I asked him.

"He tore a muscle and had to leave the trail for a while."

Many hikers, especially the younger ones, spent time each morning stretching their muscles. They'd push against trees, pull up their legs, and contort themselves into pretzel knots, preparing their bodies for a hiking day. My preparation each day was to put on my pack and start walking. By the time others were sufficiently stretched out, I was a mile down the trail. Stretch had torn a shoulder muscle while doing pushups in preparation for his daily hike.

We enjoyed a lively evening, socializing with about forty other guests. A women's church group was there on a retreat, and we discovered that we had met part of their group the night before at the Liberty Springs tent site on Franconia Ridge. Apparently the women had been given a choice of tenting or staying at the hut. We assured the women at Galehead that they had made a smart decision; the night before on Franconia Ridge had been miserable. Fargo and I had set up our tents on wooden platforms and spent a cold, miserable night just trying to stay dry and warm. I'd put on every article of clothing, including my rain gear, and several times I lit my cookstove, hoping for some meager warmth. The wind howled all night and cold rain battered my tent. The group of ladies tenting at the same site had the misfortune of spending the night on that cold and stormy ridge while their counterparts were warm and dry at Galehead Hut.

While we talked with the guests, the staff took a radio call. The ladies' group leader back at the Liberty Springs tent site had fallen and broken her leg; a rescue crew was on its way.

Fargo, Gerty, and I slept on the hardwood floor of the dining room that night, and I was thankful simply to be warm and dry.

We could not leave the next morning until our work was finished. After the guests had eaten breakfast and checked out, we shook out dozens of blankets and swept the entire hut. The chores were a welcome change from laboring up and down mountains with a heavy pack. We finished at nine o'clock and collected pay in the form of breakfast leftovers.

We had hoisted our packs and were ready to leave when we spotted two familiar figures coming up the trail toward the hut. I recognized Franklin and Einstein; they'd met each other back at Delaware Water Gap and had hiked together since then. They had learned from a southbound hiker that Apostle was just ahead of them, and so they had left camp early that morning to try to catch up with me.

I was delighted to see my friends again. We dropped our packs and took time to catch up on all the trail chatter, joining them for another round of food before starting our day on the trail.

The AMC huts in the White Mountains offer a hiker special. For two dollars, we could eat whatever soup was left from the previous night's meal—all the soup we wanted, as long as the supply lasted. When we left Galehead, we planned to hike seven miles to the Zealand Falls Hut, resupply on their soup, and end our day at a campground in Crawford Notch.

The seven miles to Zealand Falls were rainy and slippery. This hut is a delightful place to stay, with a beautiful falls nearby, but we'd seen enough water. We wanted only to be inside and dry. The five of us soon devoured all the cornbread and bean soup remaining from the night before.

Before we left the hut, I mooched a garbage bag from a croo member, emptied the contents of my backpack, and lined it with the bag. The rain had been constant and blowing, and my pack cover couldn't keep the contents dry. The garbage bag was one of my better decisions; it did protect my few possessions from the almost constant rain during the next several weeks.

After our soup break, we had eight miles to Highway 302 at Crawford Notch; we'd been informed that these were the easiest miles in the White Mountain stretch. At the road crossing, we'd head three miles down the highway to the Crawford Notch General Store and Campground. Gerty and I decided to see how quickly we could do these miles. Our plan was to make the campground in record time, then send a vehicle back to where the trail crossed the road and pick up the other three who lagged behind us.

For the next two hours Gerty splashed and skidded over rocks and rivers at a ridiculously reckless pace, and several feet behind him charged one equally ridiculous Apostle. I was determined that he would not out-hike me—unless, of course, I fell and broke every bone in my body. We foolishly risked life and limb, but, oh, what a thrill it was to emerge two and a half hours later at the road crossing—with me right on Gerty's heels.

We attempted hitchhiking the three miles to the campground, but no one would pick up two hikers walking along the road in the pouring rain. When we reached the camp store, Franklin greeted us at the front door. While we were walking the three miles in the rain, the other three had come to the road crossing and the first passing car had picked them up. They rode to the campground while we walked in the rain.

"Thanks for picking us up, Franklin," I complained.

"We waved when we passed you, but you were already close to the store, and we didn't want to interrupt your challenge."

Exactly five bunks were still available in the bunkhouse, and so we were soon five happy hikers. A laundry room and a shower house added to our bliss. All evening we lounged, eating and talking and attempting to dry out our backpacks. Outside, the cold downpour continued. I didn't care about the rain. I was dry, and I was among friends.

Mt. Washington lay ahead of us. At 6,288 feet, that mountain would be our second highest climb on the trail, second only to Clingman's Dome back in the Smoky Mountains. Our next stop would be the Lakes of the Clouds Hut, just 1.5 miles short of the summit.

The towering mountain endures the world's most extreme weather conditions. Mt. Washington sees snowfall every month of the year. The highest wind ever measured on planet Earth occurred at the summit on April 12, 1934, measuring 231 mph. The main building on top of the mountain is built to withstand gusts up to 300 mph, and all other buildings are chained to the ground. Storm systems seem to meet on this summit and result in extreme weather conditions. If snow and wind and storms do not deter the visitor, fog will often obscure the views.

The forecast was lousy, with weather warnings out for the mountain. We awoke to a damp, misty morning at the campground. Franklin and Einstein had already planned to take a zero day to recover from several long and difficult days and to wait for better weather before climbing Mt. Washington. Fargo was torn between hiking with me or heeding the dire forecast and staying at the bunkhouse. I remarked that if my hike had been dictated by weather forecasts, I'd probably still be in Georgia. Eventually, he decided to stay behind; if the sun happened to come out, he'd try to catch up with Gerty and me.

We two caught a ride back to the trail and started our climb, gaining several thousand feet in elevation in just two miles. At Webster Cliffs, the clouds gave way to sunshine and we enjoyed a splendid view over the valley and the three-mile road walk we'd done in the previous evening's rain.

Mt. Webster and Mt. Jackson were between us and soup at the next hut, the Mizpah Spring Hut. (Fargo had renamed it the Bar Mitzvah Hut.) Thinking about that soup as we hiked, I tried to guess what kind it would be; I was craving chicken noodle. So I was happy to find that the soup of the day at Bar Mitzvah Hut was turkey noodle. Gerty and I each had two large, steaming bowls of soup and several pieces of cornbread and, refreshed, tackled the remaining six miles upward to Lakes of the Clouds Hut.

About this time, the sun had also peeked out down at the campground. Fargo soon realized the error of his calculations. He was now behind his hiking partner and, in addition, had lost his connection to da missus back in Scansin. He'd been using my phone to keep in touch with home; now that I was gone, how would he keep up with the progress of his house sale?

He took off in pursuit of Gerty and me, and made it as far as the Bar Mitzvah Hut before stopping for the night. By then, we were six miles ahead of him at Lakes of the Clouds. Although he made a valiant attempt to overcome that six-mile gap, it would be 230 miles before we met again.

I'd just crossed Mt. Franklin at 5,004 feet when the sky opened up and dumped cold, hard rain. The trail became a rushing torrent, and I splashed through water streaming around and over my feet.

I'd almost reached Lakes of the Clouds Hut when the rain stopped and a rainbow pierced the gray clouds and arched over the mountainside. For a rain-drenched hiker, it was a beautiful reminder of God's promise to never again destroy the earth with a flood. There would be times in the next several weeks, though, when I wondered if God had excluded Maine from that promise.

Trail Journal, from Lakes of the Clouds Hut:
I can't begin to describe how I hate getting rained on, so I won't. One of these days I expect to wake up covered in moss and sprouting mushrooms.

Hikers know Lakes of the Clouds Hut as "Lake of the Crowds." Its popularity is not surprising; the hut sits dramatically on the rocky mountainside just below Mt. Washington's summit, looking out over lesser peaks and drifting clouds. This hut is the largest of the eight, built to accommodate ninety-two guests, and it was completely full when I arrived.

A croo party was scheduled for that night at the next hut, Madison Spring, which had closed for the night. The croo from Lakes of the Clouds was also invited to the party, so our hut that night was staffed by former workers filling in for the regulars. They were delighted when Gerty and I showed up wanting to do a work-for-stay and even more excited when they discovered that I had twenty-five years of restaurant experience.

Hand-washing dishes for ninety-two guests was more than I'd bargained for. Gerty and I joined the guests later for a question-and-answer session about our thru-hike. We did eat well; and later that evening, I unrolled my sleeping bag and slept on the same tabletop where I'd eaten just a few hours earlier.

At least our work was done that night and we could leave early in the morning. Only 1,200 feet remained to summit Mt. Washington, but when we arrived we found the mountaintop shrouded in heavy mist. No views today.

Inside the Summit House, I noticed a plaque memorializing people who had been killed in various mishaps on the mountain. It listed over one hundred persons who had died there, noting name, age, and reason for demise. Not the most pleasant way to start another hiking day on a dangerous mountain range.

We left the summit, crossed the cog railroad tracks, and headed for Madison Spring Hut. Much to my relief, the trail passed below the summit of Mt. Clay, Mt. Adams, and Mt. Jefferson. Along the trail, we passed croo members returning from their party at Madison Spring Hut the night before. I hoped the temporary help back at Lakes of the Clouds would hang around for a while, because these young folks did not look ready for prime time.

At Madison Spring Hut, everything was still in slow motion. It had been quite a party. Apparently, soup had not been on the menu last night; we were told no soup was available. "What do you mean, no soup?" I asked. "Every other hut has had soup for us."

"I think we had chicken noodle soup several nights ago, but it would take time to heat it up," the girl replied. But those were magic words; we would wait. The rain had started again and we were in no mood to continue hiking soaked and soupless. We spread our wet clothes across tables and settled in and waited. And waited.

Our reluctant hostess at last realized the only way to get rid of the two pesky hikers was to give them their soup. It was worth the wait. Life just runs better on hot chicken noodle soup. We navigated a descent of almost 4,000 feet, forded seven streams, and put Mt. Madison behind us.

Our fifteen-mile day was completed when we arrived at Pinkham Notch, where New Hampshire Rt. 16 cuts through the mountains. Pinkham Notch Visitor Center offers a bunkhouse, camp store, and dining room. We would again have a bed and a shower. In the last five nights, I'd slept on a wooden tent platform, a hardwood floor, a tabletop, and two bunk beds.

I took my shoes into the shower with me, as I'd done earlier that week. Since they couldn't possibly get any wetter, they might as well be clean.

During a delicious meal in the dining room, Gerty and I discussed our reasons for doing our thru-hikes. His wife had recently informed him she wanted a divorce. He was finding his peace on the trail. Why follow a five-step program to peace when you can just as easily shoulder a backpack and walk five million steps to peace and freedom?

The dining room opened early the next morning, so we finished off a huge breakfast to store as much energy as possible for the day. We walked through another wet and foggy morning, over Rt. 16, up the Wildcat Ridge Trail, to the top of Wildcat Mountain, gaining two thousand feet of elevation over two miles.

I'd heard of thru-hikers quitting their trek in the White Mountains, and I'd always been puzzled. How could one quit so close to the goal? Now I understood. This was no longer hiking; this was difficult rock climbing, made even more difficult by wet and slippery rocks. Three times during my week in the White Mountains, hikers fell, broke bones, and had to be rescued.

Gerty and I finally rounded the top of Wildcat Peak E. In blowing wind and rain, we hiked past the Skyride gondola, a chairlift available for folks wishing to enjoy the view from Wildcat without the workout we had just suffered.

Wildcat has five peaks—A, B, C, D, and E—and we crossed them all. I'd been concerned that the Presidential Range in the White Mountains might not have enough mountains for each president to have his own namesake, but apparently there is no need to worry.

We crossed all five peaks and arrived at Carter Notch. Ahead was an afternoon of more climbs: South, Middle, and North Carter Mountains. But we needed soup before attempting more climbs. Carter Notch Hut is the last hut in the Whites. The morning had been miserable with cold rain, and we needed to get inside and warm up. By the next day, we would be in Gorham, where I hoped a package waiting for me at the post office would have my winter gear. I'd been warned about the possibility of bad weather in the mountains but was still surprised by just how miserable July could be.

Today's treat was bean and pasta soup. That was a new taste for me, and just confirmed that you can put any two ingredients in broth and call it soup. But the hot mixture brought new vigor to my tired and wet body, and we continued our all-day slog over more mountains.

The Appalachian Trail through the White Mountains is notoriously difficult to follow. Instead of trail signs indicating "Appalachian Trail," different sections of the trail were given alternate names. A hiker who does not know the name of the section he's currently hiking can easily take a wrong turn. Many frustrated hikers have taken the matter into their own hands and carved AT directions on signs. Or sometimes hikers leave their own handmade signs for those following them. These impromptu guides probably saved many thru-hikers from needlessly getting lost.

Just beyond North Carter Mountain was Imp Campsite. We'd been battered by the weather and drained by climbs for thirteen miles, and I wanted to get out of my wet clothes. The Imp Shelter offered us sanctuary. The front of the building was partially enclosed, affording even more shelter.

One old gentleman had also taken refuge there. He was on a section hike, but the weather was so miserable he had spent several days at the shelter. On the previous evening, a rescue party had brought a man with a broken leg to the shelter and waited for daylight to carry him out. It took twelve paramedics to transport the injured man across this slippery and rocky trail.

The eccentric guy seemed genuinely pleased to have the company of two thru-hikers during his solitary stay. He had just finished cooking his meal, and I thought the mice would be delighted; he had spilled half his food over a large area.

There were only the three of us, so I set up my tent in the shelter and ditched wet clothes and slipped into my sleeping bag. Again I lit my stove inside the tent and soon had a warm and cozy spot. The elderly gentleman kept up a steady stream of conversation; sometimes Gerty answered, sometimes I did, and sometimes he answered himself.

Outside, the wind howled and mist swirled around the shelter as darkness fell. I made a journal entry, noting that it had been another cold, wet, foggy, windy, muddy day in the White Mountains, very nasty up along the ridges. But I could hike through just about anything as long as I had hopes of being warm and dry at the end of the day. I had survived another day, and I was content.

Our section hiker was singing, his tenor serenading the wind and the rain. *Mariah*. It's a lilting and haunting melody about days of love when the sun was always shining. The song could not have been about New Hampshire, since the sun almost never was shining out here. I wondered if our tenor knew the mountain ahead of us was Mt. Moriah.

At six in the morning, I donned still-wet clothes and left the Imp Shelter. We were eight miles from the highway that would take us into Gorham, New Hampshire.

Once over Mt. Moriah, we rolled downhill. Somehow we managed three river crossings. Our guidebooks showed footbridges across the rivers, but there were none to be seen. They were submerged under the swollen waters. We waded across, and although the water was never above our knees, maneuvering around rocks and against the strong currents was challenging. And the rain was still coming down.

Reaching U.S. 2, we still had a road walk of 3.6 miles to Gorham. Happily, someone took pity on us and gave us a ride into town.

At the edge of Gorham is The Barn at Libby House. The Barn is a popular hiker hostel. Gerty and I agreed that after the unrelenting misery of the Whites, we deserved more luxury than the hostel. Scattered along a mile on the outskirts of town are numerous hotels, shops, and restaurants. The Royalty Inn seemed an appropriate place for two beaten-up hikers.

As I walked toward the rooms stretching behind the main building, I realized I had been here before. The front of the inn had been remodeled, but the rooms were the same. I'd forgotten that I had ever been in Gorham before, but now I'd stumbled into the same motel where our family had stayed many years ago on a trip to New England. Our family was young, and time was still moving slowly. So much had happened since that trip. Now the children were grown and had moved on and Mary was gone. I had grandchildren. . . .

Grandchildren? I felt as if I'd barely had time to enjoy my children. The memories brought a sadness; I wanted to go back in time and enjoy my family more, and I would do things differently. I had spent so much time preparing for the future that I had neglected to enjoy the present. Now that present was the past. What had happened to all those years?

The room Gerty and I shared was only two doors down from the room our family had rented. I recalled the morning we left the motel. We were packing up to leave and were heading to Maine. I had backed our van up to our front door. The window in the room next to ours was open. Our van was an oil burner, and the smoke from its exhaust set off the smoke alarm in the next room. The maids couldn't figure out what had happened. I told Mary and the kids to get in the van quickly so we could disappear before I set off more alarms.

"But shouldn't you let them know why the alarm's going off?" Mary said.

"No, I'm too embarrassed. What does it matter? I'll never be back here again."

But here I was, again.

Between downpours, Gerty and I dashed to the post office and picked up my box with food and winter gear. At Burger King, we consumed large quantities of flame-broiled goodness, then stopped at a Dunkin' Donuts and topped off our feasting with several of those small cakes. One more stop to replenish our supply of hiking snacks, and we were back in our room, drying out our clothes.

Gerty had started his hike long before I had left Springer Mountain, and he was a stronger hiker than I. Yet I had caught up with him. I asked him how that was possible; his explanation told me a lot about the man.

Hiking through Virginia, Gerty was crossing a small footbridge when he heard a noise underfoot. Curious, he investigated and discovered a kitten meowing forlornly beneath the bridge. If he left the kitten there, it would probably die. Instead, he rescued it, making a nest in the hat that hung around his neck. Gerty carried the kitten for a day, struggling to keep it in the hat while the kitten constantly tried to climb out.

He attempted to give the kitten to other hikers, with no success. Several advised him just to turn it loose; if it died, it died. Gerty could not do this. He reversed direction, hiked twenty miles back to a town, and tried to find a home for the kitten. No one wanted the little thing; folks just told him to abandon it. He would not. He had started to bond with the kitten, and could see only one other solution. He would keep it himself.

Gerty took a taxi to the nearest airport, where he rented a car. He then drove to his home in Maine, asked a veterinarian friend to keep the kitten for him until he finished his hike, drove back to Virginia, returned the car to the airport, had another taxi take him back to the trail, and then continued his hike. The total cost for his new kitten, named "Troll," was close to $660. That explained how I had caught up with him.

I could not imagine why any woman would leave a man with such a tender heart. When I called Ina that night to tentatively set a finish date for my hike, I told her Gerty's kitten story and how amazed I was that a woman could leave a man who does something like that. Her reply was, "That's probably why she left him, *because* he does things like that."

Huh?

Leaving town the next morning, we stopped at The Barn at Libby House, looking for a ride back to the trail. In an oversized easy chair, my friend Padre sat soaking his foot in a bucket of Epsom salts.

"What happened, Padre? I thought I wouldn't see you again. You were headed to the finish line."

"Well, the day I told you that, I hiked thirty-five miles. But we've had so much rain, my feet have just been too wet for too long. My toe's infected. It'll be several days before I'm ready to hike again. Don't worry. I'll catch up with you soon."

Back on the trail, Gerty and I crossed the Androscoggin River and began our last day of hiking in New Hampshire. If all went well, I'd enter Maine sometime later that evening. The sky had finally cleared up, and behind me I could see the mountain range I had crossed. Those same mountains had hidden in rain and fog for most of my time there, but as I hiked the last miles toward Maine, the Whites were silhouetted in blue and green against a clear, sunny sky.

Today was also my last day of hiking with Gerty. His kitten had altered his schedule and he needed to do some big mileage days if he was to finish by his deadline. I'd kept up with him on that one headlong dash to Crawford Notch, but I wouldn't be able to match his pace all the way to Katahdin.

The mountain climbs were at lower elevations now, but the trail was still slow and difficult. The last climb of the day was Mt. Success, aptly named for my finish in New Hampshire. I crawled up and down rock climbs and waded through stretches of mud. I sure missed those huts and that hot soup.

But I was about to become an ingredient in a large primordial soup myself. Years of rain and decaying matter had settled and created a swampy bog almost at the top of Mt. Success. Narrow boards formed a walkway over the area, but the waters had risen with the large amount of rain, and several of the boards were now under water. I tap-tapped with my poles, trying to stay on the straight and narrow. But I slipped. That is, one hiking pole slipped off a board, and I lost my balance and sank into the oozing peat-filled bog. In a panic, I reached out and grabbed a board, and slowly dragged myself from the muck clutching me. "Congratulations, Mom and Dad. It's a boy," I muttered, as I lay there covered with mud and mire.

After regaining my balance and composure and scraping off as much of the goop as I could, I finished crossing Mt. Success. I was now a genuine born-again hiker: I had been immersed. I had become a new creature, albeit a swamp creature. Old things had passed away—yes, New Hampshire was behind me—and all things had become new. I was in Maine!

The small blue and white sign tacked to a tree brought an incredible rush of feeling.

> Welcome to Maine
> The Way Life Should Be

At last, my fourteenth and final state! I gave that little sign a welcome kiss and stepped into Maine.

I'd hiked seventeen difficult miles, and I was exhausted. My journal entry that night admitted, "I have never hiked a harder trail in my life." And the morrow would be just as strenuous. Mahoosuc Notch was six miles ahead of me and was known as the most difficult mile on the entire Appalachian Trail.

I stopped at the Carlo Col Shelter and Campsite, less than a mile into Maine. The cabin-type shelter lay down a steep, rocky side trail. I filtered two liters of cold Maine water from a nearby stream. I had the shelter to myself and hung clothes everywhere, trying to dry out.

No one else showed up that evening. I hoped for company, but it was a lonely night; only a little chipmunk stopped by to share the shelter. Still, I was warm and dry. I again had my winter hat and my Patagonia fleece; additional weight, yes, but I had a feeling I'd need them as I hiked across this rugged and beautiful state.

I was ready for the Maine Event.

23

The Maine Event

In the quiet of early morning, I heard my chipmunk friend scurrying about. I shared my breakfast with him and stored away as many calories myself as possible. The "most difficult mile on the trail" was ahead of me that morning.

Before that notorious mile in Mahoosuc Notch, though, I crossed Mt. Carlo, the three peaks of Goose Eye Mountain, and the south peak of Fulling Mill Mountain. Between the mountain peaks are the sags, low points filled with murky water, wet and decaying plants, and sphagnum moss. I'd dropped in to visit one of these bogs the day before; and, much to my dismay, I made a return visit this morning.

Crossing a board over a sag on Goose Eye Mountain, I took a misstep and once again tumbled into the oozing mess. My backpack halted my plunge, and I used the board path to pull myself out of the gooey slime. Leaving a trail of filth, I climbed a rock and shook and scraped off as much of the moss and fragile alpine vegetation as possible. I soon found a creek along the trail that, in comparison, looked clean and pure. I jumped in with clothes and shoes still on, hoping to shed more of the swamp. A change of socks, and I was ready for more adventure.

Imagine the letter V, with Fulling Mill Mountain forming one side and Mahoosuc Arm forming the other side. Mahoosuc Notch is the bottom of that V. It's a mile long, it's narrow, and it's filled with a jumble of boulders, many as large as cars or even houses, that have fallen from the opposite cliffs. I'd read hikers' accounts of traversing the notch, but nothing had prepared me for this most difficult mile on the Appalachian Trail.

There was no path; the white blazes came sporadically along the mile, but they served only as assurance that I was still following the AT. Each hiker must find his own route over, under, or around the boulders.

Those strong and brave enough can sometimes jump from rock to rock. I did jump from several boulders, using my Grand Canyon safety scale, but I was substituting "moose" for "death." A moose trapped in the notch had broken its leg in a fall.

We'd been reading the story in hiker comments in the shelter registers. Hikers had tried to get park officials to put the moose out of its misery, but the official policy seemed to be to let nature take its course. Register entries voiced vehement disapproval of this course of inaction. One hiker attempted to do the job himself, with his own knife, but apparently the moose disapproved of that plan. And so the unfortunate animal had slowly died of starvation. I passed the skull and bones, all that was left of the huge creature.

Someone had strung Buddhist prayer flags nearby. Was the moose a recent convert? Or was the gesture simply a tribute to its suffering?

When I wasn't jumping, I was squirming under boulders, pushing my backpack ahead of me. Little streams flowed under the rock piles, and sometimes I even discovered large chunks of ice, well-protected from the summer sun. A cool mist filtered up between the rocks; the notch was air-conditioned.

When I at last reached the north end of the notch without breaking a leg or having a house-sized boulder fall on me, I found that the second and third "most difficult" miles were up Mahoosuc Arm. I stood at the end of the notch, looking upward at an almost vertical trail, and shook my head. *It's impossible to go up there.* But there was nowhere else to go. Grabbing tree roots, searching for toeholds, and clawing for fingerholds, I pulled myself upward over the next two miles.

By four o'clock, I was exhausted and I'd only covered nine miles. I stopped at the Speck Pond Campsite, overlooking Speck Pond. In Ohio, a "pond" is a small body of water, usually under an acre in size. In Maine, a "pond" can be anywhere from several hundred to several thousand acres and often several square miles in area. Thunder rolled over the pond. Moving inside, I set up my tent on a wooden platform with a view of the water, placed rocks on the corners of the rain fly, and retired for the evening.

Trail Journal, Speck Pond:

I am very tired and smell like a swamp. One exciting thing happened this morning. I went over 1,900 miles. Only 274 Mainely hard miles to go.

Since it was still early, I studied my guidebook, planning the next several days. The next day was Sunday, and I'd hardly seen anyone for two days; I needed a town stop. Fifteen miles up the trail, I'd cross East B Hill Road. Andover was another eight miles down that road. My guess was that East B Hill Road was not a major thoroughfare and I'd have little chance of getting a hitch for those eight miles into town. Perhaps I'd have cell service on top of one of the mountains, and I could call ahead for a ride.

Early Sunday morning, I trudged up Speck Mountain to an elevation of 4,180 feet. Then the trail dropped to 1,498 feet at Grafton Notch. It was a roller-coaster day, with climbs to mountain peaks followed by drops to the sags between, where boardwalks crossed more oozing bogs lying in wait. I hiked those areas with extreme caution.

Baldpate Mountain was bald, devoid of trees or foliage. Rock cairns marked the path up and over its West and East peaks and then over Little Baldpate Mountain. At the summit of East Baldpate, I stopped to take in the views. Maine is a state of spectacular beauty, with range after range of mountains dotted by ponds.

On East Baldpate, I had cell service and called Pine Ellis Lodging in Andover, hoping to persuade someone to pick me up at the road crossing. A woman answered the phone.

"Ma'am, this is the Apostle Paul, calling from atop Baldpate Mountain. I would like to stay at your house tonight."

"You have to be kidding," she replied. "I can't believe this."

"What can't you believe? Do you have room for me at your place tonight?"

"Yes, I do. But it's your trail name that shocked me. I was sitting here, reading a book about the Apostle Paul, and the phone rang, and it's the Apostle Paul wanting to stay house tonight. It's just . . . such a strange coincidence.

She agreed to have someone pick me up at the East B Hill Road at 5:00 p.m. "Oh, by the way," she added, before she hung up, "my husband's name was also Paul. He passed away from cancer not long ago." Even out here in the middle of nowhere, God was still throwing "coincidences" at me.

At Pine Ellis, my hostess and I sat at her kitchen table and shared our losses. Her husband had lived only a few months after his diagnosis, and her heartache and grief were still raw. I assured her that healing would happen; we just never know *when*. Memories of our lost ones will always be with us, but the acute, overwhelming anguish will lessen at some point. We do find life on the other side of grief. I had left the shackles of my grief in a puddle of tears on top of Eph's Mountain three weeks before.

Many folks remain stuck in grief because they can't comprehend why God would take their loved ones. We get angry with God and question why He would subject us to such terrible loss. But if it were up to us, when would we ever allow God to take our son or daughter or spouse? The answer, of course, is that we would never choose it. We don't want to die and we don't want our loved ones to die. If the choice of when to die were left up to us, this world would be filled with sick people.

Each of us lives in a small slice of measured time, inserted here between eternity past and a never-ending life hereafter. From the moment of your birth, death becomes inevitable. Your little slice of time is so fleeting. Whether you live on this planet ten years or eighty is insignificant to God. What is significant is your choice of paths that will lead you to the end of your time here.

For those who do not believe in God, my thoughts on life, death, and eternity will make no sense. If you came here to read an adventure book, just skip ahead a few paragraphs while I talk with those who have suffered a devastating loss in life.

We question, *Why, God, why?* Each of you must answer one question for yourself: Is God in control or not? If you believe He is in control, then He knows the whys and whens and wheres of your loss. If you don't believe God is in control of these difficult situations, if you believe all that happens to us is random and beyond God's powers—well, then, you still need to skip ahead a little further.

If you could comprehend heaven and the bliss your loved one is experiencing, and if you also had the power to bring that person back to earth, would you? When you can finally say, *No, I would not bring her back*, your journey to the other side of grief has begun. Perhaps instead of lamenting our misfortunate loss of loved ones, we should wonder why God chose them as fortunate enough to join his celestial city.

If you've blue-blazed to this paragraph, welcome back. It's good to have you with us again.

Rejuvenated by a hot shower, I walked to the Andover General Store and Diner to resupply. My first Sunday in Maine ended with a pint of Hershey's chocolate ice cream on the Pine Ellis front porch and conversation with other hikers lodging there.

At five in the morning, I was back at the diner. Huge breakfasts started my days with an extra burst of energy, but these mountain climbs and difficult trails exhausted me by day's end. That day, I crossed Wyman, Moody, Old Blue, and both peaks of Bemis, struggling through nineteen miles. At Bemis Mountain Lean-to, I set up my tent, too weary to write more than one paragraph in my journal. Updating my daily miles in my guidebook, I added a one-word description of the day. "Wow!"

The sound of raindrops against my tent that night was a sign of things to come; rain would be my constant companion for the last two weeks of my hike. Early the next morning, as I wiped the water off Big Agnes, I was already thinking about finding a dry room for that night. Eighteen miles away, the trail crossed Rt. 4; at that point, I would still have a nine-mile hitch into the town of Rangeley.

I was crossing the Bemis Range, walking over an area of smooth and rounded rocks, when a noise startled me. I stopped when I caught sight of a mother grouse just a few feet in front of me. She was foraging for food under the bushes at the edge of the rocks, her four little chicks scurrying after her as she bustled and scratched. When I looked up and started down the trail again, a large fog bank was rolling down the hillside to meet me. After 1,900 miles, I was still fascinated by these amazing vignettes in nature and still thankful for my good fortune to witness such scenes.

Ten hours of stream crossings, stretches of well-marked trails, walks over long slabs of solid rocks, and wet and muddy paths brought me at last to Rt. 4, my thumb in the air. Before this AT hike, I'd never hitchhiked in my life; now, it was my mode of transportation on the highways. Fortunately, the folks in Maine weren't as judgmental as I had been in my previous life, and this dirty, wet, bearded hiker soon had a ride into Rangeley.

Rangeley is a small tourist town surrounded by 110 lakes and ponds, a town that caters to snowmobilers, skiers, and fishermen. I stopped at the lovely Rangeley Inn and asked for their cheapest, no-frills hiker rate. The young man in charge actually had one such room; it did have a bed and a shower, and that was luxury enough for me.

I found a restaurant and enjoyed a huge steak dinner. These town stops with good eats and extra calories always made for a stronger hiking day. I also stopped at a grocery store for supplies for the next several days.

More mountains and more rain. The next day took me over three large climbs, Saddleback Mountain at 4,120 feet, The Horn, and Saddleback Junior. When I wasn't laboring up a mountain, I was fighting treacherous mud at the lower elevations.

Toward evening, I was hiking alone through a cold and miserable rain on Lone Mountain. The wind howled around the mountainside and tried to shove me about. I was still two miles from Spaulding Mountain where I'd planned to stop at the shelter, but I was exhausted. Along the trail, ripe blueberries grew in abundance, and I stopped to gather and eat many handfuls of the delicious morsels. My arrival at the shelter was delayed a bit more, but even in the cold and blowing rain, I could not resist an evening snack.

At Spaulding Mountain Shelter, I quickly erected my tent in front of the building, and then went inside to catch up on the news in the register. Many entries spoke of a very large rabbit that visited this shelter. The stories sounded wild and unbelievable, and I wondered if perhaps some mind-altering substances had contributed to the unlikely tales.

My water was filtered and I was dry, inside my tent for the night. Something bumped up against the canvas. What was going on here? I flipped back the tent flap and was face to face with the largest rabbit I've ever seen. Had I eaten psychedelic blueberries or some other plant that caused hallucinations? Could this creature be real? Quite unalarmed at my presence, the huge thing turned slowly and hopped away. I'm not exaggerating when I say it was four times bigger than any rabbit I've ever seen back in Ohio. I never imagined there would be a night that I kept rocks within reach . . . to protect myself from a rabbit.

As I left the shelter in the morning, a voice behind me on the trail shouted my name. I turned and my first glance fell on a white flute protruding from a backpack.

"Good morning, Padre. How's the toe?"

"The toe's fine, but I need to get into a shelter and dry out. I was trying to catch up with you, but got caught in the storm up on Lone Mountain last night." Padre had tied his hammock to two trees and spent a cold and miserable night in the rain on Lone Mountain. "Let me warm up and get something to eat, and I'll catch up with you."

"Nice sticks you have there, Padre." He explained that he had, indeed, lost his girl's ski poles; now he had somehow acquired an unmatched pair of Leki poles.

I hiked ahead while Padre stopped at the shelter. I was struggling over slippery rocks on my way up Spaulding Mountain, when a sound stopped me in my tracks and brought tears to my eyes. Haunting notes from a flute drifted through the mist on the mountainside. I'd often heard Padre play a melody on his homemade flute. That morning, however, as I stood alone in the Maine woods, the sound pierced my soul.

Never in my life had I worked so hard toward a goal as I had struggled to finish this hike. I just wanted to reach that sign on Katahdin and go home. But I'd been so engrossed in the physical difficulties of the hike that I hadn't given much thought to what would happen *after* Katahdin. Two hundred miles from where I stood, Mt. Katahdin waited, with that sign and the finish line.

Then what?

The notes from the flute, dropping through the mountain woods, sang the song of my life on the trail. This trail had become my life. My fellow hikers were my family. I'd discovered peace and a sense of normalcy out here. My body had gone to previously unknown limits of exhaustion, but my mind was on a path of freedom.

Now the floating melody stirred emotions I didn't know existed. I wept as I realized how much this trail experience meant to me; I cried for what had been, what was, and what was about to end.

The last notes of the flute drifted away. It was time to start walking again.

I'd been alone in these woods for the last hundred miles, so I was happy when Padre caught up with me. Our big climbs of the day were South and North Crocker Mountains, both over 4,000 feet. By the middle of the afternoon, we'd crossed four mountains, forded four streams, hiked over slippery rocks and through muddy paths, and stood at the edge of Rt. 27, five miles from Stratton. Huddled under pine trees, seeking shelter from pouring rain, we had no difficulty convincing ourselves that we needed to go into town. Hitchhiking was unsuccessful, but I had cell service, and the owner of the Stratton Motel agreed to drive out and pick us up.

All evening and night, the rain poured down, but we laundered our clothes and ate a delicious meal at the White Wolf Inn.

Padre and I hiked in the rain for the next two days. The rain had turned the trail into a miniature bog. Undergrowth along the trail was so thick that we could not walk alongside the path; there was no choice but to slog through mud and running water.

Crossing a small mountain road at the base of Little Bigelow Mountain, I reached a major landmark in my journey. In the middle of Long Falls Dam Road, someone had painted the number 2,000. The few cars and log trucks passing through probably never saw it on the pavement; or if they did, they wouldn't guess its significance. But any thru-hiker crossing that road certainly knew what that 2,000 meant.

Several southbounders had highly recommended a stop at a hunting and fishing camp near Pierce Pond. Harrison Fish Camp served a lumberjack breakfast that included twelve pancakes, sausage, eggs, juice, and coffee. A makeshift bridge over Pierce Pond Stream brought us to the primitive but wonderful camp in the middle of nowhere. Padre and I rented a cabin, and that evening I journaled by the light of a kerosene lantern while my clothes hung drying on the front porch. Life was good.

The lumberjack breakfast was bliss. The twelve pancakes were the best I'd ever eaten and were gone in no time.

Three miles beyond Harrison Camp, I stood on the banks of the Kennebec River. The level of the Kennebec is controlled by a dam, and in years past some hikers have attempted to ford the river at low levels. One hiker lost his life attempting to cross, and so the official route across the Kennebec is now a canoe. The white blaze is painted on the floor of the canoe that ferries hikers from one bank to another. Anyone fording the river now is blue-blazing, although that choice was not a consideration for me. With the abundant rainfall, the river was now twelve feet deep where hikers used to walk across.

On the south bank of the Kennebec where I stood, a signal flag was provided to summon the canoe. I waved the flag, and across the river another flag acknowledged my call. A canoe pushed into the river, and my ride was on its way.

Beyond the Kennebec, the trail crossed U.S. Rt. 201 at Caratunk. I loved these little Maine towns and regretted that I could not stay and explore. It was still early in the morning, and my goal was to reach Bald Mountain Brook Lean-to. That would be an eighteen-mile day, and would put me within a day's hike of Monson. Padre and I reached my goal at six that evening, but it turned out my goal was not his goal.

"Let's try for Moxie Bald Lean-to," he said.

"That's over four miles away, and we'd still need to cross Moxie Bald Mountain. It's impossible," I lamented.

"We can do it in one and a half hours. Just keep up with me."

Why do I fall for these challenges?

Once again, I risked life and limb trying to keep up with someone. But Padre was right. We made the Moxie Bald shelter and found a lovely setting. The small and primitive building perched on the shore of a placid pond. The shelter came equipped with rain, but wasn't this a standard amenity at all Maine shelters? A rainbow arched over the neighboring mountains. Rocks jutted into the pond, and Padre relaxed on the rock formation and played his flute in the last of the evening light.

The notes of the flute and the glow of the rainbow both faded away, and another day in Maine was finished.

Monson, Maine, is the last outpost of civilization for hikers facing the 100-Mile Wilderness. This stretch of untamed Maine is much like the previous hundred miles, but it lacks towns and resupply points. Hikers are advised to leave Monson with a ten-day supply of food. I had planned for seven days on this last stretch of my journey. That also meant I could take a much-needed zero day in Monson.

It was a rocky, eighteen-mile hike to Monson, with several tricky river fords. The current was especially swift on the West Branch of the Piscataquis River. A small island split the river. I waded toward it, through rapidly flowing water that reached above my knees, praying for safety. Fortunately, I did have a man of the cloth behind me to recall any last words I might utter, should things go badly.

The trail followed the gorgeous river for several miles through the woods, crossing the waters again where the river widened and was shallower.

Years ago, the AT passed through Monson, but a relocation had taken the trail four miles west of town. The old trail still existed as a blue-blazed trail, and anyone but a purist could cut off three miles of hiking by using the old route. I was sure that Fargo would not have a difficult decision to make here. The shorter, blue-blazed trail might even make it possible for him to catch up with me.

When the trail crossed Maine Rt. 15, I attempted to call Shaw's Lodging in Monson, but I had no reception. The rain was coming down, and I resigned myself to a four-mile road walk into town. A young couple took pity on me and pulled over to pick up this rain-soaked and dirty hiker, and graciously dropped me off in front of the boardinghouse.

I booked a room for two nights, showered, and went downstairs to wait for Padre. Padre was a stronger hiker than I, but whenever a town was within range, no one could catch me.

Breakfast at Shaw's is a glorious event, and I happily experienced it twice, since I was taking my last zero day here. Each hiker at the table is simply asked, "How many?" The answer determines the size of breakfast served. A "Three" got you three of everything: eggs, bacon, sausage and pancakes. There was no limit on the number. I thought "Six" was about right for me, but I was too embarrassed to go that high, so when our server circled the table, I just ordered "Three." Halfway through the meal, I got the server's attention and held up three more fingers for the last half of my breakfast.

It was a beautiful day in Monson, the first day without rain in . . . how long? I almost couldn't remember a day without rain. I set out on my errands. My final food box was waiting at the post office, and I stopped at a store for glue and tape. My shoes were coming apart, casualties of the daily battle with rocks, roots, mud, and water, and I hoped to hold them together for the trek through the 100-Mile Wilderness. I spotted a library and stopped in to use their computer. I'd been isolated from all world events since Fargo had abandoned me.

On my way back to Shaw's, a booming voice came down the street. Fargo was coming down Pleasant Street, waving his arms wildly.

"Hey dere, Apostle, I finally caught up wit ya. I gotsta say, doh, dis trail's a humdinger, believe you me."

"It's great to see you again, Fargo. How's da missus? Did your house sell? Let's get you checked in and go find something to eat."

I relaxed on my zero day in Monson, visiting with Fargo and other hikers. Fargo and I discussed our plans for the 100-Mile Wilderness and Katahdin's summit. He had his usual concerns and worries about this final trek, but I assured him that if he stayed with me, we would summit eight days from now on Wednesday, August 13.

Back at Shaw's, I sat with other hikers and caught up on trail news while I attempted to work a glue-and-tape miracle on my shoes. Within reach were a slice of pizza and a pint of chocolate ice cream.

I knew I was one fortunate man at Shaw's that night. All my needs were met. I certainly had enough to eat, I had a soft bed, and I was dry. It had not rained that day (although I would hike in rain for the next seven days). And I was among friends. Tomorrow I would start the 100-Mile Wilderness, with its trials and difficulties and final push to the finish line. But that was tomorrow. Tonight at Shaw's, all was well.

24

Trials and Tears

After a "three" breakfast, it was time to head into the wilderness. Padre caught a ride back to Caratunk to pick up a mail drop; he'd catch up with us later. The mail drop was actually his floppy straw hat. Padre had left it back at Pine Ellis Lodging, and our hostess had graciously mailed it ahead to the Caratunk post office.

Back at the trailhead, I asked Fargo if he wanted to hike back and do the three miles he had cut off by blue-blazing into Monson. He declined; that would put another six-mile gap between us and he remembered the last time he'd let that happen. Furthermore, he reminded me, he had hiked the *traditional* route into Monson.

The sign announcing our entry into the 100-Mile Wilderness warned us not to underestimate the difficulty of what lay ahead. It's the longest stretch of wilderness on the AT, and, for some reason, I had imagined this section of the trail would be a hundred miles of easier hiking, with time to enjoy the sheer beauty of Maine. Now I realized there were still more mountains to climb, and those southbound hikers had not been exaggerating—this trail was very, very difficult. Yes, I should have known better, but I *had* underestimated the 100-Mile Wilderness.

River fords were unusually dangerous; the waters were high and currents swift, a result of all the recent rain. We forded four rivers. The wildest one actually turned out to be the safest crossing; a rope strung above the swift current helped to steady us as we waded across.

By noon, the rains had started again and continued all afternoon and evening.

We stopped at Long Pond Stream Lean-to and quickly shed our wet clothes. A group of French students on a section hike camped nearby. Fargo and I relaxed in our sleeping bags, and watched and smelled and envied as the group's sponsors cooked huge bowls of steaming spaghetti. This scenario could turn out to be either a horrible torment or the best thing ever.

Finally, those wonderful words, "Do you guys want any leftover spaghetti?"

You would never have guessed that Fargo and I had just finished our own evening meals and had eaten an enormous breakfast that morning. We showered them with thanks as we gulped down the treat.

"Do you want me to cook more? We have plenty."

Our mouths full of spaghetti, we shouted our affirmative. Soon two more large bowls of hot spaghetti slid our way. I asked if there might be any Parmesan cheese. Sure enough, a bowl of grated cheese appeared.

The gift of a bowl (well, two bowls) of spaghetti had quickly taken me from the misery of cold rain and muddy trails to a high plateau of satisfaction and contentment.

———

The rain drummed steadily all night, and morning brought no hope that it would end. I gasped and shivered as I climbed into my wet clothes.

We planned to hike twenty miles that day. As usual, I'd set a goal for myself and was soon hiking far ahead of Fargo. In three days, I wanted to be at the White House Landing Wilderness Camp, a private camp on Pemadumcook Lake that can be reached only by boat. The camp is a mile off the trail and difficult to find, since trail maintainers in this section do not permit any private directional signs on the AT and hikers have to follow a primitive path through private timberlands. But I'd heard southbounders rave about the one-pound hamburgers at the camp, and I was determined to be one of the fortunate hikers who found their way to the lakeshore.

Once at the shore, visitors sound an air horn, summoning a boat from the camp that transports guests across the lake to White House Landing. The camp was still three days away, but the juicy one-pound burger dangling in my future was now every bit as much motivation as monetary bonuses had been in my previous life. And I did need motivation to get through this mud-filled trail.

There was no way I'd reach my goal of twenty miles that day. White House Landing by Saturday night also seemed doubtful. By two o'clock, I'd climbed four mountains but had covered only eleven miles. Every inch of those miles had been through cold rain, and I was completely drenched, was chilled to the bone, and had lost all feeling in my hands. Partway up

Chairback Mountain, the trail passed in front of Chairback Gap Lean-to. I could go no farther. I'd hit a wall. Mentally, emotionally, physically, I was worn out.

I wanted to get out of my wet clothes and somehow warm up. Hot food would help, but I needed water, and the spring at this shelter was down a steep, rocky hillside. I started down, but my foot slipped on a slick rock and I fell, tumbling forward in a complete head-over-heels somersault. A moss-covered rock softened my landing, but for a moment as I pitched down the slope, I thought my hike was over.

The stinging in my elbows gradually subsided, and I continued my search for water. Heavy and constant rains had overwhelmed the spring, making it indistinguishable from the surrounding swamp waters. I filled my water bottle and cooking pot with liquid that already looked like soup.

I headed back uphill. At the same place I'd slipped on the way down, my foot now caught on a root stretched across a rock. My tired body had no fight left; I went down hard, sprawling on the rock and spilling the water from my cooking pot.

I had an emotional meltdown. I was at the end of my tolerance for this misery. Pulling myself up from the rock, I shook my fist at the heavens, and yelled, "God, You're not looking out for me anymore, are You?"

I'm a little embarrassed now about my tantrum. The foolish and silly statement came out of sheer frustration, and I knew it wasn't true. I had no serious injuries; those falls could have easily broken one or every bone in my body. Of course He had protected me.

My expensive GORE-TEX rain gear had suffered three significant rips. I decided the holes no longer mattered; they might even be beneficial, allowing more moisture to leave than what might creep in.

Finally back at the shelter, I attempted to light my stove and boil the swamp water. My fingers were so cold that I could not move them to ignite the lighter. I finally resorted to striking the lighter with the side of my hand, but by the time I switched on the gas on my stove, the lighter had gone out. When I tried to light it again, only a few sparks flew from the tip.

Desperation set in and suggested a foolish plan. I turned the gas valve open on my stove and let the lighter's feeble sparks ignite the escaping cloud of propane. It was the one plan that actually worked that day. My desperate act also singed all the hair from my hands and filled the shelter with the aroma of burnt hair. My hands were too cold to feel a thing. I had fire; that was the only thing that mattered.

While the water boiled, I removed my wet clothes and pulled on my dry Patagonia long johns and my warm fleece. When Fargo arrived at three o'clock, he needed no convincing; his day was also done. By four, we were in our sleeping bags for the night, happy to be out of the never-ending cold rain.

My clothes and shoes were still wet in the morning. And cold. There was nothing to do but pull them on and hike off in the rain. I wanted to make East Branch Lean-to by that night, a 20.7-mile hike. Between me and East Branch were Hay Mountain and White Cap Mountain; both were over 3,000 feet, but they were the last two mountains of such elevation until I reached Katahdin.

All day I plodded over mountains, fighting the muddy trails, determined to do the 20.7 miles that might make possible a hamburger at White House Landing on Saturday night. Toward evening, I crossed White Cap Mountain in a blowing, misting rain. Later, the trail passed directly in front of Logan Brook Lean-to, and a familiar figure in a sleeping bag propped himself on his elbows and grinned at me.

"Fargo, what are you doing in there? I thought we were going to the East Branch Lean-to, so we can make it to White House Landing by tomorrow night."

The truth was, at that moment Fargo did not care about East Branch or White House Landing. He'd arrived at Logan Brook shortly before and had met a southbound couple there. Now he was engrossed in telling them trail stories, and their interest in his stories would keep him there for the night. When I arrived, he was in the middle of the Wapiti murder story from back in Pearisburg, Virginia. I'd heard him tell it many times, and every telling was more gruesome than the last.

I let Fargo know that I intended to go another 3.5 miles to East Branch. He assured me he would catch up with me the next day. As I left, I encouraged him to spice up the story even more. "Add a bear to it," I suggested.

I finally arrived at East Branch Lean-to at eight o'clock. I was soaked, half-frozen, and mud-splattered, but I'd achieved my goal and that was very satisfying. Earlier that day, I'd also crossed the 2,100-mile point and now had only 68 miles remaining on my journey. I peeled off my wet clothes, ate a quick meal, and went to sleep with visions of one-pound hamburgers dancing in my head.

Cold and wet clothes will wake you up faster than coffee. I had only 21.7 miles to my hamburger. Little Boardman Mountain, just over 2,000 feet, was the highest climb of the day. My shoes were still soaked from the previous day's hike, so there was no need for careful stepping on the flooded trail. Throwing caution to the chilly wind, I splashed and stomped out those 21.7 miles by four o'clock.

Maher Tote Road, leading away from the trail to the shores of Pemadumcook Lake, was not much more than a grassy path. At the edge of the lake, I sounded the air horn and saw a speedboat, my ride to White House Landing, leave the opposite shore. I arrived at five, just in time to join other hikers for supper.

I relished that one-pound hamburger and congratulated myself on reaching my goal.

I rented a bunk in a small cabin by the lake and washed my clothes in a washtub outside. In the evening light, I paddled a canoe away from the shore and watched a beautiful sunset over Pemadumcook Lake. The storm clouds had passed, and from my canoe on the quiet lake I caught my first glimpse of my final goal, the mighty Mt. Katahdin. Its name came from the Penobscot Indians and means "The Greatest Mountain."

A seventy-four-year-old man shared my cabin, and in two days he hoped to finish his hike of the entire Appalachian Trail. I'd complete my hike in one season; he would complete his hike after fifty years. Satisfaction in reaching goals does not always lie in the speed with which we achieve them; sometimes the satisfaction rises from overcoming obstacles and gaining wisdom in our journeys. How often do we dream of a goal, finally reach it, and then wonder, *Is that all there is?* Don't forget to live on your journey.

I devoured a stack of blueberry pancakes at breakfast the next morning, took the boat across the lake, and found my way back to the AT. Fargo was walking down the trail from his campsite three miles short of White House Landing.

"Good morning, Fargo. Want to hear about the one-pound hamburgers and the blueberry pancakes?" I believe his answer meant no, but I described them anyway.

Fargo and I took a break at the top of Nesuntabunt Mountain, where we could see Mt. Katahdin in the distance. Fargo left before I did; I was enjoying that view. Several minutes later, I took off in pursuit, but he was nowhere in sight. I was surprised; apparently he had speed that had not previously shown itself.

Since I had only sixteen miles to the Rainbow Stream Leanto, I hiked slower that day. Later in the morning, I heard someone behind me. It was Fargo.

"What happened to you?" I asked. I'd been certain he was ahead of me.

"I got turned aroun' up on da mountain und went down da udder side again."

"Hey, Fargo, if you do that often enough, you'll make up for all those miles you skipped by blue-blazing."

The AT crosses the West Branch of the Penobscot River on a pedestrian walkway on the Abol Bridge. Halfway across, I again had a view of Mt. Katahdin looming over the landscape. Only two days and fifteen miles separated me from that mountain peak and a lifetime goal.

At the north end of the bridge is the Abol Bridge Campground and camp store. Stopping at the store, Fargo and I rented tent spaces in the campground. Another storm was brewing, so we set up our tents quickly.

On our way back to the store to buy food, we saw two familiar figures crossing Abol Bridge. Einstein and Franklin were also headed to the campground. I'd never imagined this final scenario; I'd be summiting Katahdin with three hiking partners that had contributed so much to my AT experience. In the camp store, we read an entry in the hiker journal that told us Padre had stopped the day before and would be summiting that day.

For several hours, the four of us sat under the awning of a deserted RV parked in the campground near our tents. It was the perfect time to reflect on our journeys. In two days, four middle-aged men who had been brought together by the trail would be reaching their ultimate thru-hike goal. I was certain that my three friends had experienced, learned, and changed as much as I had. The trail does that to a person.

Occasionally, a campground employee passed on a golf cart and warned us to move away from the RV and its protective awning. Private property, he kept insisting. But we had spent too much time in the woods; the concept of private property held little significance for us that day. We had no intention of leaving our sheltered meeting place, and since the rain was again pouring down, the would-be enforcer had no desire to leave his covered golf cart to remove us.

I did not sleep well that night. Perhaps it was the rain pounding my tent or the steady rumble of log trucks crossing the Abol Bridge. More likely, it was a thought I could not ignore: tomorrow would be my last full day on the Appalachian Trail.

Just past the camp store, the trail continues into the woods. We stopped at an information board close to the path and reserved our shelter for that night.

Baxter State Park, where Katahdin reigns, was donated to the people of Maine by Percival P. Baxter, who wished the land to remain "forever wild." The park is very restricted, with a limited number of shelters, and spots in those few shelters are usually booked far in advance.

Since thru-hikers cannot know when they will arrive at the park, several shelters near the Katahdin Stream Campground are reserved for thru-hikers only. As hikers arrive at the information board at the Abol Bridge, they reserve a spot in one of these shelters, ten miles ahead on the trail. A maximum of twelve campers each night are permitted one-night stays in this area called The Birches. From there, hikers have less than six miles to the summit of Mt. Katahdin.

Ina was driving to Maine from Ohio to climb Katahdin with me. She would not be permitted to take one of the thru-hiker spots at The Birches, but I hoped to find a shelter in the Katahdin Stream Campground for her.

Fargo, Einstein, Franklin, and I hiked together, at a leisurely pace, since we had only ten miles to hike that day. This stretch included the last two river fords of my trek. The unceasing rains had made these river crossings dangerous, and a sign informed hikers that a new, blue-blazed trail had recently been opened to bypass the river crossings. Four hikers approached that bypass, but only three took it. One stubborn purist chose instead to risk his life and his entire hike.

I rock-hopped over the first river crossing and remained dry. *Only one more ford, and it's done.* That's what I thought. But it wasn't that simple.

My heart sank as I approached the last crossing. The current was swift, and a ford seemed impossible. A log stretched between two large rocks, bridging the narrowest part of the stream. But the water churned through here with a roar, and the log was less than six inches in diameter. Could I walk across that? I carefully put one foot on it, then the other. The log quivered beneath me as I took a step, and I retreated back to the rock to evaluate the situation. *Are you willing to die to remain a purist?*

I'd asked myself the question back in Maryland, during a storm, and the answer then had been *yes*.

I walked upstream, searching for an easier crossing. No luck. I must either cross at this place or give up my purist hike and take the safe, blue-blazed bypass. My two goals of finishing this hike and remaining a purist were within reach, and I did not want to give up either one. *I got here by stubbornness and persistence, and I will get across this river.*

Back in the woods, I found a small but sturdy log and dragged it to the river. I positioned it beside the log already spanning the rushing water, one end on the rock on which I stood, the other end in the water halfway across the river. I now had a V-shaped log bridge. Would it work?

Hurling my hiking poles to the other bank of the river, I was committed. With hands on the original bridge and feet on the log I had added, I inched across the water, arching myself over the rushing current.

Halfway across, I had stretched my body as far as possible and knew I would have to jump the remaining distance. I launched toward the other side of the river, my arms found the rock, and I pulled myself up onto it. I wanted to shout in victory. I know it was foolish and dangerous, but . . . I'd done it! Yes! I was still a purist hiker.

I grabbed my poles and went in pursuit of my friends.

Every thru-hiker planning to summit Mt. Katahdin is required to sign in at the campground office. Each hiker is assigned a number, thereby giving an accurate count of thru-hikers finishing the trail. On Springer Mountain, I signed in as hiker 391. At Harpers Ferry, I had moved to number 191, having passed two hundred of my fellow hikers somewhere along the way. I'd soon find out how many others I had passed on the second half of my hike.

At the ranger station, I asked about a possible shelter for Ina. Unfortunately, all of the fifteen shelters at the Katahdin Stream Campground were full.

While I was talking to the ranger, I heard a commotion brewing outside and a familiar voice came through the screen door.

"Are you Fargo? Is Apostle in there?" Ina was coming up the lawn toward us. She'd heard enough about my buddy Fargo to recognize him. I ran out and greeted my friend and introduced her to Fargo, Einstein, and Franklin.

"Come in the office, Ina, while I sign up for the hike tomorrow. And we have a problem. I don't know where you'll stay tonight. I wasn't able to get a shelter for you."

"Oh, that's not a problem," she said. "I stopped at the entrance to the park and booked the last shelter they had." Ina's arrival had been perfectly timed; someone had just cancelled a reservation, and she snatched the spot.

I signed in for my climb up the mountain. I would be hiker 91 to finish the trail this season. I had passed another hundred hikers.

How was it that number 91 followed me all along the trail? God's promise of protection for my hike came from Mary's beloved Psalm 91, read on the very day I started walking. All coincidence? Perhaps. Or maybe it was yet another reminder from God that all was well and in His hands.

At the shelter, I prepared my pack for an early morning departure. Outside, the rain poured down, much like every other day for the last month. The forecast for the next day, though, predicted sunshine. The first rays of sunlight to hit America each morning touch Mt. Katahdin. I wanted to get an early start to witness the union of morning light and mountain peak.

"Someday never comes." Or so the saying goes. Endless waiting for *someday* can be frustrating, but the somedays of dreams can actually come to pass. Set goals and hike confidently toward them, one step at a time, and you will fill your life with many realized somedays.

August 13, 2008, was my someday. Even as recently as the last day of March, less than five months ago, when I walked the first mile on the Appalachian Trail, this someday seemed impossible. But now it had arrived; someday was *today*.

At 5:00 a.m., Ina and I left for the final 5.2 miles of my thru-hike, the climb up the mighty Mt. Katahdin. The storm clouds had passed, and stars sparkled in the night sky. Those stars faded and faint morning light grew as we made our way up the mountain. We crossed Katahdin Stream over a footbridge; a waterfall roared nearby. For several miles, the trail was much like Mahoosuc Notch, except these house-sized boulders were vertical. We slowly pulled ourselves upward with the assistance of rebar rods jutting from the rocks. On one precarious slope, a rope dangled to assist hikers up the slick surface.

I had advised Ina to get in shape for this hike, but she had not understood how strenuous this climb would be. Now she was breathless, trying to keep up with me. Einstein passed us, then Fargo and Franklin. "We'll wait for you up there," they promised. Ina apologized for slowing me down and encouraged me to keep pace with my friends.

"This is the hardest thing I've ever done," she admitted. I didn't confess to her that even after climbing 299 other mountains, I also found The Greatest Mountain extremely difficult.

We climbed above tree level and the sun shone on the panorama of Maine's beauty rolled out below us: green mountain ranges and hundreds of ponds and lakes. We looked down on soft, fluffy clouds that sometimes drifted between us and the views.

At last we reached the tableland, a level plateau. The trail threaded its way between slabs of broken rocks and passed Thoreau Spring, named for Henry David Thoreau, who explored Mt. Katahdin in 1846 and wrote a book called *The Maine Woods*. Thoreau Spring was exactly one mile from that sign at the summit. Occasionally, we heard a shout of exhilaration from the mountaintop, as another hiker realized his dream.

I could see the famous sign in the distance. It jutted upward from the rocks, marking the end of my hike. Then a cloud descended and enshrouded both the sign and a group of hikers already assembled there.

I had only a few hundred feet to go.

Back in Damascus, Virginia, I'd met Pathfinder, who told the story of his own hike after his wife's death. "I got within ten feet of the sign and couldn't finish. I broke down and cried," he'd told me. In Damascus, his statement had puzzled me; I just wanted to finish my hike and go home.

Now I stood in sight of that sign, and I understood what had happened to Pathfinder. I understood, because I felt it myself. Our lives had both experienced brutal endings. We found peace and healing here, and the trail became reality and family. Now this too was about to end. We stood at the brink of another good-bye. The very thing that I had so wanted to finish was now done . . . and I did not want it to end.

Fargo, Franklin, and Einstein had finished and stood off to one side, waiting for me. A group of day hikers had gathered around the sign. I hung back, waiting. I had earned the right to have that sign to myself, and I waited for the other hikers to move away. Franklin noticed and understood.

"Guys," he said, addressing the day hikers, "that hiker over there has walked close to 2,200 miles from Georgia to finish here. Let's let him have the sign to himself for a few minutes."

The other hikers stepped aside, making way for me, applauding as I approached. I dropped my backpack and laid my poles across it, then grabbed the sign and sobbed. I fell to my knees, still holding the base of the sign, tears falling, and thanked God for safety and healing.

After a few moments, I regained enough composure to pull out a Hershey bar and a Coke. I celebrated the only way a thru-hiker knows to celebrate—with calories. My trail friends and I took a group photo at the sign.

And just like that . . . it was over.

Top, 100-mile wilderness sign; *center*, trail up Katahdin; *bottom*, Apostle at sign

Epilogue

One by one, each leaving in his own time, we drifted away from that sign on the mountaintop and slowly made our way back down Katahdin. I was reminded of high school graduation, when I walked out of that school and thought, *It's over. Now what do I do?* Once again, I had no job and no idea what to do. In my prayer at the sign, I'd also asked God for wisdom as I sought new beginnings. I wondered if I'd be able to put into practice all that I'd learned in the wilderness.

Back at Katahdin Stream Campground, I found myself behind the wheel of a car for the first time in many months. Franklin and Einstein had already left, but as I passed a small pavilion, I noticed Fargo sitting there, waiting for his ride. I stopped the car, and we exchanged addresses and said good-bye.

As I climbed back into the car, Ina said, "Fargo had tears running down his cheeks when he walked away."

There were two of us with tears in our eyes. I got back out of the car and called my friend's name. He turned around, and I said, "Hey, Fargo, give me a hug." With tears streaming down both our faces, we embraced.

We were just two average men who had shared life on a difficult, 2,176-mile hike from Georgia to Maine. We'd met and become like brothers. We were family.

As the car bounced down the rutted dirt road leading out of Baxter State Park, I was caught in a swirl of emotion. What had kept me working so hard had now ended. Back in March, I'd driven the dirt road up Springer Mountain, dodging potholes on my way to the unknown. That unknown became the rhythm of waking up early, hiking long miles, struggling over mountains—always striving toward my goal. Now here I was again, on another rutted road leading into another unknown. I was unemployed. Katahdin was behind me. I needed new goals.

Several hours later, I was speeding down the Massachusetts turnpike when I spotted the overpass carrying the Appalachian Trail over the highway. I had crossed that overpass and watched the traffic, thinking ahead to the day when I'd be in one of those cars, finally heading home. Now I looked at the walkway and thought back to my days on the trail. That narrow pathway had been my path to freedom; it had taught me and changed me.

God had honored His promise to be with me, and now I needed to honor my promise and give folks the message He had asked me to deliver.

Back in Holmes County, my first stop was at the hillside cemetery where Mary was buried. With tears running down my face, I knelt in front of her memorial stone.

"I did it, Mary. I thru-hiked the Appalachian Trail. It was so much harder than I ever imagined, but I did it!"

I told Mary how much she had meant to me and how much our family missed her. My children had been without both a mother and a father these past five months.

"Mary, I'll tell you all about my hike when we meet again. Now I'm going home to see our new grandson."

A number of people had followed my hike, reading my entries on the Trail Journals website. I soon received invitations to speak about my adventure. The first meeting was at a local restaurant with a group of area seniors. Following my presentation, a lady sitting behind me tapped me on the shoulder and asked if I knew the gentleman beside her. He was stooped with age, with two canes lying across his lap. He looked familiar, but I could not put a name to the face. My jaw dropped when the lady told me he was a retired evangelist from Nebraska.

He was the same man who had scared me half to death many years ago with rapping knuckles and shouting about Jesus's imminent return. I reached out and took his feeble hands in mine . . . and examined his knuckles. To his bewilderment, I replied, "I'm checking your knuckles for calluses. Do you have any idea how badly you scared me that night so many years ago?"

I smile even now, realizing the incredibility of our meeting. God sure does move in mysterious ways. God was reminding me that the message He gave me is real, and I needed to get to work and get it written for other folks.

My hike had to be about more than just walking two thousand miles. When I decided to do the hike, I needed a greater purpose for quitting my job and changing my life so drastically. One of my goals was to remind men to appreciate what they have today—don't take your family and your wife for granted. It really is true; we never realize what we have until we no longer have it. How it would change our lives if we could fully *see what we see* in our families and marriages, be grateful for what we have, and make gratitude part of our daily living!

Using my story on the trail as a vehicle, I also wanted to write a book that shows readers that the Christian life doesn't have to be boring. To my Christian friends: If people observe your daily life, would they say, "I want what he has"? We Christians should be the happiest folks in the world, with what we know about life in the hereafter. Why are we often seen as the most downtrodden, dismal, and judgmental people around? It's no wonder the world doesn't want what we offer. Maybe we need to remind ourselves of what we really do have.

When I started this hike, I never imagined how difficult it would be. Had I known, I would never have attempted it. The trail is much like our lives. We never know what difficulties we'll encounter on this earthly pilgrimage. What we are assured of, however, is a finish line.

That does sound rather strange, doesn't it? The biggest event of our lives will be the finish line, when we end life's journey. Yet we don't like to think about the end. We don't want to be reminded that we will die, because we often are afraid of what lies beyond death. Fear of that great unknown prompts us to try to ignore the matter.

Remember the free meal in a log home in Virginia? The owner spoke about salvation and offered us books if we wanted to read more. That night, he handed me a small piece of paper with a short message. That message spoke to my spirit, and I want to share it with you. Here's my paraphrase of that message:

> Supposing that we've traveled all these miles together, and I've never told you about God and the reality of a future judgment. If we meet someday at that final judgment, I don't want you to say to me, "You *knew* about this, and you didn't tell me?"

Here's what the Apostle Paul—the real one—says about the importance of this choice. He sums it up clearly in Romans, a letter he wrote to the church in Rome. These may be the most important words you'll ever read. You can take this message and never open it, and figuratively hang it from a nail on a board fence, just as Motormouth did with his spiritual book that night in Virginia. Or you can hang your eternal existence on these words, if you choose.

For some reason, God wants to have a relationship with us. I don't pretend to know why, but I suspect it has something to do with love. However, there's a problem between God and us. The problem is sin. God just absolutely cannot tolerate sin.

In Romans 3:23, the Apostle Paul tells us that everyone *has* sinned. Romans 6:23 says the price we pay for a life of sin is death. So there you have it: everyone has sinned, and the punishment for sin is death.

But our friend the apostle also has some good news for us. Romans 5:8 says that God demonstrated how much He loved us by allowing His Son Jesus to die for us on the cross. That death on the cross paid the price for our sins.

The defining question is this: What must we do to be saved from death? Once again, the real Apostle Paul gives us the answer. Romans 10:9 says that if we speak with our mouths that Jesus is Lord and we believe that God raised Jesus from the dead after He was crucified, then we'll be saved.

It can't be that easy, you might be thinking. *I thought I had to jump through all kinds of hoops and follow all kinds of rituals to be assured of eternal life.* My friend, it is indeed that simple. Paul says in Romans 10:13 that everyone who calls on the name of the Lord will be saved.

You see, there truly are two pathways in this life. One is the path to destruction and everlasting death. The other is the path that leads to an eternal life with God in a place called heaven. These paths run somewhat parallel to each other in our earthly life; however, there is the problem of crossing from one path to the other. Don't look back. You cannot change what is behind you. To change your path and change your life, you'll need a bridge. You're at that bridge now. The cross of Jesus can take you from the path of death to the path of life. The cross, that great symbol of Christianity, beckons you to give up whatever is keeping you on the wrong path. Cross the bridge, and find a peace you've never imagined and a journey with God that is indescribable.

Nailed to a cross, Jesus paid a great price for your life. Choose wisely, my friend. You can mock that cross if you wish, or you can say, *God, forgive me.* Words do have meaning.

It's time to finish this adventure. What a journey it's been! From the highest mountain to the lowest valley on the Appalachian Trail, my summer of 2008 is a story of peace and healing. I hiked with a partner, God, who is the originator of love. God's love will comfort you too through valleys of despair and will lead you to your own mountaintop of peace and freedom.

Acknowledgments

Although it may seem idyllic and liberating to quit a job, sling on a backpack, and leave all worries behind, my story was not quite that simple. The journey I undertook, the adventures I lived, and this book were all made possible by many wonderful people in my life.

My family has anchored me through the years. Mom and Dad have always given us a quiet Christian example. Although I joke about my many sisters, I would not want to give up any of them. My mother-in-law, who has traveled the path of grief many times herself, has a strong trust in God and a positive attitude that have been an inspiration to me.

My children not only lost Mom, but Dad was also unavailable for a season. Melissa and Tom, Rodrick and Jill, Kristin and Trevor, a great big thank-you for the things you did and sacrifices you made to make my hike possible.

Thanks to Dutchman Hospitality in Walnut Creek, Ohio, the parent company of my restaurant, and the owners who made it possible for me to spend all the time I needed with

Mary during her illness and the last months of her life. Thanks also to my friends and co-workers at Dutch Valley in Sugarcreek, Ohio, for their support, not only during Mary's illness, but for the seventeen years I managed the restaurant. Thank you to my co-worker and friend Ina for coordinating food drops, driving me to Springer Mountain, and picking me up at the end of the trail.

Elaine Starner organized my thoughts and ramblings and helped make possible my dream of a published book. Her insights and her belief that God spoke with me on the trail were much appreciated as this book took shape.

A special thanks to my editor Vicki Crumpton and the team at Revell for their dedication to publishing *Hiking Through*. God promised to get this book were He wanted it, and with your efforts that will now happen.

A special thank you to all my friends and hiking partners I met along the AT. It's impossible to name everyone, but you are also family.

God was with me every step of the way, just as He had promised. I am humbled that He knows me well and still loves me.

Finally, to all my readers, thank you for reading this book. I am honored that you took the time to read my story. My prayer is that you have been blessed in some small way by the journey we've taken together. I would be delighted to hear your response to anything you've read in these pages. You may post your comments on my website at www.hiking through.com.

God bless you all.

Paul Stutzman

Meet Paul Stutzman at
www.hikingthrough.com
See pictures from his hike
Read his blog
Post your own inspiring adventure story
And More